Comic-Con and the Business of Pop Culture

Comic-Con and the Business of Pop Culture

WHAT THE WORLD'S WILDEST TRADE SHOW CAN TELL US ABOUT THE FUTURE OF ENTERTAINMENT

ROB SALKOWITZ

New York • Chicago • San Francisco • Lisbon • London • Madrid • Mexico City • Milan • New Delhi • San Juan • Seoul • Singapore • Sydney • Toronto

1 2 3 4 5 6 7 8 9 0   DOC/DOC   1 8 7 6 5 4 3 2

ISBN   978-0-07-179702-3

MHID 0-07-179702-5

e-ISBN 978-0-07-179703-0

e-MHID 0-07-179703-3

McGraw-Hill books are available at special quantity discounts to use
as premiums and sales promotions or for use in corporate training
programs. To contact a representative, please e-mail us at bulksales@
mcgraw-hill.com.

This book is printed on acid-free paper.

For Eunice

CONTENTS

Comic-Con and the Business of Pop Culture

FIVE DAYS
IN JULY

"You're a futurist, and you love comics—why don't you write a book about the future of comics?"

Over the years, a lot of people have asked me that question, but this time it carried special weight, since it came from Denis Kitchen, the respected former comics publisher turned literary agent and a longtime personal friend.

It seemed like a casual suggestion, but the more I thought about it, the more it seemed like a serious, even essential, project. Not only are comics a personal interest, but the industry and its current problems illustrate a theme that has been at the center of my work: how advances in digital technology, globalization, and changes in audience demographics are disrupting old business models. The tribulations of this one sliver of the pop culture world also exemplify the biggest challenge facing *all* creative enterprises in the twenty-first century: how to balance the trend toward consolidation and centralization in the business with the radical democratization of access toward creative tools, media, and audience engagement.

So I took up Denis's challenge and began the most intense and demanding project of my career so far: an effort not only to make sense of a complex and dynamic business when everything seems to be changing moment by moment, but also to bring my personal and professional interests together in a way that would appeal to business readers and comics fans alike.

The motives for undertaking this quixotic project are simple. Comics are fun. I've loved them since I was a kid, and I have amassed quite a collection, along with a ridiculous amount of trivia knowledge that comes with the obsession. Writing about them barely seemed like work.

Comics as a medium solve a vexing problem of the information age. At a time when so many shiny things are competing for our attention and demanding our time, comics hit fast and hard. Their design is unique and compelling; the copy is brief; everything is there on the page in one view. Comics excel at telling certain kinds of stories that have proven especially durable and engrossing, but they are handy for delivering all sorts of content and information. They are a big part of the future of communications and a key ingredient in the twenty-first-century media mix, though they often escape our notice. Issues that are now being resolved within the small and insular comics industry will ripple through the global entertainment world and affect the way billions of people consume content.

And comics are big business. They sit at the crossroads of art and commerce. Their unique style and subject matter power Hollywood blockbusters and *New York Times* bestsellers. Scan the lists of all-time box office champions, all-time bestselling video games, top-rated TV shows, and best-trafficked blogs and websites. Comics are all over them. But as an industry, they face many of the problems of the twenty-first-century economy: how to mobilize a massive fan base with diverse and sometimes contradictory interests, how to negotiate the transition to digital distribution, and how to translate the magic they muster on the page to new and disparate media channels.

If any proof were required, just look at Comic-Con International San Diego (hereafter known as Comic-Con or just the Con), the sprawling pop culture festival that takes over San Diego for a week every July and contributes an estimated $163 million to the local economy. Comic-Con draws upwards of 130,000 people (more by some estimates) and sells out almost instantly, with millions more following the proceedings online or through news reports.

My wife, Eunice, and I have been going down to San Diego since the late 1990s, first as attendees and then as part-time event staff. We don't wear costumes or speak Klingon, but we love the craziness, the spectacle, and the energy of so many people all in one place having the time of their lives. We've seen Comic-Con mutate from a "gathering of tribes" into a pop culture singularity: an electrifying, exhausting convergence of comics, movies, TV, video games, fantasy art, fashion, toys, merchandise, and more.

In addition to being an entertainment spectacle and a complete madhouse, Comic-Con is a laboratory in which the global future of media is unspooling in real time. While I was attending the 2011 show, it occurred to me that there could be no better framework for discussing business issues affecting the multibillion-dollar entertainment industry; the various fields of publishing, technology, communications, and distribution; and the changing relationship between pop culture and the global audience than simply walking around Comic-Con and reporting on what I saw.

It turns out that this is an ideal time to shine a spotlight on these issues. The summer of 2011 will go down in history as "peak geek": the moment when comics and nerd-based culture reached a point of total saturation. Characters in CBS's top-rated sitcom *The Big Bang Theory* proudly sport comics-themed gear, hang out at their local comics store, and banter about comics-oriented themes. DC's relaunch of its comics line in September 2011 created a buzz around superhero comics that brought new fans into the fold and jumpstarted the nascent digital channel. The announcements of new movies, TV shows, and web series with ties to comics and comics-based genres are ongoing. Graphic novels continue to win awards and flood the shelves of bookstores and libraries. As 2011 gave way to 2012, there was a palpable quickening on the technology front, with new long-anticipated breakthroughs and convergences occurring almost daily. Just about all the changes that industry watchers have been predicting for years seemed to be manifested simultaneously, while the past melted inexorably away.

Comics are the hamster running in the wheel at the center of this gigantic media contraption. Once despised as subliterate and corrupting, they now command the money and attention of some of the largest corporations on earth. But the hamster is sick—and the symptoms are probably familiar to any content- or marketing-based business that is trying to succeed in the new media environment. Sales have been in free fall, but digital distribution risks cannibalizing the industry's retail channel. Piracy threatens the value of intellectual property assets. Consolidation is changing the traditional management structures: the biggest comic book publishers are tiny divisions of media conglomerates, while independents struggle to survive and wait for their properties to be optioned in other, more lucrative media formats.

Meanwhile the core audience is aging, and conflicting expectations are putting pressure on publishers. Positive market trends are showing signs of slowing. A wave of transformative technologies, creative strategies, and business developments that has been building for a decade is starting to break, and it is highly uncertain whether comics will surf to new heights or get dragged down in the undertow.

The flavor of global popular culture in the twenty-first century depends on how these issues play out. So do the fortunes of a lot of big entertainment, media, and technology companies that have bet big on comics-styled programming and properties. American comics are the product of a unique, idiosyncratic industry: one that is almost entirely reliant on individual creative talent for its success. Like miracle drugs harvested from a remote and exotic rainforest, the supply of high-quality source material is finite, and it is difficult for today's corporate custodians of comics intellectual property (IP) to replicate the specific conditions in which their prized content properties were originally cultivated. Get the formula wrong and the fans stomp off disgusted, leaving owners with a lot of silly characters in costumes. Get it right and magic happens. The vitality of the medium depends on the continuation of this complex relationship among creators, content owners, and fans during a moment of profound business and technological change.

Because of this uncertainty, it is impossible to speak of "the future of comics" as one thing only. Comics are moving in several directions at once: toward the wide-open spaces of broad transmedia saturation, digital distribution, and globalization, and toward the narrowing horizons of fannish insularity, nostalgia, and niche-art connoisseurship. Each of these trajectories has a claim on any possible future of comics and pop culture, and each implies a very different cultural framework for how comics and comics-related media are seen, sold, created, and consumed.

Professionally, these are the things that fascinate me. Demographics, globalization, and changing technology are all forces that I have tracked closely in my work, including my previous books: *Generation Blend, Listening to the Future,* and *Young World Rising.* My sonar is already tuned to listen for these frequencies and interpret how their echoes define the shape of industries and markets.

But as a comics fan, these are the things that worry me. I would like to see the industry get this right because the art form is so unique and compelling, and because the creators who are doing great work in the medium deserve to prosper. So part of my goal in this book, in addition to looking at the wider business implications inherent in the integration of comics into the global media mix, is to see where comics themselves might be heading in a future that is fraught with uncertainty.

Though I bring some analytic tools of my trade to this study, I approach the comics and entertainment industries as an outsider. Within the pop culture business, there are conversations taking place among professionals, consultants, and serious bloggers and journalists who study the industries as their full-time job. These folks have been in the game for years. They are smart, perceptive, and articulate. They have access to inside information that informs their perspective, whereas I am only an observer. They also have skin in the game, sometimes creating "expertise bias," which comes from looking at a problem too closely for too long and becoming personally invested in particular methods and outcomes. I am not without opinions when it comes to comics and pop culture, but my livelihood does not depend on your accepting my preferred vision of the future. My perspective has advantages and drawbacks. I hope you find that the former outweigh the latter.

Then there is Comic-Con itself: a perfect lens through which to examine these issues and a simple point of entry for casual readers who are neither industry experts nor hard-core fans, and who are not that interested in futurism and business strategy. The centrality of Comic-Con to so many different subcultures makes it ideal for spotting emerging trends. It has become the locus and embodiment of the contradictory forces pulling at pop culture and entertainment in the 2010s. It represents everything that can possibly go right—and wrong—about mobilizing a vast army of enthusiasts behind your product and your brand.

I've been attending Comic-Con since the late 1990s, and I've become fairly adept at navigating the frenzy, but no one, not even an author with an agenda, can be everywhere or do everything. Like most attendees, I pick the stuff I'm most interested in and try to see about 10 percent of that. That means I missed a bunch of things that were highly relevant to this book and didn't talk to dozens of people that I probably should have. If I didn't catch up with you or mention something you think is important, it's nothing personal. Managing the Comic-Con experience is about choosing your points of entry; so is this book.

I try not to dwell on the eccentricities of fans, the costumes, or the ubiquity of celebrities, although I am not above a bit of name dropping. Yes, a lot of goofy stuff goes on at the Con. You can read all about it in most generic media reports, and you can ogle the costumes all over the web.

This book does not purport to be an authoritative history of Comic-Con or a complete view of all the activities that take place at the show. For the former, you can turn to the fantastic official fortieth anniversary Comic-Con history book that came out in 2009. For the latter, to the extent that a "complete view" is even possible, I recommend the many great bits of reporting and memoir on the web, curated by Tom Spurgeon via the "Collective Memory" links at his Comics Reporter site. For a different perspective on the events and significance of the 2011 Con, check out *Comic-Con Strikes Again*, the monograph by Douglas Wolk, published as a Kindle single in August 2011.

Finally, I must declare my interests and biases. I like comics. I think they are unique and worthwhile, even the bad ones. People should read them. It would be tragic if the art form died. I also think the people who publish comics are sometimes their own worst enemy.

I like fandom. I think it's healthy to have interests and hobbies. I think it's cool to get together in large groups to celebrate your love of geeky things. I don't really care what you're a fan of, and I'm not inclined to judge people for an overabundance of enthusiasm or knowledge about the stuff that turns them on. I use the terms *nerd*, *geek*, and *fanboy/girl* as descriptions and compliments, not as slights.

I like Comic-Con. Yes, it's crowded and an incredible hassle. Yes, it's an orgy of consumerism and commercialism and apolitical superficiality in the midst of a world full of serious problems. It's not just about comics (it never was), and it's an awkward jumble of serious artists and Hollywood celebrities, historical figures, scholars, and grown men dressed as Wolverine and Lightning Lad. Comic-Con is still a blast, an amazing bargain for the amount of entertainment on offer, and a testament to the dedication and competence of its organizers.

And finally, I am a business analyst, not a pop culture journalist. In my previous work, I have focused on the social implications of digital technology, generational change, globalization, and new business models. That's the lens through which I see the world, even when I look at a subject as close to my heart as comics.

Consequently, there will be quadrant charts, talk of "paradigms," and words like *transmedia*, alongside discussions of Jack Kirby and Robert Crumb. My aim in this book is to balance color and insight, personal passion and analytical observation. It's a tough needle to thread, and I may miss the mark from time to time. Please forgive me.

I hope this book gives readers a flavor of the energy generated at Comic-Con and conveys some of my personal feelings on why it is important to keep that energy alive through the growth and evolution of comics as an art form, a medium, and a business. Comics may not be the most important industry or the most important social and cultural trend in the world today, but comics are a vehicle for our hopes and the extension of our imagination. May they live long and prosper.

Note for Business Readers

You may have noticed that this is a nontraditional topic and a nontraditional format for a book from a business press and from an author whose platform is that of a business/technology futurist. Nevertheless, the challenges faced by the comics and pop culture industry in the 2010s mirror those facing others in entertainment, content, high tech, marketing, and communications, as I've tried to make clear in the business-oriented summaries that follow each section heading in the text. Throughout the narrative, which is intended both to inform business audiences and entertain those with a more general interest in comics and pop culture, you will find a few recurring themes that are relevant across the spectrum of creative industries:

1. **Complexities of a global, transmedia environment.** The rise of giant new, young markets in Asia, Latin America, Africa, and the

Middle East, concurrent with the spread of information networks and digital technologies, presents a huge opportunity for content creators worldwide. Visual media such as comics have the potential for universal appeal across ages and cultures, especially as we push deeper into a postmodern era of mashups, playful appropriation of design and storytelling elements across genres, and engaging, interactive delivery media. Content that originated in comics now has a life in film, video, games, fashion, advertising, toys, and so much more. Content that originated in training manuals, product brochures, textbooks, newspapers, social networks, and performance venues may now have a life in a sequential art format. How are key players across the entertainment world creating transmedia strategies to reach new audiences and cross-pollinate ideas from one medium to others?

2. **Disruptive changes in the delivery/distribution platform.** All media and all content owners are struggling with the challenges of digital delivery. On the one hand, the economics of disintermediation are compelling; on the other, the shift from a physical supply chain and distribution network to a digital model must be handled gradually or companies will cut off their existing revenue streams before replacements can come online. There are also the problems raised by piracy and control of IP assets, plus the hard-to-measure role of customer service expertise in the retail environment, which we may miss when it is gone. The music and video industries struggled with this during the 2000s; now it's the turn of comics. What have they learned, and what new problems are they encountering?

3. **Generational change within the audience and the business.** We are at a historic moment where most content is being

produced by the two older generational cohorts (Baby Boomers, born 1946–1962, and Generation X, born 1963–1980) for a younger audience of mostly Millennials (born 1981–2000). Not only does the new audience have different interests, aesthetics, and values from its elders, but it also has a fundamentally different orientation toward digital technology. Meanwhile, the cohorts driving the creative side of the business are influenced by their formative experiences in a very different phase of the history of the medium. In comics, where respect for history and continuity is critical to maintaining audience engagement, the tensions around generational change are especially pronounced and problematic. How is the industry reconciling different modes of audience engagement, and what can others learn from its successes and failures?

4. **Entrepreneurial innovation putting pressure on incumbents.** Some of the most disruptive changes in the business world over the last 20 years have come from insurgent entrepreneurial start-ups: think Amazon, Netflix, Google, and Facebook. Each of these companies came to market with a new model that forced everyone in related businesses to rethink their pricing, distribution, and partnership arrangements. The same thing is now occurring in the comics industry with the arrival of extremely savvy and ambitious digital comics distributors that behave much more like tech start-ups than like traditional comics/entertainment/publishing entities. What opportunities and challenges does this create for the industry?

5. **Tension between centralization and democratization in the creative industry.** New platforms are empowering individual

creators to reach their audience directly, and enabling the audience to cocreate its experience to a greater extent than ever before. This introduces uncertainty into an economy where huge companies have invested in top-down control and centralization of the production of IP, and are counting on proven brands to generate predictable revenue. How will those big investments play out when creative competition can come from anywhere?

CHAPTER 1

DAY ZERO:
HOTELOWEEN

t's a cold, rainy March day in Seattle, and my wife, Eunice, has taken the morning off to dial the same telephone number over and over until she gets through. Across the room, I am on two different computers trying to load a website that went live just seconds ago. The hourglass on the browser spins as the page starts to fill one character at a time, as if we were still in 1988 and connecting to CompuServe with a 300-baud modem.

Welcome to "Hoteloween," the term coined by comics journalist Heidi MacDonald for the dreadful day when the hotel reservation lines for the San Diego Comic-Con open. Though the show itself is still four and a half months in the future, the next moments are crucial. In a high-stakes game of musical chairs, more than a hundred thousand frenzied attendees are angling for a limited supply of discounted rooms in hotels near the San Diego Convention Center.

If you don't get through in the first hour, you are likely to be stuck miles away, out in Mission Valley. If you wait more than a day, you will be lucky to get a room for the "special rack rates" that apply that week, which can run over $500 per night. Before the end of March, just about every hotel, vacation rental, catered apartment, and couch in the greater San Diego area will be reserved by fans who are willing to do anything to make it to the big show.

Securing a place to stay is just one of the many hurdles facing would-be Comic-Con attendees in recent years as the show has become *the* pop culture event of the summer. Tickets, hotels, airfare, onsite registration, lines that make Disneyland look like a county fairground—all these make going to Comic-Con an uncertain, frustrating, expensive, and complicated undertaking.

What's so special about Comic-Con that it generates this much crazy activity so far in advance? After all, not many people read comics these days. Sales of the bestselling titles in early 2011 topped out at half the annual attendance at Comic-Con. Even if you're a fan, there are plenty of other conventions around the country that don't require nearly the same effort and preparation.

Yet starting around 2000, attendance at the San Diego Comic-Con has skyrocketed, breaking record after record, to the point that it now takes over downtown San Diego for the better part of a week. During those five days in July, fans have been known to line up for days, sleeping on the streets just to get a chance to see one panel. Parties go on all night. Entire blocks are transformed by giant floats, banners, and structures erected just for Con-time. Every year, the Con is accompanied by thousands of reports of different aspects of the proceedings that amount to a room full of blind men describing an elephant. Even when you separate the signal from the noise, there is still so much signal that it is impossible to get a clear reading on what just happened.

Photo by Doug Kline

Comic-Con takes over the neighborhood around the San Diego Convention Center for the better part of a week.

Comic books and Comic-Con alone are not responsible for this; comics culture is. Comics culture is the blend of superheroes, animation, movies, video games, television shows, art, fashion, toys, accessories, and personalities that has emerged as the result of a postmillennial convergence of media and the concurrent explosion of online channels for connecting fans with the objects of their fandom.

Comics culture is a tightly woven matrix of art and commerce. Extending out in one direction is the "comics as art form" continuum, in which the medium of graphic storytelling (pictures in sequence with text) is applied in all kinds of formats (comic books, webcomics, graphic novels, comic strips) and all kinds of styles (minimalist, "mainstream," fine art) to tell all kinds of stories, from superheroes to satire to autobiography to political commentary. The other path heads toward "comics as genre," where the distinctive graphic look and storytelling elements associated specifically with *superhero* comic books, such as plot-driven continuity, the creation of entire fictional universes, and the predominance of supernatural and power-fantasy motifs, have taken hold in other media like film, television, and video games.

Over the past 20 years, comics have expanded in both the artistic and commercial dimensions, moving from the fringes of the high culture and entertainment worlds to the centers of both. The comics art form has been embraced by some of the most serious and accomplished creators working today all around the world. Comics aesthetics and comics genres, especially superheroes, are mainstays of the entertainment industry, responsible for billions in revenues across various media and through various licensing tie-ins.

The appeal of comics-related subject matter, whether it is fantasy-based, humorous, or in a more literary style, is rooted in the medium's unique use of words and pictures to tell stories. Comics are catnip to consciousness. They engage us at multiple levels: through stylized visuals; through narration; through their ability to create convincing, self-contained worlds; through the way they make preposterous characters and situations more real and plausible than everyday life; and through the distortions of time and space that are possible only with the medium of sequential art.

The simplicity and accessibility of the comics medium appeals to kids who might be too young to read the words, but who can follow the story through pictures. The fanciful story lines capture young imaginations, especially when they are reinforced across media through cartoons, video games, and prose fiction in comics-type genres (fantasy, mystery, heroic adventure, and so on). Comics exert a powerful allure for older folks who remember them basted in the glow of nostalgia. Graphic novels, webcomics, and manga (Asian-style comics, typically embracing a wider range of genres) engage readers who have no interest in traditional comics subjects.

The power of the medium combines with the curious history of comics in the United States to create irresistible intrigue for certain kinds of people. Comics themselves are full of details and story points to amuse obsessives. Every artist has a unique approach to storytelling, layout, and rendering, giving the connoisseur much to appreciate. Comics are sequentially numbered, making them easy to catalog, giving them a built-in appeal for completists and collectors. Publishers and creators are the subject of gossip and lore; real insiders know the stories. Even comics fandom has a history. All of this renders the world of comics more than a hobby and more than a category of "media content." In terms of stickiness—that intangible factor that keeps the audience coming back for more, so desirable in today's attention-deficit world—the medium makes superglue seem like Teflon. That extra richness is what makes comics important in the wider spectrum of entertainment media, and what makes the adaptation and evolution of comics so problematic.

Comics fandom transcends economic class, race, region, educational attainment, and (despite stereotypes) gender. For decades before the mainstreaming of comics and nerd culture, those who remained fans beyond childhood tended to be intellectuals, autodidacts, and outsiders whose peculiar interests turned out to be well suited to the emerging information economy. A disproportionately large number of creative professionals are or were involved in some aspect of comics culture at some point in their lives. This secret army of comics fans includes sleeper cells throughout the entertainment, marketing, high-tech, and media industries who signal their affiliations by subtle and overt means, ranging from the occasional adept use of comics-tinged imagery to the advocacy of comics-oriented projects "done right" (as fans would want them) from their platforms as decision makers in creative enterprises. Fans have smuggled the aesthetics of comics into design, advertising, and fine art in addition to entertainment media. This has led to a critical mass of visibility and institutional acceptance of comics within twenty-first-century global culture at all levels.

All these unique features of the culture of comics cause people to *participate* in their entertainment rather than passively consume it. People of all ages and backgrounds want to engage with comics, discuss their favorite characters, meet the creators, and immerse themselves in the phantasmagoric landscapes of imagination that comics call into being. They do this online, through fanzines, at comics stores, and at the conventions that have spread over the past decade in the wake of the San Diego Comic-Con's phenomenal growth.

Comic-Con is ground zero for comics culture in all its forms. If you want the unique feeling of being at the center of a particular universe and are not superrich or super-well connected, Comic-Con is one of the few places anywhere that you can get it. The intensity is awe inspiring. Today, every marketing and branding expert is looking for ways to engage "raving fans." They don't come much more raving than the crowds that descend on San Diego in July. Some of the largest companies on earth spend millions every summer building megabooths, throwing parties, and giving away mountains of swag to impress and delight this superengaged, superconnected audience.

But marketers beware: comics fans are not an easily stampeded rabble of consumer zombies. Long before Twitter and Yelp and social media, this hyperaware and detail-oriented audience grew accustomed to voicing opinions on every aspect of the art, industry, and hobby. The complex relationship between creators and their audience, which plays out at Comic-Con, holds many lessons and cautionary examples for anyone trying to mobilize a mass market around their content in today's connected world.

Comic-Con in the 2010s is not just the pop culture industry in microcosm; it is the pop culture industry incarnate. Everyone and everything relating to comics and their connection to the wider entertainment industries is here, under one roof, in person. For five days in July, Stan Lee, Steven Spielberg, the cast of *Twilight*, the makers of bestselling video games, graphic novelists reviewed in the *New York Times*, the publishers of the first comics fanzines of the 1960s, the proprietors of the most-read comics blogs and news sites, hundreds of dealers and exhibitors, and throngs of hard-core fans all occupy the same space and breathe the same air. Other shows have emerged recently to challenge San Diego for sheer numbers, but they lack the pedigree and tradition that San Diego Comic-Con has after more than 40 years. Also, San Diego is a two-hour drive from Hollywood, and that makes a difference.

Hollywood has been using Comic-Con as a massive focus group and marketing megaphone for at least a decade, serving up megawatt star power in a bid for street cred with the most vocal and influential fans. The cycle of hype and spectacle has propelled Comic-Con into something greater than the sum of its parts. It has become a media event unto itself, generating crowds of gawkers from around the world.

Amid the chaos and the costumes, the glitz and the sprawl, Comic-Con is also the meeting place of the global pop media industry and the creative profession. It is where tastes are made and deals are done, where new talent is discovered and crazy ideas are unleashed on an unsuspecting public. What happens in San Diego doesn't stay in San Diego: it ripples out and influences how billions experience entertainment around the world. And everyone wants to be there.

It used to be possible to register for tickets just days before the show, or even just walk up and buy a badge at the convention center, as I did when I first made the trip to San Diego back in 1997. I had recently rekindled my childhood love of comics, which had lain dormant for nearly 15 years, and I wanted to make up for lost time by attending the king of comic conventions. I'd been to other shows as a kid—typically a few thousand fans gathering in a hotel ballroom over a weekend to swap old comics and meet a few industry pros—so I thought I had some idea of what I was in for. On a whim, I bought a plane ticket and found a nearby hotel for $80 per night.

When I entered the exhibit hall for the first time, I was stunned by the scale. Attendance that year was estimated at 40,000, and the San Diego Convention Center, before its expansion, was about 40 percent of its current size. Still, the show was huge. Everywhere I turned, I saw legendary comic artists drawing sketches and chatting with fans, or priceless collectibles for sale. I went to the Eisner Awards, a ceremony named for comics' reigning master, Will Eisner (1917–2005), honoring the year's best work and creators. At the end of the evening, I somehow ended up in a card game with Eisner himself(!) and a bunch of other industry pros at the afterparty. I went to panels and film previews, snapped photos of people in crazy costumes, hung out with other fans, and experienced an amazing sense of community and camaraderie among a crowd of total strangers united only by their common interest.

Eunice, who had had no exposure to comics or comics culture, was intrigued enough by my frenzied account of the proceedings to join me the following year. A few minutes at Comic-Con and it was all over: she took to the hobby as if she'd been bitten by a radioactive spider. These days, my interest in comics themselves is more casual, but Eunice regularly subscribes to nearly a dozen Marvel, Dark Horse, and DC titles, reads scads of online comics and comics blogs, and is crushed if she is not first in line for any *Star Trek*–related event. She's not quite as fussy about the art, the creative personnel, and the story continuity as a lifelong comic geek like me, but she is as avid and opinionated as anyone.

She is also thorough and tenacious—qualities that have become increasingly important in planning for the Con each year. Sometime around the mid-2000s, as the Con mushroomed from 40,000 to well over 100,000 attendees, and exhibitors now included Hollywood studios that brought small armies of publicists, booth staff, and VIPs down from LA, the online scramble for hotels metastasized into a crazed frenzy that crashes banks of servers and overloads phone circuits.

These days, even the simple act of registering for the Con has become a chore. The first year that the Con was sold out in advance was 2008; no passes of any kind were available to walk-up customers. The next year, the Con was sold out by November. The most desirable tickets for the 2011 convention sold out two hours before the 2010 convention closed, well before the vast majority of people ever had access to them. In 2011, thousands of desperate attendees slept out on the cold stone walkway behind the Hyatt hotel for their chance to preregister for the next year's Con when the passes were sold each morning. Starting in 2012, prospective attendees must register for an ID number months ahead of time just to have a chance to purchase memberships later.

Even in the prefrenzy days of the early 2000s, Eunice took no chances. She routinely registered for the next year's Con on preview night, once bragging that she'd scored double-digit badge numbers (that is, among the first 99 sold). I now see that she was a better futurist than I was regarding the need for preparation. But thanks to her efforts and the good relationships she has established with some important people, we have managed to cling to a decent Con experience despite a rising tide of hassles, costs, and inconveniences.

This time, even her well-coordinated assault on the Travel Planners reservation desk was to no avail. I struggled with the slow website, and Eunice finally got through on the phone, but by that time all nearby hotels were sold out. All that was left was the wait list and the nerve-wracking process of checking back at random times to see if you might catch a split-second availability created by a cancellation. Panic set in.

It took long weeks of wrangling to get our situation sorted out. In the end, through nothing short of divine intervention, we were able to get discount-rate rooms in the Marriott Marina—not only a cool and comfortable spot, but the closest hotel to the convention center. This is not a common occurrence; even long-time pros sometimes find themselves sleeping on couches or missing the Con altogether because they got caught in the hotel squeeze. Eunice, who will probably have "better safe than sorry" inscribed on her tombstone, was not content with my explanation that the Force was strong with us. She confirmed and reconfirmed and re-re-re-confirmed right up until the moment we left.

But sure enough, the path that led to this book kicked off with a most unlikely turn of events: a Hoteloween miracle.

CHAPTER 2

WEDNESDAY:
PREVIEW

On the morning of Tuesday, July 19, we headed to Sea-Tac airport for our flight to San Diego. In the departure lounge, we scanned the crowd of families, business travelers, and vacationers for the telltale signs of membership in the tribe of True Believers.

Tuesday was a bit early; the real crowds start to gather on the morning and afternoon flights on Wednesday. Still, we were not alone. There in the corner was a big guy with bushy sideburns, wearing an XXL Green Lantern T-shirt over cargo shorts and sneakers, with an art portfolio on the chair next to him. Probability of Con attendance: greater than 99 percent. A few seats down, Eunice spied a young woman with black eyeliner and lipstick, sporting a tote bag from Emily the Strange, sitting next to a pale friend with lidded eyes wearing ornate Cthulhu-themed earrings. We would spot them at the Trickster party in a couple of days, in line for the sushi bar. Then there was the thirty-something guy reading the *Watchmen* trade paperback, the young dad browsing *Newsarama* on his iPad while his kids played *Star Wars* on their Game Boys, the older guy in horn-rimmed glasses with a battered leather satchel that doubtless contained a tabbed and underlined copy of the *Overstreet Comic Book Price Guide* . . .

Over the next two days, in airports all around the world, underground rivers of fandom were bursting out into the open, forming the tributaries of a mighty torrent surging toward San Diego. When we landed at Lindbergh Field three hours later, we saw more likely suspects in the crowd filtering toward the taxi stand, pulled inexorably together like the pools of liquid metal reconstituting the "bad cop" cyborg in the final moments of *Terminator 2*.

We took a cab to the Marriott and admired downtown San Diego, decked out in banners and signs to welcome its largest convention of the year. As we approached up the circular drive in front of the two gleaming metallic towers of the hotel, workmen on scaffolds were busy attaching a 30-story banner to the side of the building advertising an upcoming fantasy-themed movie.

The Con does not officially begin until Wednesday evening around 6 p.m., when the exhibit hall opens to attendees, but Tuesday and Wednesday see a rising crescendo of activity as exhibitors set up their booths, attendees and professionals brave long lines to claim their badges and swag bags, and various organizations stage pre-parties and meet-ups ahead of the full-on craziness of the next 100 hours. The anticipation generates some anxiety among the army of service workers who work in and around the convention center area. They either know what they are in for firsthand or have heard the stories from traumatized coworkers.

Photo by Doug Kline

Hotels around the convention center are decked out with giant banners for Comic-Con week.

"Here for Comic-Con?" asked the hotel receptionist with a tight smile. When we replied in the affirmative, she reached under the counter and produced special card keys sponsored by movie studios and comic companies, laying them flat on the desk. Mine was branded *Supernatural*. Eunice's was *Scooby-Doo*.

"Can I have a *Smallville* one instead?" my wife asked, sliding the card back across the counter. I could see the hotel clerk scan her face for signs that this might be a joke. It most assuredly was not.

There were few obvious signs of Comic-Con in the hotel lobby, although we noticed a luggage cart loaded with *Star Wars* storm trooper armor. Later in the day, crews would mount gruesome zombie posters on the inside of certain elevators (with doors marked "Don't Open: Dead Inside" in the style of the *Walking Dead* comic

Elevators at the Marriott are transformed into marketing vehicles.

book and TV series). Parents with small children quickly learned to avoid these elevators and wait for the next one.

We got to our room and went to the balcony overlooking Harbor Drive and the city skyline. It was a glorious sunny afternoon, and the streets were nearly empty.

We had made it, and we were sitting pretty, with all our plans and social events set for the next six days. All that was left was for the storm to break.

Backing Into the Future

Every industry benefits from looking strategically at its market and accounting for future uncertainty.

This book is about two things: Comic-Con and the future of comics as it relates to pop culture. As we will see, these turn out to be very much related. But before we start weaving the strands together, let's take a moment to examine why the future of comics is so uncertain, and why anyone should care.

These days, comics seem to be everywhere: on every movie screen, video console, hoodie, and T-shirt. Comic-inspired toys and merchandise dominate the shelves at youth-oriented retailers like Hot Topic. Graphic novels are reviewed in the *New York Times*. Comic artists headline gallery openings and museum shows. Even the most ardent fans could never have dreamed that comics would enjoy so much attention and respect.

And yet, sales of individual comic books have shrunk to perilously low levels. There was a time in recent memory when comics could sell a million or more copies per issue. In the months leading up to the 2011 Con, "bestsellers" in a given month rarely broke 75,000, and midlist books were selling in the low 10,000s or less. This was for characters and stories that receive literally billions of dollars in exposure and promotion from every corner of the media. More than 70 million people bought tickets to the 2008 Batman movie *The Dark Knight*. Fewer than 70,000 people bought the July 2011 issue of *Batman: The Dark Knight*—the top-selling Batman title that month and the number 7 title overall, according to industry sales data.

Periodical issues (sometimes called "floppies" or "pamphlets," as opposed to "trades" or "graphic novels," which refer to bound editions) are the fundamental storytelling unit of the medium, and the immediate source of employment for most of the people on the creative side of the business. Floppies can be produced on a regular schedule (usually monthly) and sold at an affordable price. At 18 to 24 pages of content, they are usually long enough to tell a satisfying chunk of story, develop characters, and give space for the artist to show off some technique in narrative art, illustration, and page composition. The characters, story lines, and universes that today have so much value in other media were built up in this format, issue by issue, month by month.

Longer and shorter formats are also viable, of course, just as symphonies and jingles can be great pieces of music, but they are not songs. Can you imagine a pop music industry without songs as the primary format? Can you imagine a construction industry without bricks? Today, we are closer than ever to a future of the comics industry that does not include comic books.

Comic books in the 2010s are like the run-down "historic district" of a city whose growth is all at the edges. The whole apparatus for the creation, publication, and distribution of comic books these days seems little more than an expense required to keep the intellectual property assets current and the trademarks up to date. Even the unlikely return of peak-era sales of DC and Marvel titles would barely rate a footnote in the annual reports of those companies' corporate owners (Time Warner and Disney, respectively).

How did comics find themselves alone in this dark alley, so late at night?

The short answer is that the retail distribution system for comic books is tied up in a fist-sized knot and has been for the last two decades. Starting in the 1980s, most comics publishers discontinued newsstand sales, where unsold issues could be returned for a refund, in favor of a "direct market" system that shipped comic books exclusively to specialized comic book stores on a nonreturn-able basis. Initially this worked out well for everyone: comics fans got the convenience of a one-stop shop and a better-quality product; publishers realized higher margins and better sell-through (no returns!), and could charge higher prices for books targeted to hard-core enthusiasts who hungered for denser stories and art, and more production value, than the old mass newsstand readership.

But it turns out there is a problem with distributing your product exclusively through independently owned retail stores run by and for your products' biggest fans. Despite the efforts of some active and visionary retailers, the odor of overgrown adolescent males hangs heavy over many comic book shops, creating a forbidding environment for women, kids, and casual fans who might have an interest in the material but don't want to put up with the clannishness and know-it-allism of the old-school comic book culture. *The Simpsons* character Comic Book Guy and his shop are, unfortunately, too close to the truth to be considered a parody of many actual comics stores. And if you don't go to comics stores because you don't like the real-life Comic Book Guy, it's very tough to buy and become a regular reader of comics.

At the same time the distribution channel for comic books was narrowing, the subject matter of the most recognizable titles became increasingly insular. Even as the culture moved toward a broader acceptance of comics as art and literature, the "mainstream"* industry dug deeper into the genre of superheroes, telling longer and more convoluted stories that depended on readers knowing years or

---

* I put the term "mainstream" in quotes throughout the text to avoid confusion, because in the comics industry, it means the opposite of what it means elsewhere. That is, the term "mainstream comics" usually refers to those featuring superheroes—a genre catering to a specialty market of fans—whereas "alternative" or "independent" comics have a wider range of subject matter and potential audience appeal.

decades of the characters' histories. Why? Because this was what the regular customers at the comics shops wanted to read (and what the fans-turned-pro who staffed the big companies wanted to produce), so it was what the retailers ordered—often to the exclusion of more adventurous independent titles that could appeal to a wider audience. Fans of the *X-Men* movies or the highly accessible *X-Men: Evolution* animated series who dared venture into a comics shop were faced with more than a dozen ongoing *X-Men* series and hundreds of graphic novels and collected editions. Most of them made the reasonable calculation that it was not worth the time or the money to join the boys' club.

This whole story is so well known within the industry that professionals rarely bother complaining about it anymore. Bloggers, creators, publishers, and independent fans have beaten the horse to death, then performed a voodoo ritual to exhume the carcass and started beating the zombie horse. However, despite nearly a quarter century of griping, the disaster that is always just around the corner for comics has never quite arrived.

The closest the industry came to collapse was in the mid-1990s, when a speculator-driven market bubble burst and took out a handful of publishers, hundreds of retailers, and all but the largest of the wholesale distributors. Even mighty Marvel Comics, the longtime market leader, teetered on the edge of bankruptcy. But then, new sources of revenue came swooping in to save the day: bookstore sales, manga (Japanese comics with huge toy, game, media, and fashion crossover that appealed to girls and tweens), merchandise licensing, and Hollywood dollars to bring comics to the big screen.

The boom in all of these areas has allowed the industry to ignore grievous structural problems in the distribution of its core product for the past decade and a half. It has also enabled publishers to postpone difficult decisions about the move to digital format that was disrupting the business of *all* media, from music to movies to books. But now there are troubling signs that the reprieve may be over.

It was against this backdrop that I attended a half-day conference on the Future of Comics, sponsored by the industry group ICv2. I was interested to see how the comics industry was talking about itself and its future—not just because I was contemplating writing about it, but because comics needs some good strategic thinking if it is to survive the uncertainties ahead.

This event was by no means the highlight of the convention and was not typical of the other activities that go on. However, I am going to take some time to discuss the proceedings because the issues that were raised provide a useful context for many of the weekend's subsequent activities and conversations. Think of this as the orchestral overture to the opera that follows. Skip it if you find it boring; it will still be here if you get confused later.

ICv2 has been around since the 1980s and is the authoritative source for market data on comics sales, industry trends, and media crossover. This year's event, presented under the auspices of Comic-Con, was held in one of the conference rooms of the Marriott. About 100 industry mavens and media watchers plunked down the $200 registration fee to absorb a program that included a state-of-the-market report from ICv2 honcho Milton Griepp, followed by panel discussions on the state of comics in Hollywood, "transmedia" properties, and the migration from paper to digital.

Despite the pop culture subject matter, this was every bit an industry conference, with keynote speakers muttering into feedback-prone microphones, glitchy PowerPoint presentations, attendees doodling on the complimentary notepads, and panelists introduced by monotonous recitations of the biographies that were printed in the conference program. I attend plenty of these events for all kinds of businesses, often on the other side of the podium as a speaker; the sense of familiarity in the proceedings was both reassuring and disconcerting.

Griepp led off the session with a data-rich address that underlined the perilous financial condition of the comics market. Sales of individual comics in the United States average around $270 to $300 million per year for books usually priced at $2.99 to $3.99 at retail, available mainly at the country's estimated 1,800 to 2,000 independently owned comics stores. Graphic novels (an umbrella term for any bound edition, whether it is a collection of previously printed materials or an original work) account for another $300 to $315 million, and digital comics clocked in at $6 to $18 million, for a total market of about $625 million.

According to ICv2's numbers, sales declined across the board from recent highs in 2008—not surprising, considering the general state of the economy. The problem is that floppy sales really can't go much lower. Most midlist titles are barely viable. Even at $3.99 per copy, books that sell less than 3,000 units at retail are hard-pressed to cover the costs of printing, distribution, and retail markup, not to mention the paychecks for the writers, artists, letterers, colorists, and editors who produce them.

Publishers typically expect to make the money back when the poor-selling individual issues are collected in deluxe trade editions, sold through wider channels at prices ranging from $10 to $12 for basic black-and-white paperbacks to ultra-fancy "Ultimate" or "Omnibus" hardcovers that can retail for $75 or more. These have become so ubiquitous that large numbers of readers skip the monthly books altogether and "wait for the trade" to get the entire story line collected in a more convenient format.

Since the mid-1990s, sales of trade editions of comics, whether original graphic novels or collections of previously published material, boomed—mostly because they were distributed on a returnable basis through bookstores rather than specialty comics shops. These new outlets gave publishers a way around the fist-sized knot of the comics store direct market, especially once high-traffic big-box bookstores like Borders and Barnes & Noble started featuring trade editions in prominent in-store displays that encouraged impulse purchases.

That's why the next item in Griepp's presentation hit especially hard. The graphic novel market had been staggered by the reversal of fortunes of the national bookselling chains, which were suffering from online competition, internal management issues, and the general economic downturn. After more than a decade of steadily increasing sales, graphic novels were down more than 5 percent in 2010—before the worst news for the bookstore chains really started to hit. Then, just days before the 2011 conference, Borders had gone into final liquidation after circling the drain for months. This caused much lamentation and rending of garments in the comics business because Borders had been such a pivotal player in the graphic novel explosion, and it was unlikely that Amazon or other online retailers could create the same kind of impulse-buying momentum. The demise of Waldenbooks, Borders's downmarket cousin, left comics without an important presence in the nation's shopping malls, where the chain served as a gateway for many young readers who would not have seen them elsewhere.

Griepp revealed that the industry had suffered another blow with the collapse of the market for manga, the Japanese-style comics that had proved so popular with tweens and young girls and had brought new blood into the world of comics/pop culture fandom. Once fueled by the breakout success of crossover proper-ties like Pokémon, Sailor Moon, Dragonball, and Naruto, manga in the United States has now gone a half-decade without a big hit. Young readers have moved on, and one of the largest publishers, Tokyo Pop, closed its doors in 2010. Another large player, Bandai Entertainment, would announce that it was leaving the manga business and restructuring in 2012. This is another area where the collapse of Borders and the teetering health of other book chains really hurt: most manga sales come through bookstores, not com-ics shops.

Finally, Griepp reported that digital comics showed remarkable growth in the first year in which the medium met its ideal hardware platform in the Apple iPad. Of course, growth is inevitable: digital comics were starting at zero. Neither big publishers nor indepen-dent creators had been able to drive much revenue on the web, but the advent of convenient reading devices and a secure transactional delivery model have set the stage for a veritable gold rush. ICv2 presented some rudimentary data about the state of the digital mar-ket and the emerging ecosystem of digital providers and platforms. There would be more on that later in the program.

Griepp concluded his downbeat recitation to a smattering of applause, then quickly introduced the next panel before too many attendees could slip out to the restroom or hit the coffee table at the back of the room.

The second group on the stage consisted of agents who repre-sented comics and comic creators to the wider entertainment world, helping them get movie deals and licensing agreements. This is where the action in comics has been for the better part of the past decade. The success of the *Spider-Man* and *X-Men* franchises in the early 2000s set off a feeding frenzy in which Hollywood studios frantically waded into every corner of the comics publishing world to option as many properties as possible.

Comics have been fodder for the movies as far back as the 1930s, but the current cycle is different in both its intensity and its duration. This time around, Hollywood hasn't merely skimmed the surface with blue chip properties like *Batman* and the *Fantastic Four*; it delved deep into the stacks to find titles to exploit. Over the past decade, cult favorites (*V for Vendetta, Sin City, Scott Pilgrim*), second-stringers (*Iron Man, Green Lantern, Elektra*), obscure indie books (*Road to Perdition, Whiteout*) and critically acclaimed classics (*Watchmen, The Spirit, American Splendor*) all got the star treatment, with A-list casts and directors and amazing visual effects.

The results, both commercial and artistic, have been mixed. Still, for years agents and studio reps prowled the Comic-Con exhibit hall with contracts at the ready, like Armani-clad Prince Charmings cruising the orphanages and poorhouses looking for Cinderellas to take to the Grand Ball. For a while it seemed as if any cartoonist with a pulse and a few issues scattered on his Artists' Alley table held a short-odds ticket in a high-stakes race.

Considering the disparity between comics publishing money and Hollywood option money (not to mention the fame and fortune that awaited if a film was actually produced), a lot of creative types with no special interest in comics decided that the fastest route to Tinseltown was through Graphic Novel Gulch. The 2000s saw a whole slew of new publishers arrive on the scene whose entire business plans seemed to focus on getting their titles made into movies or TV shows. This gave the comics space a veneer of vitality and glamour despite the deep decay in sales and readership, and it made Comic-Con ground zero if you harbored ambitions of being the Next Big Thing in the entertainment world.

The message from the agents on the panel was that the big Hollywood party may not be over quite yet, but it's probably a good idea for you to finish those drinks and remember where you left your coat. Deals are getting harder to come by. Projects are no longer being green-lighted on spec; you need a full script and some name talent attached. Producers are beginning to believe that the reservoir of bankable ideas is running dry, and the big marketing benefits of catering to the crowd of comics cognoscenti are starting to yield diminishing returns. Why gamble on a $200 million-plus special effects budget for an iffy, second-tier comic book property when you could strike gold with the next Judd Apatow goofball comedy?

As we sat in the Marriott conference center in mid-July, three enormous comic-inspired blockbusters had already opened (Marvel's *Thor* and *X-Men: First Class*, and the unfortunate DC/Warner space opera *Green Lantern*). Two others, Marvel's *Captain America* and *Cowboys and Aliens* (based on a little-known 2006 graphic novel), were set to debut two days later at the Con, with Steven Spielberg and Peter Jackson's *Adventures of Tintin* waiting in the wings and the big guns of *Batman*, *The Avengers*, and *Spider-Man* trained on the summer of 2012. Movie studios were setting up million-dollar booths in the exhibit hall next door, and the movie buzz around Comic-Con was at stun-level volume. Truly it felt like the party was still in full swing. But in Hollywood, nothing is as it seems. If studios become more selective or, worse, decide en masse that comics are yesterday's news, huge swaths of the comics industry will be decimated.

Next up, after a much-needed break, was a panel on digital comics featuring top-level representatives of publishers, distributors, retailers, professionals, and online companies.

Cowboys and Aliens, the Universal/ Dreamworks movie based on a graphic novel, had its world premiere at the 2011 Comic-Con.

You would think that digital comics would offer a neat way out for the industry. Comics need to expand their audience; the web and app stores provide easy means of access. Tablets, which are now becoming mainstream consumer devices, are a great way to read comics—in fact, comics may be the "killer app" that drives market demand for tablets and high-end e-book readers. Digital delivery does away with the expense of printing and distributing paper copies, potentially breaking the cycle of increasing cover prices without cutting the throats of creators or publishers. Digital comics never go out of stock. Online channels like the Apple iTunes Store, Amazon, and Netflix are already well established in the minds and habits of consumers, so comics publishers don't need to reinvent the wheel to get their products into the hands of paying customers. Digital delivery even solves the problem of where to keep all those old comics once you've read them.

And yet, in the Bizarro world of the comics industry, all these pluses are actually minuses. Once again, it comes down to the retail channel and its advocates, who assume that any sales of digital comics will come directly out of their bottom line. Comics retailers are in such dire straits that the loss of even 20 percent of their regular customers to digital sales would put many of them out of business, taking the entire direct market down with them. Publishers are still dependent on the retail channel, no matter how sick and dysfunctional it has become. They can't burn that bridge until they are safely across it, but they can't take more than a few steps without setting it on fire.

During most of the 2000s, comics publishers saw themselves as having little to gain and a lot to lose by taking the plunge into digital, especially if this zero-sum dynamic with respect to the direct market applied. Because most of the big players were reluctant to make their comics available in digital format through legitimate channels, the fleet of pirates who scanned the printed books and put them online, usually on BitTorrent sites, had the seas to themselves. Readers who were ready and willing to pay for digital comics had no one to give their money to; the publishers themselves needlessly risked creating a whole generation of consumers who expect digital comics to be free.

Even into the 2010s, digital sales were minuscule relative to sales of paper copies (about 1 to 3 percent, or $6 to $18 million in a $625 million market, according to ICv2). The only titles making waves as digital releases were licensed properties with no real footprint in the direct market, such as *Transformers* and *Pocket God*. The technology and the business issues were complex, and many of the old-school fans who occupy editorial offices at the comics companies did not believe in their hearts that traditional comic readers were all that interested in giving up the "collectible" paper floppies.

It took outside players to bring order to the digital market. In the late 2000s, a few companies started building apps to format comics for mobile devices and sell them through various app stores, using security that tied the files to the applications so that they couldn't be shared. These start-ups were ideally positioned when the tablet boom hit. In the months prior to the summer of 2011, the leading digital distributor, ComiXology, had made a series of announcements about distribution deals, new programs for retailers, and alliances with systems and device makers. ComiXology's cofounder and CEO, David Steinberger, at age 40 one of the youngest people in a room devoted to discussing the future of comics, waxed enthusiastic about the company's widening horizons, the mushrooming number of titles available for download on the site (now over 4,000), and its strategy to bring retailers into the fold through an affiliate program.

ComiXology has had only modest success in real terms so far, but there is evidence that the company is making some headway in changing minds around the industry. Still, everyone in the room, which was full of people who were dependent on brick-and-mortar retail sales, was careful not to suggest that digital migration meant the end of the direct market, and pointed proudly to various efforts to keep retailers in the game. "Do you think Sony Music gave a shit about keeping mom-and-pop record stores in business?" someone on the digital comics panel asked. A murmur of approval rippled through the audience.

With a workable model potentially in place, the current controversy at the time of the 2011 conference was around "day and date digital release"—that is, making the digital versions available simultaneously with the printed copies. Although a few smaller publishers were experimenting with day-and-date as far back as 2008, the real action is with the market leaders, Marvel and DC, and their reluctance to fully embrace digital as a primary channel made it more risky for others to stick their necks out.

Just before the summer, DC announced its big move—making all 52 books in its linewide "New 52" relaunch available for day-and-date download starting September 1; Marvel followed suit with a day-and-date strategy for its bestselling "Ultimate" books, and, later in the fall, announced that its entire line will be available same-day digital by April 2012. In the final months of 2011, there was a spate of announcements and a lot of optimism about "record-setting" digital sales (estimated at around 10,000 units for top sellers), but very little actual data.

The next challenge is pricing. To avoid competing with retailers, the price to download a digital comic online can't be lower than the price for print, despite the huge cost efficiencies of digital distribution and the fact that readers don't "own" their digital comics in the same way that they do the paper issues. A price of $2.99 or $3.99 to download a single issue is too high a barrier for a lot of readers, especially those who are accustomed to paying nothing on pirate and BitTorrent sites. Publishers are terrified of dropping digital prices below print prices for fear that retailers will retaliate by canceling orders, but there won't be enough digital readers until the price drops. The fist-sized knot strikes again.

So at a time when so much other uncertainty hovers in the air, the transition to digital distribution has become an existential crisis. If Hollywood money and the bookstore channel dry up before publishers have successfully migrated their audience (and their revenue stream) to digital, they will be stuck with the same dysfunctional retail system and an acutely shrinking, aging audience. In that scenario, comics within pop culture are headed toward a dead end: at best, a hipster "ghost world" of connoisseurs and collectors, where high-end graphic novels and limited editions flourish outside the view of the mass audience, or at worst an "infinite crisis" where big publishers endlessly recycle their superhero fables for a stagnant, graying fan base until they eventually consolidate and collapse.

The alternative to this bleak prognosis is captured in the jargony term *transmedia*, which was on the lips of every industry insider at the conference and the Con. Transmedia content refers to creative properties that exist in multiple media forms in the marketplace— for example, comic book characters and stories that are adapted into movies, video games, webcasts, and cartoons. In the context of the current industry conversations, taking comics transmedia does not just mean bringing them to these various platforms; they're already there. It means managing that process strategically. It means creating bridges between the disparate media audiences and genre subcultures, with easy points of transition, on-ramps to complicated story lines, and market mechanisms that promote crossover without out seeming like gimmicks.

Until very recently, publishers exploited their content on a project-by-project basis, taking in the money on options and licenses and perhaps attending to the quality of each individual product, but not thinking too hard about the big picture. As a result, there are lots of brands, from characters to big-name creators to entire "universes," that are being managed opportunistically rather than strategically, squandering revenues that could be realized from cross-platform synergies. Even successful one-off projects can dilute the richness of the creative assets and confuse an audience that recognizes the characters from other media. Opportunistic management also leads to a lot of poorly realized efforts to bring comics to other media, or other media assets to comics (such as comic book adaptations of movies and video games, or comics done by brand-name celebrities), without considering the comparative advantages of each particular media type.

If comics can successfully navigate the path to transmedia ubiquity, their future as popular entertainment is assured. But this means getting a lot of things right: balancing the demands of Hollywood and the commercial hype machine with the integrity of the comics medium and its unique strengths; managing brands and franchises across multiple channels so that fans of the characters and stories can enjoy a more coherent experience as they go from movies to comics to video games and the web; and tapping into the potential audience of billions around the world who are already primed for comics' imaginative spectacle. Most of all, it means telling stories gracefully regardless of medium, so that each different version feels natural and authentic to fans and general audiences alike.

The final part of the ICv2 conference addressed this question. Moderated by Heidi MacDonald, one of the most perceptive observers of the comics industry from her perch as editor of the influential "The Beat" blog, the varied group of panelists landed on the problems of media integration and unifying the audience for comic properties, then got into a very inside-baseball conversation about cross-platform marketing, licensing deals, creator-led challenges to corporate ownership of IP, and technologies for "transmedia search" (for example, being able to find all instances of Marvel characters across different media types in the iTunes store). All of these issues would surface in much more concrete and accessible ways over the course of the convention. Still, of all the discussions at the "Future of Comics" conference, this one struck me as the most genuinely futuristic.

By this time, the conference was beginning to feel way too much like work. Energy in the room was draining away. The cartoonist next to me was putting the finishing touches on an elaborate psychedelic doodle that sprawled over the back of his conference-issued notepad. Everyone, me included, was starting to anticipate the blast of pure adrenaline that would hit as soon as the doors of the exhibit hall flew open, just a few hours hence. Enough with the bad news—it was time to party!

Setup

Even promising concepts can vanish overnight in the face of changing economics and technology. The key to survival is identifying your core creative value and differentiation.

Immediately after the conference, I made my way to the convention center in hopes of catching a few hours in the exhibit hall before the official start of preview night. Over the years, these last few moments of calm before the floor is inundated with a hundred thousand attendees have become my favorite time of the show. In that final edgy hour, the enormous reservoir of energy that will be dissipated over the coming days is at its crest, ready to burst forth when the doors fly open. It is an exhilarating feeling.

In past years, it was possible—though not, strictly speaking, permitted—to get onto the floor with a staff badge or a generic exhibitor badge, and resourceful folks could usually find someone to provide a loaner in exchange for hauling a few boxes and helping with setup. Recently though, the Con has been stiffening up security in an effort to discourage exhibitors from handing out badges to preferred customers or friends who are eager to get an early run at the exclusive show merchandise.

This is no small matter. More and more companies have been offering special-issue toys, comics, posters, and other swag in limited quantities at the show—many of which are deemed extremely desirable by collectors and often sell on eBay for multiples of their purchase price just hours after they sell out in the exhibit hall. This manufactured scarcity is like a narcotic to the acquisitive hobbyists who descend on the show willing to brave long lines and hours of waiting for that Con-exclusive Millennium Falcon toy or comic book with a special 1-in-100 cover variant. The Con reasonably tries to keep these items from being bought up by insiders before the floor opens to ordinary attendees. Security and line control have thus become more present and overbearing with each passing year.

This year, early access to the hall required a complex system of color-coded badges, stickers, and wristbands. Eunice had obtained a "temporary setup" sticker to help our friends, and I had managed to score a bona fide exhibitor badge. After providing suitable credentials to the red-shirted Elite Security team guarding the door, I stepped into the hall through the northernmost entrance.

Photo by Doug Kline

Dealers tempt collectors with rare, one-of-a-kind collectables, available only at Comic-Con.

The convention floor expanded endlessly before me. I took a moment to appreciate the long view down the mostly empty thoroughfare toward the far end of the hall, more than 540 yards in the distance. Elaborate booths and banners rose in all directions, making it impossible to see past the center of the vast space. No matter how many times I've attended the show, this first glimpse of the hall always stuns me with its sheer overwhelming scale.

The first time I attended San Diego Comic-Con in 1997, the exhibit floor, then known as the "dealer's room," occupied the three large sections of the convention center (Halls A, B, and C) that existed at that time. With about 40,000 attendees and hundreds of exhibitors, it was the largest comic convention I'd ever seen.

Over the next few years, the convention center expanded, nearly tripling the available space, and Comic-Con itself grew even faster. When the doors opened in 2002, the first year that the exhibit hall extended the entire unpartitioned length of the convention center from Hall A to Hall G (more than 500,000 contiguous square feet), there were audible gasps even from veteran attendees and exhibitors. The convention is now so big that the observation deck on the mezzanine level does not allow you to see it all in one view.

During most hours of the convention, the exhibit floor is totally mobbed, making it difficult to navigate the aisles despite efforts to widen them over the years. In the center of the hall, the big booths sponsored by publishers, movie studios, video-game companies, and networks are elaborate multidecked affairs featuring full-sized props from movies (the Batmobile, a life-sized X-Wing Fighter), gigantic video screens, rows of computers or game consoles to demonstrate products, and specialized "attractions" that fans can walk through or participate in. These pavilions are so large and distracting that it is sometimes impossible to get into them, or even fully appreciate them from the outside, when the crowds are surging.

I walked the central aisle, past the rows of vintage comic dealers in the "Golden and Silver Age Pavilion" area. Handfuls of people, mostly other dealers and their friends, were already pawing through the long white boxes or conversing in front of tables piled with pages of original comic book art. These dealers used to be the main attraction, catering to collectors who were looking for key back issues or speculating on "undervalued" items that were expected to increase in price because of their scarcity, importance, and excellent condition. For reasons we will discuss later, that part of the comics hobby is diminishing in importance, and the dealers' presence on the floor has gradually shrunk; they have been pushed to the edges by the big media exhibitors and priced out by rising booth rates.

I turned up main aisle 1600 by the B/C entrance and headed toward the enormous DC Comics pavilion. Occupying a big chunk of the center of the hall, the booth consisted of a large, carpeted space surrounded by and bedecked with floor-to-ceiling full-color banners depicting the company's iconic characters—Superman, Green Lantern, Batman, Wonder Woman—in their latest incarnations, drawn in the distinctive pins-and-needles style of DC's copublisher, artist Jim Lee. Tables and podiums lined the edges of the booth, soon to be manned by creators and editors waiting to meet fans and prospective new talent. A few suspended monitors at the center of the booth ran clips from animated series and schedules of appearances and signings that would be taking place over the next few days. A small army of polo-shirted staff was busy with the final touches. This was the last time in five days I'd see it so empty.

My destination was the Exhibit A Press booth, a considerably more modest setup directly opposite DC at the intersection of two main aisles, in a red-carpeted area of the hall reserved for independent and self-published comics. Exhibit A Press is the enterprise of cartoonist Batton Lash and his wife, Jackie Estrada, who publish a comic called *Supernatural Law*, chronicling a legal firm whose clients include vampires, monsters, and other strange crea-

The DC Comics booth draws fans in the exhibit hall.

tures. Lash came up with the idea in 1979 and has managed to extend the premise for more than 25 years by combining clever wit, endearing characterization of the central cast, and a clean, classic comic art style that emphasizes storytelling and readability over superfluous detail.

Sometime around 1999 or 2000, Eunice and I befriended Lash and Estrada and eventually became their helpers (and sometimes hosts) at both San Diego Comic-Con and the Emerald City Con, a much smaller show held in our hometown of Seattle. This turned out to be a fruitful association. In addition to being warm, friendly folks with whom we can share an unself-conscious enthusiasm for all things comics, Batton and Jackie have cultivated a vast network of connections within the comics industry. Lash, gregarious and instantly recognizable in his fastidiously tailored vintage vest, tie, and pocket square, greets all and sundry in his broad Brooklynese.

He is ubiquitous at industry functions and parties, and he is on a first-name basis with just about everyone on the convention circuit, from fellow independent creators to A-listers like Frank Miller and Neil Gaiman.

Estrada, who is one of a handful of people to have attended every Comic-Con since its start in 1970, is the longtime administrator of the Eisner Awards, the comic industry honors that are handed out annually at a banquet on Friday evening, about which more later. Several years ago, she recruited Eunice and me onto her staff, which involves helping to set up the room, unboxing and positioning the award statuettes, helping attendees to their seats, and manning the VIP registration table for industry pros and guests. Our service earns us staff badges and an opportunity to rub elbows with some of the bright lights of the comics business.

For the past decade, we have inaugurated our convention with a Tuesday night dinner with Batton and Jackie, then arrived early on Wednesday to help them set up their booth. This time, because I attended the ICv2 conference, Eunice had to fly solo on the setup.

Fortunately, the setup was fairly simple this year. Exhibit A no longer publishes a periodical comic book; *Supernatural Law* moved online to Webcomics Nation in 2005, releasing a few pages of new story twice a week. The only new product the company had for this show was a slender, self-published trade paperback compiling a complete story arc from the online strip. This joined an assortment of backstock graphic novels, T-shirts, and a few boxes of back issues on the display stand facing the aisle. Also on the countertop were a series of Batton's small original color paintings of famous movie monsters (Bride of Frankenstein, Phantom of the Opera, Creature from the Black Lagoon, and so on) on miniature easels, along with some more expensive originals.

Photo by Jackie Estrada

Artist Batton Lash at the Exhibit A Press booth, keeping his product visible at Comic-Con.

Selling art and merchandise is how exhibitors pay for the booth space, so it is important to keep a selection on hand. But really, physical product is vestigial to Exhibit A's new mission in the twenty-first-century comics marketplace, which is to attract attention to the story content using its main assets: Lash's recognizable personal brand and the company's super-prime location on the Comic-Con exhibit floor.

The changing fortunes of Exhibit A are typical of the more complex digital, media-saturated environment, which makes it at once easier and more difficult for independent creators with personal visions to reach a wider audience. *Supernatural Law* (also known as "Wolff and Byrd—Counselors of the Macabre") was part of a boom in self-published comics that got going in the late 1980s and continued to find a market through the 1990s. Along with Jeff Smith's

Bone, Carla Speed McNeil's *Finder*, Terry Moore's *Strangers in Paradise*, and many others, *Supernatural Law* attempted to stake out a space between the standard superheroics of DC, Marvel, and Image Comics and the artsy fringe of "alternative" comics coming from publishers like Fantagraphics, Last Gasp, and Drawn and Quarterly. The concepts were varied, accessible, and usually well done. Typically involving some combination of fantasy, mystery, science fiction, adventure, and humor, the titles reflected the kind of genre mix you'd find in mass-market paperback books or network television. The stories were rich without the crust of "continuity" and whiff of juvenilia that hovers over superhero comics, and the art was accessible to anyone who could appreciate the better-crafted newspaper comic strips like "For Better or Worse" or "Funky Winkerbean."

For a moment in the 1990s, this movement, which dubbed itself the "new mainstream," seemed to be the locus of creative energy in comics. Self-publishing pioneer Dave Sim authored manifestos exhorting cartoonists to free themselves from the tyranny of publishers and take ownership of their properties and their careers. Peter Laird and Kevin Eastman led the way in the early 1980s, when they parleyed their oddball self-published title *Teenage Mutant Ninja Turtles* into a multimillion-dollar media juggernaut. Their rapid rise (and subsequent fall) drew attention to the creative energy percolating at the edges of the comics industry and made independent publishing a viable business strategy for creators with ideas that didn't fit neatly into existing comic genres. In a growing economy and a comics industry that was on the way back from a nearly fatal collapse driven by speculation and overexposure in the early 1990s, the "new mainstream" offered an alternative to help burnish the reputation of the medium and expand the audience beyond the hard core of superhero readers.

Sometime in the early 2000s the air went out of the balloon. Rising printing costs and consolidation in the comics distribution system made it harder for indies to compete on the shelves. Diamond, the last surviving major comics wholesaler, culled poorer-selling independent titles from its monthly "Previews" catalog, cutting off the indies' access to the direct market. Even for those that made the cut, retailers grew skittish about ordering books that did not cater to the hard-core superhero fans. At the same time, the natural audience for "new mainstream" titles found its entertainment desires satisfied by dense new episodic genre shows like *Buffy the Vampire Slayer*, *Lost*, and *Supernatural*, which tap into the same kind of sensibility and appeal as comics.

Some of the indies petered out or finished their planned story arcs. A few of the titles went on to greater success in collected editions. Many were optioned for films, providing their creators with a much-appreciated payday, even though the vast majority of these projects never came to fruition. Larger publishers like Image, Dark Horse, Oni, and Slave Labor Graphics embraced the "new mainstream" concept and in some cases absorbed previously independent titles and creators within a more conventional publishing arrangement that still allowed creator freedom and creator ownership.

Exhibit A is one of the last holdouts. Lash and Estrada realized the utility of moving to the web relatively early, despite the absence of a clear revenue model. They recognized that the value of *Supernatural Law* was in the characters and the intellectual property of the stories, not the monthly book. If they were lucky, maybe a TV deal might be in the offing. But while Exhibit A has courted offers for years, so far nothing has seen the light of day. Meanwhile, the fiercely independent Lash takes work from Archie and Bongo (publishers of *The Simpsons* comics) to supplement the income from his own creations.

Still, come Comic-Con, Lash and Estrada unfurl the Wolff and Byrd banners, unpack the T-shirts and backstock graphic novels, and don the vest and pocket square to greet the fans. Whatever the ups and downs of the business, Lash still has pictures to draw and stories to tell. And in a world where new channels for content and story are opening up every day, you never know who might come calling, as long as you leave the door open.

Welcome to Comic-Con
Pop culture is big business and getting bigger.

"Attention exhibitors!" boomed the PA system. "Please move all pallets out of the aisles and return to your booths. The exhibit hall will be opening momentarily."

Around the hall, nervous energy reached a fever pitch. The staffs at the large booths bustled about, putting the final touches on their displays and exhibits. Artists neatened up the stacks of comics and original art at their stations and settled into "meet the public" mode. Forklifts retreated from the floor, mounded high with the last stacks of empty boxes and discarded packing materials.

I made a final survey of the hall, taking in the last unobstructed views of the mega-media booths and noting where to find particular artists and dealers. It was a Sisyphean chore. No matter how closely one studied the map or wandered around, there always seemed to be a few booths or even entire aisles that remained hidden until they revealed themselves on Saturday or Sunday afternoon.

The posted opening time for the exhibit hall was 6 p.m., but for the past several years, in a savvy exercise of expectation management, the Con has opened the doors a few minutes ahead of schedule. At about 10 minutes to the hour, the PA boomed again: "Attention exhibitors: Comic-Con 2011 is now open!"

The line of registered attendees, which ran all the way down the length of the convention center, up the steps, through an endless string of switchbacks and velvet-cordoned "crowd management" areas, through the upper level, and down the massive staircase behind the rear entrance to Hall C, slowly unwound, disgorging tens of thousands into the hall. Almost immediately, a steady stream of people began pouring onto the floor.

The PA system exhorted, "Please, no running in the aisles," an announcement that could apply only to these opening minutes, when high-speed mobility was a possibility. The first people on the floor, who had been waiting in line for most of the day, if not longer, paid no attention. They sprinted to stake their claim on an exclusive toy or poster, a limited-edition comic, or a celebrity signature. Others filtered in with a dazed zombie walk, then stopped dead in their tracks a few steps inside the door. I saw what I presumed to be a family of four—dressed in matching Batman, Batgirl, Robin, and Bat-Mite costumes—transfixed in the entryway, eyes darting around the room from corner to corner, unable to process the scale of the hall and the bewildering array of spectacles on display.

In less than half an hour, the entire gargantuan space was heaving with the frenzied energy of a stadium-sized crowd. There was a collective quickening of pulse and hyperventilation. People pawed the merchandise, ogled the costumes, snapped photos, explored the elaborate booths, and queued up in lines that spontaneously generated around the hall as the stocks of swag drew low.

By 7:00, the center aisles were clogged, even as thousands more were still making their way onto the floor. Fire marshals eyed the crowd nervously, muttering into walkie-talkies and making notes on clipboards. Preview night attendance was capped at a fraction

A small portion of the 500,000 square-foot exhibit hall, seen from an observation deck.

of the total number of four-day registrants because there was no other programming on Wednesday night to pull people out of the exhibit hall and into the dozens of meeting rooms for panels, game tournaments, film screenings, or autograph signings. There would be more people at the Con over the weekend, but the floor would never feel quite as crowded and intense as it does in the first hours of preview night.

In 2001, when preview night first opened to all four-day attendees, it was mostly an opportunity for collectors to scope out the prices and inventory at the dealers' tables and start conversations that might lead, a few days later, to the purchase of a particularly pricey back issue or piece of original artwork. By 2005, exhibitors were reporting sales on preview night that matched levels previously only seen on Saturday afternoon, the traditional height of the Con. People wanted to get their purchases out of the way before the programming started, in case they had to spend time waiting in lines or doing other activities that would take them off the floor. Preview night was no longer an afterthought; it had become *the* critical time for buyers and sellers of collectibles, either vintage or new. Lines grew longer, and the crowds initially overwhelmed the convention center's ability to handle them, leading to a lot of frustration and wasted time.

This year, the Con seemed to have crowd management down to a science. There appeared to be enough security and volunteers, adequately trained in both procedures and etiquette, to keep things moving without seeming too much like a police state. This was combined with a willingness, or perhaps resignation, on the part of attendees to accept more regimentation, given the challenges of having so many avid, amped-up fans in one place, some of whom were armed with uncomfortably lifelike swords and weaponry.

The need for all these rules, systems, and enforcement mechanisms makes logical sense considering the scale of Comic-Con in the 2000s. However, as the thinning gray ponytailed elders of the Con will tell you, it was not always this way.

The San Diego Comic-Con dates back to 1970, when organizers led by Shel Dorf (1933–2009) and a few hundred fans first assembled at the U.S. Grant Hotel to meet special guests Jack Kirby and Ray Bradbury, watch vintage horror films, buy and sell back issues, and, in later years, attend a Saturday night fan banquet that was open to all attendees. In that early age of comics fandom, San Diego vied with big conventions in New York to be the center of the comics universe. It got a boost in 1976, when a fledgling studio called Lucasfilm showed up with a slide show introducing its new movie, *Star Wars*. The shrieks of geek orgasm that shook San Diego that year echoed out across the cosmos—an early indication of the force of Comic-Con buzz that would so intoxicate Hollywood marketing departments decades later.

Fandom grew more numerous, confident, and sophisticated through the 1980s and 1990s, and the Con grew with it. By 1985, Comic-Con had moved to the Convention and Performing Arts Center, and the crowd of about 6,000 was enough to freak out star writer Alan Moore, who never attended another comic convention in the United States.

Comic-Con became the site of a film festival, a gaming tournament, an academic conference, a retail trade show, and a meeting place for dozens if not hundreds of fan organizations whose members rarely got together in person. Somewhere along the way, the Masquerade costume parade that was traditionally held on Saturday night overspilled its levees and flooded across the entire breadth and duration of the Con. The "cosplay" antics of fans dressed as their favorite characters became a staple of media reports of the Con in this period, giving the show the Mardi Gras-like reputation it enjoys today.

I was not alone in discovering Comic-Con in those years. In 2002, attendance jumped more than 10,000 from 2001: in the midst of a severe economic downturn and the lead-up to the wars in Iraq and Afghanistan, people needed an escape from reality, and they knew where to find it. The next year, the exhibit hall expanded to its current size, taking up the entire lower level of the convention center from Hall A to Hall G, which formed a gigantic contiguous, cavernous space crammed with every manner of pop culture diversion. The media were starting to take note. Big features appeared in *Entertainment Weekly, Variety,* and *USA Today,* as well as on network news and business shows.

By 2005, Con attendance crossed the 100,000 mark. Whatever virulent strain the nerds had been cooking up in their parents' basements had gotten loose in the general population. This was the era when even hardened professionals and veteran attendees went weak-kneed at the sight of the crowds, the lines, the endless aisles of booths and tables, the costumes, the noise, the celebrity star power, the crazed over-the-top hype, and the increasingly exclusive parties for A-listers thrown by Hollywood studios and big media outlets.

Each year, new voices arise to declare that Comic-Con has lost its way, sold its soul, jumped the shark. Each year, it sells out faster and the quest for hotel rooms grows more frantic. Each year, Eunice and I pack our bags and wonder, how could they possibly top last year? And each year, they find a way.

CHAPTER ③

THURSDAY:
LIFTOFF

O n Thursday morning, Comic-Con begins in earnest. The focus
shifts from the nuttiness of the exhibit hall to the crowded
schedule of programming that takes place in meeting rooms
throughout the convention center and the adjoining hotels. This is
where Comic-Con performs the alchemy that unites fans with the
objects of their affection while reminding creators of their power to
inspire imagination.

Programs fall into several categories: *spotlights*, in which one
creator (often a special guest of the Con) is interviewed or holds
forth on his life, work, and personal interests; *panels*, featuring
anything from a group of experts to the entire cast of a movie or
TV show, discussing a topic of interest; *workshops*, where professionals discuss and demonstrate their techniques; *meetups*, where
folks with common interests can get together in person; and *events*,

like film screenings, Klingon mating rituals, or a performance by the Cirque du Soleil. The academic programming track associated with the Comic Arts Conference also features seminars and presentations of research papers. Almost all the programming allows for interaction between fans and creators, usually in the form of Q&A.

Program experiences come in all shapes and sizes. At the media-crazy high end of Comic-Con, thousands of people can line up for hours to get a glimpse of Robert Downey, Jr., or Angelina Jolie talking about how much they love old Marvel comics as they pimp their next action film; Sylvester Stallone might announce that his pal Bruce Willis has decided to drop by as a surprise guest on the panel; someone dressed as ET can ask a question, in character, of Steven Spielberg if he gets to the microphone fast enough. Much of this mayhem takes place in Hall H, which has become synonymous with Comic-Con's mind meld with the entertainment industry. More on that later.

The "mainstream" comics panels, hosted in the midsized auditoriums by DC, Marvel, Dark Horse, and Image, feature big announcements about upcoming story lines and creative teams. Occasionally, they dissolve into screaming matches between a bellicose editor and a room full of disbelieving or disappointed fans. Smaller publishers hope for a favorable spot on the schedule—usually between bigger, more popular programs, so that they'll be guaranteed a captive audience of folks who don't want to lose their seats for the next panel.

In the more human-scale meeting rooms on the mezzanine level, kindly looking old men in blazers and cardigans, who days ago were riding golf carts around their retirement communities and are still a bit overwhelmed, sit for detailed public interviews about the "Golden Age of Comics" (the 1940s and 1950s). They slowly come to realize that hundreds of people still fondly remember the work they did back in their salad days, drawing pictures for funny books as they tried to climb the ladder as commercial illustrators. At the end of the panel, they choke back tears as a representative of Comic-Con hands them an Inkpot Award recognizing their contributions to a great American art form while an audience of several dozen middle-aged men stands and claps with earnest reverence.

Then, down the hall, a crowd explodes in a flurry of ecstatic tweets as the director of a new science fiction series announces that he brought a reel of previews, bloopers, and behind-the-scenes footage just for fans at Comic-Con. "Anyone want to see Scarlett Johansson's wardrobe malfunction? No cameras, please; we wouldn't want this all over YouTube (smirk)."

And so on, in nearly two dozen parallel tracks across the length and breadth of the upper levels of the convention center and the larger ballrooms of the nearby hotels, for four solid days. Capacities of the rooms range from a few hundred for smaller-scale panels to the cavernous Hall H, which accommodates more than 6,500. In recent years, even Petco Park, the 46,000-seat home of the San Diego Padres, across the street from the convention center, has been pressed into service for special evening events.

The programming schedule is released a couple of weeks before the start of the Con and is yet another source of anxiety for attendees. The 2011 Events Guide handed out at the Con ran to nearly 200 pages; the iPhone app takes several minutes to load up the schedule, even with a fast connection.

Given the specialized tastes of pop culture fans, there are always difficult decisions. In addition to straightforward time conflicts, there are logistics and opportunity costs to consider. It is physically impossible to get from, say, Ballroom 6A at the south end of the convention center to the offsite Hilton Bayfront in less than 15 minutes, so forget going from the fans vs. pros trivia contest to the Venture Brothers panel that starts immediately after.

Then there are the crowds. People will line up for hours and sit through two or three preceding programs in which they have no interest to catch one popular event later in the day. If you want to see a hot or highly-buzzed program, it may take a day of standing in line and sitting through meaningless demonstrations of 3D animation software, previews of generic cop shows, and discussions of the religious symbolism in modern representations of vampires that are scheduled earlier in the same room. Is it worth the hassle to get a glimpse of Bruce Campbell or Kevin Smith, or would you be better off trying for less popular panels and spending the rest of the time in the exhibit hall? Decisions, decisions!

Eunice downloads the daily schedule grids as they are posted on the Comic-Con website, prints them out, and pores over them with a highlighter. I use the Con's mobile app. By the time Thursday rolls around, we are each prepared with our order of battle, fallbacks and second choices, and communication plan. Naturally, it all falls apart as we push through the unimaginably large crowd and set foot in the exhibit hall. The first full day of Comic-Con has dawned, and sensory overload has already begun.

Larger than Life: Superheroes and the Future of the Man of Tomorrow

The owners of comics' most recognized properties must balance brand stewardship and creativity as they vie for the attention of generations of fans.

Despite the unprecedented breadth of content and styles available today, American comics are still primarily identified in the public consciousness with superheroes, the crown jewels in comics' pantheon of creative properties. That extends to Comic-Con, where costumed characters traverse all media and even protrude into real life by walking the aisles of the show floor in their colorful multitudes. For better or worse, the future of comics in popular culture is intimately tied to the future of the superhero.

To be into superheroes, you have to suspend a lot of disbelief. The genre asks readers not only to accept the existence of all kinds of supernatural forces, from aliens to magic to mutations that miraculously result in extraordinary abilities, but also to envision a world in which human morality and behavior, not to mention fashion aesthetics, are very different from our ordinary experience. Crucial plot points often hinge on facts and history that are unique to the "universe" that the publisher has created, sometimes over decades, with which fans are simply assumed to be familiar.

All these leaps of logic come naturally to kids, especially when they are facilitated through dynamic, colorful artwork and simple text. In the 1960s and 1970s, when most of today's regular superhero readers were youngsters, superhero comics were at their seductive best. They were cheap. They were on newsstands everywhere. Amazing storytellers like Jack Kirby, Stan Lee, Steve Ditko, Chris Claremont, and John Byrne were at the peak of their powers. The imprint that these comics made on kids of that era was often permanent. The characters and story lines developed during this period form the core of the superhero canon and have been mined over and over again for current-day comics, movies, video games, and animated cartoons.

When comics moved from the newsstand to the direct market, they took their audience with them. The kids of the 1960s and 1970s grew into the teens and twenty-somethings of the 1980s and 1990s and demanded that the superheroes of their childhood mature (or at least develop) along with them. As the superheroes evolved to cater to a more sophisticated fan base, they lost the accessibility and the ubiquity that had brought in the previous generation of readers.

Today there is a growing divide between the aging cohort that reads superhero stories in comic book form and the younger generation, whose primary exposure to costumed crime fighters is likely to have been through other media. This gap is unsustainable—not just because it is unhealthy to rely exclusively on an aging audience for a pop culture product, but because the stories that fuel the transmedia popularity of superheroes can be told convincingly only in comic book form, at least in the first instance.

Costumed superheroes that originated in other media have simply not generated the same kind of mystique as those created in the pages of comics. Even licensed characters that have become successful movie franchises—*Spider-Man*, *X-Men*, *Batman*, and Marvel's *Avengers* cycle—are using plots that originated decades ago in the comics, and they run out of steam after three films at most. Many attempts to bring superheroes to live-action media fail because the film medium is too visually literal to carry off the suspension of disbelief that comics can routinely achieve. Grandeur on the page translates too easily into pomposity on the screen; few people will end up as fans of *Daredevil* or *Green Lantern* if they know those characters only from the movies.

The superhero concept is not unpopular, as any quick scan of box office receipts and video-game sales will tell you. However, many of the genre's defining features have become stale and predictable, which accounts for the inability of even the most successful concepts to sustain franchises beyond a certain point. The whole idea of masked avengers righting wrongs does not connect with audiences in the visceral way that it did in the early days, the 1930s and 1940s, or again in the 1960s and 1970s, when superhero comics were fun and widely accessible. In the long run, the only way the superhero concept can stay viable across all media is through the continued episodic production of good stories in the sequential art format—that is, comic books, whether paper or digital. That will happen only if the owners of the popular characters find a way to expand their readership by rediscovering the connection between superheroes and the wider audience rather than just the hard-core fans.

The big publishers understand this, but are stuck in a dilemma. The popular, household-name superheroes like *Spider-Man* and *Superman* are more than characters. They are brands, properties and licenses whose value is based on their familiarity. They can't change much without risking their value as recognizable icons, but without changing, they can't hold reader interest.

DC and Marvel manage their universes of superheroes through an increasingly centralized bureaucracy of executives, editors, and creative directors, sometimes plotting out story lines in detail years in advance. Artists are selected for their personal styles and have some latitude for creative expression, but writers are hired (and fired) purely for their ability to bring predetermined story lines to life and keep fans coming back issue after issue.

The tension in the mainstream industry comes from balancing the increasingly centralized creative strategies of the corporate publishers with a medium whose artistic success depends on the power of individual creative voices and imaginations. The first item on our Thursday programming agenda was a spotlight on a writer who has built his career on exploring the relationships between iconic mainstream superheroes, the audience, and the culture according to his most singular voice and vision: Grant Morrison.

. With his wide-ranging intellect, rock star charisma, and conspicuous financial success, Morrison has one of the great personal brands in an industry dominated by larger-than-life personalities. He is a polarizing figure among fans and professionals alike, inspiring equal parts awe, jealousy, and disdain. And, oh yes, lots of attention. He is undeniably a major talent with a head full of big ideas. If you are capable of being convinced that characters with supernatural powers who fight crime wearing long underwear and capes can have profound cultural significance, Morrison is the guy who could convince you. And if you are open to the possibility that one of the most intriguing and thoughtful literary figures of the twenty-first century makes his living writing stories featuring corporate-owned characters in the most commercially oriented, "mainstream" areas of comic book publishing, exposure to Morrison's best work and commanding presence might just convince you of that as well.

Grant Morrison is a living embodiment of the contradictions that bedevil the future of the superhero genre. He has delivered a string of megahits over his three decades as a comic book writer, while simultaneously building a reputation as one of the most avant-garde figures in the industry. His early work on titles like *Animal Man*, *Doom Patrol*, and the graphic novel *Batman: Arkham Asylum* distinguished him even among a cohort of highly accomplished peers like Neil Gaiman, Warren Ellis, Garth Ennis, and Mark Millar, who followed the visionary Alan Moore across the Atlantic in a "British Invasion" (Morrison is Scottish) of the American comics industry in the 1980s. In his baroque masterpieces *The Invisibles* and *The Filth*, Morrison successfully smuggled the sensibility of William S. Burroughs, the most transgressive postwar American literary figure, into the pages of DC Comics.* For that achievement alone, he would be worth paying attention to.

And then he wrote *Justice League*. And *X-Men*. And *Superman*. And *Batman*. And a bunch of operatic superhero sagas that played dice with the DC universe over the course of many months and piles of issues. Not only was this work solidly within the corporate comics mainstream, but Morrison eventually became part of the brain-trust that plotted out company strategy, helping to generate the marching orders that other creators had to follow.

Morrison's superhero stories are always ambitious and often well crafted—if you like superheroes and care about their worlds. And that's a big if. *Seven Soldiers of Victory*, Morrison's 2005–2006 epic that unfolded in seven interconnected miniseries, featured unfamiliar versions of obscure DC heroes in a reimagined fictional continuity. It rivals the work of Thomas Pynchon in its narrative complexity, but it is impressive in the context of the tricks it plays with characters and situations that are familiar only to dedicated fans. Stuff like this exemplifies the problems that superhero comics have had in reaching a wider audience in recent decades. The best of the genre is genius if you know the code and gibberish if you don't.

It is hard to get away from the fact that much of Morrison's superhero work is a lot less interesting than he is. Like one of those celebrity chefs who specialize in reinventing comfort foods, Morrison himself may be inspired by the flavors of exotic herbs and mushrooms, but he dishes out mac and cheese.

---

*The series were published by DC's adult-oriented imprint Vertigo and were not marketed to kids.

He makes no apologies for this; rather the opposite. Morrison sees superheroes as figures in a modern mythology—manifestations of a primal subconscious of the human species that, in previous eras, have been called saints, legends, and gods. Telling their stories is important, meaningful work that can, if done properly, tap into the mainline currents of the cultural moment. In Morrison's conception, superheroes have a future to the extent that they maintain this mythic aspect and don't get sucked too far into the morass of realism—something that he believes soured the stew in the aftermath of gritty mid-1980s game changers like Frank Miller's *Batman: The Dark Knight* and Alan Moore and Dave Gibbons's *Watchmen*.

He expounded on these ideas, and on the arc of the superhero through the history of comic books, in his 2011 book *Supergods: What Masked Vigilantes, Miraculous Mutants and a Sun God from Smallville Can Teach Us About Being Human*, released around the time of the Con. I was looking forward to his balancing act between talking seriously about these ideas and serving as a marketing mouthpiece for DC's imminent high-stakes relaunch of its entire comic book line.

"I'm not sure I want to see him," said Eunice, who reads several of Morrison's titles on a monthly basis. "He seems like he'd be arrogant."

"Just check him out," I assured her. I'd seen Morrison at panels over the years, and I always came away amused by how he handled questions from fans ranging from, "Will Colossus be coming back in *X-Men*?" to, "Why do humans feel the need to wear clothes?" (someone actually asked this)—sometimes back to back, or even from the same questioner. Though he clearly does not lack confidence, he comes across as simply a curious guy with a lot on his mind. The working-class Sco'ish accent helps, too.

Writer Grant Morrison (seated) greets an admirer at a signing in Scotland.

We arrived 20 minutes before the start of the panel, partly expecting not to get in, but to my surprise, there were still plenty of seats around the room. Maybe it was too early in the day, and people were still busy in the exhibit hall. Maybe it was because there would be no shortage of opportunities to hear Morrison during the Con. He was slated to be on several DC panels and to hold a bunch of signings, as well as conducting his traditional mutual interview with Deepak Chopra (!) on Saturday afternoon. The fact that Morrison is probably the only person working in comics who could pull that off says a lot about why people love him and hate him.

Lights dimmed in the 500-seat room, and the sprightly Morrison took a seat on the stage. There was no moderator, so after the briefest introductory remarks, he went right to Q&A. Though he fielded the usual quota of oddball questions and sycophancy with charm and respect, it was clear what he wanted to talk about: Superman and the New 52.

Several weeks before the Con, DC Comics had announced a major reboot of its entire superhero universe, relaunching 52 new comics, with first issues appearing in September 2011. Most of the time, publishers use these reboots as a way to establish new story lines and new creative teams, giving them the sales push that comes with having a number 1 issue on the stands. Reboots, along with the annual "crisis/crossover" events that sprawl over dozens of titles for months, are the epitome of the "change everything/ change nothing" paradox that the big publishers face on a constant basis. The New 52 initiative was notable because it included the most venerable titles in the DC catalog: *Action Comics, Batman, Superman,* and *Detective Comics,* which had run in continuously numbered series since the 1930s and were pushing toward their one thousandth issues. That raised eyebrows, suggesting a greater degree of commitment (or desperation) on the part of one of the industry's "Big Two" publishers.

Morrison was center stage in this effort as the announced writer for Action Comics #1—the comics equivalent of directing a remake of *Citizen Kane.* Action Comics #1 is the comic book that introduced Superman in June 1938, launching both the superhero concept and the American comics industry. There is no more culturally significant, iconic comic book in existence. Restarting that particular series for the first time in more than 70 years as part of an overall revamp of Superman was considered a very big deal.

Morrison took up the challenge with gusto. He announced that his goal was to return the character of Superman to his historical roots as an outsider, a rebel, and a champion of the oppressed. This was what gave the pulpish, sketchy, science fiction–oriented conception of writer Jerry Siegel and artist Joe Shuster such visceral power in the dark days of the Great Depression. America yearned for someone who would stand up to the bully, the racketeer, the wife beater, the crooked politician, the corrupt cop, the greedy businessman who treated his workers like dirt. Superman, an immigrant to this planet who donned the mild-mannered attire of Clark Kent just to fit in, was the revenge of the little guy: the nerd who wasn't going to take it anymore.

In succeeding years, Superman morphed into a national symbol: selling bonds and riding bombs; the center of a "Superman family" of pals, relatives, and pets; a go-getting yuppie; a strict and disapproving father figure; and a transcendent icon. The shifting personas of Superman matched the rhythms of American culture as the depression gave way to the war, the 1950s, the 1960s, and beyond. But somewhere along the line, the icon fell out of sync with the public.

Back in 1986, when DC did its first major renovation of the character, the beloved, slightly goofy Superman of the 1960s and 1970s was given a nostalgic send-off by star writer Alan Moore in a classic tearjerker called "Whatever Happened to the Man of Tomorrow?" How times have changed. Despite an eventful 25 years that saw our hero die, be reborn, change costumes, get a bad haircut, get married, and see his archenemy Lex Luthor elected president, the Superman of the 1990s and 2000s is unlikely to be either missed or fondly remembered when his backstory is swept into the dustbin of obsolete continuity. It wasn't the fault of the creative teams; it just wasn't Superman's time. The go-go, gadget-driven 1990s and the tense, terror-splattered 2000s belonged to Batman, the self-made entrepreneurial crime fighter and the no-nonsense dark detective, not the idealistic immigrant exponent of truth, justice, and the American way.

Morrison believes that is about to change. In *Supergods,* he cites a theory by futurist Iain Spence that ties oscillations in youth culture taste and style over the years to changes in solar activity in 11-year cycles. Based on this, Morrison thinks we are heading into a new cycle that not only favors the Apollonian Superman/Sun God over the dark, nocturnal Batman, but also suggests that we are due for a return to first principles. Consequently, he is hoping that his revival of the primal Superman will catch the changing mood of American youth and propel this particular piece of superheroic mythology out of its Fortress of Solitude and back into cultural relevance. He wants to "occupy" Action Comics with a more transgressive and unruly Superman, and recent events show that his timing may be spot on.

I agree with Morrison's conclusions, though I take issue with his methodology. In my view, American culture does have patterns and cycles, but they are driven through the much more earthly dynamics of generational change. The authors Neil Howe and the late William Strauss first put forward this idea in their 1991 book, *Generations: The History of America's Future 1584–2069.* In their model, four basic generational types—Civics (builders and keepers of social institutions, including the World War II "Veteran" generation and perhaps the current-day Millennials), Adaptives (socially minded linear thinkers who breathe humor and humanity into those institutions, such as the Silent Generation born in the 1920s and 1930s), Idealists (dreamers who call for spiritual renewal and secular crusades, like the Baby Boom generation born between World War II and the early 1960s), and Reactives (pragmatic individualists and entrepreneurs, like Generation X, whose members came of age in the 1970s and 1980s)—march through history in an orderly procession, each enjoying periods of rise, dominance, and decay. The tenor of the times depends on which of the generations is in adulthood, adolescence, or maturity.

It turns out the big events of American history, including wars, economic booms and depressions, spiritual upheavals, and periods of corrupt politics, all correlate with specific alignments of generations and occur predictably in cycles. Using this model, Strauss and Howe, writing in the early 1990s, were able to accurately forecast the 1990s economic boom, Bill Clinton's election and impeachment, a terrorist attack on the United States at the turn of the century, and the subsequent overreaction of the reigning baby boomer–dominated administration.

In my previous work, I've applied this analytical framework to the issue of technological innovation and adoption, but it also fits quite nicely around the history of comics. While Grant Morrison points to 11-year oscillations in youth culture between, essentially, hippie and punk aesthetics, the Strauss and Howe model covers an arc of 75 to 80 years. And according to that framework, the pendulum is swinging back to the generational milieu of the late 1930s, characterized by a clash of strident ideologies, political crisis, economic distress, and the emergence of a frustrated young Civic generation seeking an outlet for its creative, socially conscious ambitions. This earlier period is known to comics fans as "The Golden Age," when the concept of the superhero first took hold.

In other words, we have returned to the cultural moment of the Siegel and Shuster Superman, just as Morrison is promising to return him to us. If he and his colleagues who are spearheading the DC New 52 initiative, are right—and initial sales results have demonstrated that they might be—the timing may be perfect to refresh the original mythology and restore a clichéd trope to mass-cultural relevance. As an artistic proposition, the benefits of that may be debatable, but as a driver of the continued salience and market viability of the comics medium, it would be just super.

Camp Breaking Dawn and the Twilight of the Boys Club
Diversifying your content mix to attract a broader audience might generate controversy, but it is critical to long-term success.

When we left Morrison's panel, we realized that it was already past lunchtime and we hadn't had much to eat since the night before. At Comic-Con, it's easy to lose track of things like food, sleep, and healthy levels of alcohol intake.

We stepped outside the convention center into the beautiful San Diego afternoon. The sidewalk in front of the convention center was a steady procession of fans carrying the gigantic, colorful Warner Brothers swag bags, rugged-looking exhibitors stepping outside for a smoke, fans adjusting their costumes, pierced dads in baggy shorts pushing strollers, and harried staff and security people directing traffic.

We walked south toward the new pedestrian overpass that spanned Harbor Drive and connected the convention center area with the restaurants and bars of the Gaslamp Quarter. That trajectory took us right past Camp Breaking Dawn, the encampment of thousands of fans of the tween girl vampire franchise *Twilight*, who were lined up starting in a maze of velvet ropes under tents outside Hall H and ending somewhere very far down the walkway along the harbor, behind the convention center.

Twilight, in case you've been sleeping in a tomb for the past half-decade, is the insanely popular young adult series by author Stephenie Meyer, featuring a love triangle between a teenage girl named Bella Swan, her brooding vampire beau Edward Cullen, and werewolf bad boy Jacob Black.

Meyer's unconventional take on the whole vampire thing (the fact that vampires sparkle in daylight instead of turning to dust, and that they spend most of their time moping around and looking cool instead of tearing people's throats out) has not earned her much love from horror/fantasy enthusiasts who like their brew a little bit stronger. I must admit that I have not cracked the cover of any of these books and don't have much interest in doing so. I wouldn't watch the movies for free if they were the only available entertainment on a 12-hour plane flight. I'm not sure I'd watch them if the alternative were a week's stay at Gitmo.

And you know what? Who cares! I'm a 44-year-old guy with no kids. I am not the audience for *Twilight* in any way, shape, or form. But I'm all for any material that generates enough passion to get a completely new pop culture audience to stand in line for 40 hours and sleep on concrete for two nights just to bask in the presence of the actors who portray these characters in a film. That enthusiasm is the rocket fuel that drives the industry and the artform forward, and it doesn't pay to be too picky about where it comes from.

As we were walking past, the camp was in the process of decamping. Hall H would be opening in moments, capping days of camaraderie and informal celebrations for the thousands penned in on the patch of land between the south end of the convention center and the Bayfront Hilton. Since Tuesday night, the entire scene had been one long sleepover party of thousands of excited teen- and tween-age girls (and their moms, big sisters, boyfriend wannabes, and the occasional hapless-looking dad). In a burst of amazingly good PR, some *Twilight* cast members showed up on Thursday morning to serve breakfast to the campers, mingle, and sign autographs.

Tents are set up outside Hall H to accommodate the tens of thousands of fans waiting overnight for events like the *Twilight* panel.

Photo by Jackie Estrada

The Twilighters first made their presence felt in 2008, when the line for the panel featuring heartthrobs Robert Pattinson and Taylor Lautner stretched for nearly a mile. Those at the front had been camping out in sleeping bags and chaise longues for days. What made this group remarkable was not only the tenacity and intensity of its fandom, even by Comic-Con standards, but its demographics. This group was about 95 percent female, most of its members under 25 and many under the age of 16.

I don't think it will come as a big shock that, for most of the history of comics fandom, conventions have not been distinguished by high numbers of females of any age. That began to change in the 1990s, when strong and emotionally authentic female characters like *Xena: Warrior Princess, Buffy the Vampire Slayer,* and the cheerful Goth-girl personification of Death in Neil Gaiman's popular *Sandman* series activated the recessive fan gene on the X chromosome. The trend accelerated with the mainstream popularity of manga, which had developed numerous styles over the years to appeal to all genders and was sold in bookstores, beyond the boys-club direct market comics shops. The rise of the Internet poured gasoline on the fire, creating spaces for feminerds to come out of the woodwork and share their passions. Many of today's best online comic and fantasy-genre news sites and discussion groups were started by, and remain powered by, women.

Today, there are increasing numbers of proud girl geeks of all ages; I count myself fortunate to be married to one. Crowds at conventions and even some comics stores now reflect a much more equal gender balance. As for the comics industry itself, not so much. But that's a different conversation.

There are big differences between the mature, established, mostly Generation X women, who developed their interests through actual comics and comics-related media (and can be every bit as marinated in the minutiae of continuity as the hardest-core male superhero reader), and the younger cohort, who are largely drawn into the worlds of fantasy and pop culture through manga and young adult fiction: not just *Twilight*, but also *Baby-Sitters Club*, *Diary of a Wimpy Kid*, and, of course, *Harry Potter*. But at least girls and teens are coming into the social and participative world of fandom rather than just sitting on their couches playing Xbox.

You would think that male comics fans would have no problem with women getting into both the hobby and the business. Traditionally, guys who are into comics and related subcultures did not suffer an overabundance of female attention during their adolescence. Now that they are grown-ups, they might see the advantages of having women around who share their interests and passions. Indeed, most of them do. But there remains a hard core for whom arrested adolescence extends beyond the persistence of childhood interests. These are the boys who put the "no girls allowed" signs on the doors of their clubhouse, and those signs are there still.

Perhaps this is why the *Twilight* phenomenon activates such intense passions among the Comic-Con crowd. Back in 2008, when the Con was "invaded" by thousands of young, female *Twilight* fanatics, some guys caused a ruckus by walking the floor with signs and T-shirts reading, "Twilight Is Ruining Comic-Con!" That attitude has gone underground, but it has not gone away. Sure, a lot of the hostility is wrapped around objections to the series itself and its lightweight treatment of the supernatural (fans take this stuff very seriously). But it's telling that many of the same folks who pitch a fit over a couple of twinky, sparkly boy vampires mooning over Bella Swan have no problem with unorthodox treatments of the material that feature mostly naked girl vampires and sexually depraved demons, as can be seen in many modern horror comics. Commitment to the purity of subject matter is apparently only skin deep.

Like all reactionary cultural movements, the anti-*Twilight* sentiment at Comic-Con is rooted in the primal fear that tribal territory is being threatened by outsiders (leavened in this case by a generous helping of sexual anxiety). Young men of the Millennial generation are routinely outdone by their female peers across a wide range of academic, social, and professional achievements. Hardly a month goes by when we don't see one of those "young men in crisis" stories on the cover of a magazine.

Camp Breaking Dawn is a concrete example that even in the traditionally masculine world of fandom, girl nerds can outperform boy nerds when it comes to demonstrating support for their pop culture obsessions. Through their numbers and their visible presence, they are forcing their tastes into the conversation, regardless of the disdain of purists.

Mainstream comics publishers could tap into this audience and make their offerings more female-friendly by cutting down on gratuitously offensive characterizations of women in their books, or perhaps by employing more female creators. But current evidence suggests that publishers see this as a zero-sum game: cut out the cheesecake and you'll alienate the proven audience of male readers—and why risk that? Or perhaps the creative decision makers are simply the products of the same culture as their audience. Whatever the cause-and-effect relationship, most comics demonstrate through their design and marketing that they view male readers as essential, and any women who want to read along are welcome as long as they don't insist on any of that icky frilly-girly stuff like you find in *Twilight*. Typically, female comics fans who speak out on this issue from a feminist perspective are roundly and rudely shouted down, sometimes from the podium.

It's hard to imagine a more self-defeating strategy for the long-run health of the industry. Women today are the loudest and most compelling voices in fandom; young girls are making some of the most popular self-published comics. Decades from now, *Twilight* will be fondly remembered (or ironically inflected) nostalgia for millions of middle-aged women, some of whom will be able to look back on the shared communal experience of sleeping out for days at Comic-Con and having had the time of their young lives. At the fifty-ninth Comic-Con in 2028, I am sure a reunion will be on the program calendar. Maybe one of the (by then) corpulent, middle-aged ex-teen idol stars will get a day pass from the rehab center to attend.

And where are the millions of young fans of *Ben 10* and *Generator Rex*, two popular tween boy–oriented properties with much closer affinities to comics and comics culture than *Twilight*? You can't buy a monthly comic book called *Ben10* or *Generator Rex*, even though the properties belong to Warner Brothers Entertainment, parent of DC Comics, and were created by comics industry veterans. Where, indeed, is the next generation of male comics fans to take over from their nerd-pioneer forebears? I think I saw a few of them playing Game Boys and putting on their best "Can we go now?" expressions as dad pawed through the white boxes in search of that elusive copy of *Avengers* (1963 series) #135.

When it comes to the changing gender balance in the future of pop culture and fandom, the writing is on the wall . . . in blood. And it sparkles.

Strange Synergies: What Do Sitcoms, Buddy Cops, and Talking Dogs Have to Do with Comics?

In the transmedia age, adapting storytelling techniques from one medium to another can unite diverse audiences.

After returning from lunch, we decided to indulge a guilty pleasure and attend a panel on the sitcom *Wilfred*, which had just debuted on the FX network weeks before the 2011 Con. These kinds of miscellaneous programs fill out the Comic-Con schedule throughout the weekend, creating some controversy among purists. Many of them are straight-up marketing pitches for shows that don't have anything at all to do with comics. *Wilfred,* an edgy but otherwise conventional sitcom, has only one contrived point of contact with comics culture: costar Elijah Wood is best known to the world as Frodo Baggins in the *Lord of the Rings* trilogy, as well as for a creepy cameo appearance in the 2006 Frank Miller film *Sin City.*

In *Wilfred*, Wood plays a washed-up and depressed young lawyer named Ryan with a crush on his attractive neighbor and an unusual relationship with the neighbor's dog. Where everyone else sees an ordinary mutt, Ryan (and the audience) sees a slovenly guy in a cheap dog costume, played by Australian co-creator Jason

Photo by Doug Kline

Actor Jason Gann entertains at the *Wilfred* panel.

Gann, who seems to channel the anarchic energy of mid-1970s John Belushi. Hilarity ensues.

Back in 2002, Gann and co-creator Adam Zwar came up with the concept in a short film directed by Tony Rogers. The short won the 2002 Tropfest and later went on to be screened at the Sundance Festival in the United States. It eventually got picked up for two seasons on Australian TV (in a slightly different version, costarring Zwar), then came to the United States courtesy of *Family Guy* producer David Zuckerman, who also participated in the San Diego panel. This kind of bootstrap do-it-yourself story, which is often punctuated these days with a star turn as a viral video on YouTube, has become a standard on-ramp to a mass audience in the transmedia age.

The panel was quite entertaining. The producers screened an unaired episode of the show, then Gann, Wood, actresses Dorian Brown and Fiona Gubelmann, and the rest of the ensemble charmed the crowd during the Q&A. The room frequently shook with laughter.

As far as the FX marketing department goes, it must have been "mission accomplished." Fans who came to see Wood discuss his previous comics-related work and the upcoming *Hobbit* film may have been disappointed with the young actor's reluctance to talk about his other projects, but they probably left with a good impression of the new show. If the producers were lucky, some of these vocal opinion leaders would post about their discoveries on their blogs, Twitter feeds, or podcasts, creating a groundswell of credible word-of-mouth recommendations. This is a necessary but not sufficient step for *Wilfred* to hit the Comic-Con jackpot, where the San Diego buzz propels a borderline show to mass success.

Wilfred is by no means the first rider on the Comic-Con publicity bandwagon, nor the one with the most far-fetched link to the fan base. Comedies, cop shows, and oblique "mystery" programs share the bill with network and cable offerings that have much more straightforward connections to the world of comics, such as the WB hit (and Comic-Con favorite) *Smallville*, based on the Superman mythos. J. J. Abrams brought *Lost* and *Fringe* to Comic-Con, where great word-of-geek-mouth helped propel them from cult to mass appeal. Perhaps the biggest success story of recent times is Tim Kring's *Heroes*, a late addition to the NBC lineup that benefited from orgasmic levels of fan response when it premiered at Comic-Con in 2006.

The fantasy and supernatural subject matter of these shows endears them to fans of comics culture, but the connection is actually much deeper. Episodic TV resembles comics in that both media rely on serialized storytelling with a core cast of characters who develop yet remain fundamentally unchanged. Each individual episode or issue must stand alone to provide a point of entry for newcomers, but form a part of a larger story line to keep people coming back week after week.

Most prime-time TV programs weren't always like this. From the 1950s to the 1980s, very few shows had any kind of continuing story lines from episode to episode. Even heavily plotted dramas, police shows, or science fiction series like *Star Trek* (the original series), which may have had recurring characters or occasional cliffhangers, rarely referred to prior events or offered any coherent sense of their characters' histories and motivations.

The revolution that transformed episodic storytelling first took place in the pages of Marvel Comics in the 1960s, when Stan Lee and his collaborators (principally Jack Kirby and Steve Ditko) wove long story arcs over dozens of issues and multiple titles, each of which also provided a satisfying individual reading experience and usually wrapped up the primary plot points in a single issue. In case anyone wonders why Stan Lee, the kindly old charmer with his name on every licensing deal, is so famous and well regarded today, that's why. The bold artwork and wild flights of imagination and fantasy of the Marvel Silver Age gripped readers, but this sense of integrity to the entire comics universe (provided partly by Lee's consistent writing and editorial voice) kept them coming back for more and buying anything with a Marvel logo on the cover. Before he became a brand unto himself, Stan Lee was one of the most important brand innovators of the twentieth century.

Chris Claremont, who wrote the wildly successful *X-Men* books for Marvel starting in the late 1970s, elevated the continuity aspects of comics storytelling to rarefied heights under the universe-building stewardship of then-Marvel editor in chief Jim Shooter. *X-Men* was not just about good guys and bad guys, or mutants trying to fit into a world that was prejudiced against them; it was an ongoing soap opera with handfuls of overlapping subplots and long-simmering conflicts bubbling along under the surface at any given moment. Like a soap opera, it sometimes got so tangled in its own mythology that casual readers couldn't make heads or tails of any given issue, but hard-core fans kept demanding more story, more X-titles, and greater complexities.

By the early 1990s, when top *X-Men* books were selling millions of copies (many to speculators, but that was unclear at the time), folks in the American TV industry started to take note. Series like the crime drama *Wiseguy* experimented with multiepisode story arcs. *Star Trek: Deep Space Nine* and *Babylon 5* were among the first to use arcs that spanned entire seasons. Soon they were joined by cult classics in a variety of genres, like *Buffy the Vampire Slayer*, *The Adventures of Brisco County Jr.*, and many more. As collected editions (graphic novels for comics; DVD boxed sets for TV shows) became a more common mode of distribution and people could sit down and consume the entire story arc at once, the trend really took off. Today, the continuity-oriented mode is the rule across most of television, and shows that rely on a reality that "resets to default" every episode are the exception. Even a sitcom like *Wilfred* features episode-to-episode continuity that built, it turned out, to a rather troubling finale to season one.

Longtime comics fans are accustomed to this kind of storytelling. They expect it, and they have gravitated to television shows that provide the same sort of density. Well-executed shows in this style that have no connection to comics whatsoever are now discovering that they are attracting comics fans, who tend to be vocal advocates for stuff they like. Consequently, you see networks and producers bolting comics-oriented extras like illustrated online interactive games and graphic novels to properties like *Breaking Bad* in an after-the-fact effort at transmedia integration to mobilize this audience.

The feedback loop has only gotten stronger as innovations in packaging and presentation from the television programming have made their way back to the comics industry. When Joss Whedon's popular *Buffy the Vampire Slayer* and *Angel* series went off the air in the early 2000s, Whedon conceived of doing additional "seasons" as comic book originals. Dark Horse Comics, which pioneered this approach, has duplicated it successfully with other titles. The "season" motif has taken off with other publishers as well, even when they are not adapting TV shows, as a good compromise between the ongoing series (hard for new readers to jump into) and the miniseries (with a built-in expiration date). Marvel Comics adopted this approach for a whole slew of new offerings in 2012.

We've also seen attempts at synergy where the brand strength of a well-known television series or popular creator gets carried over to the comic book adaptation and vice versa (such as DC chief creative officer Geoff Johns writing episodes of *Smallville*). This convergence points toward a very obvious transmedia strategy for both comics and episodic TV (or episodic webcasts in the case of a property like *The Guild*, which has successful live performance and comics manifestations).

But there are a few caveats. Whedon has an unusual talent: he is multilingual when it comes to media, telling his stories as well in comic book form as in television and using each format to its greatest advantage. The path that writers travel between comics and Hollywood has widened from a goat trail to a four-lane highway, but it is littered with wrecks on both sides of the divide. For every Joss Whedon or J. Michael Straczynski (*Babylon 5*), who understands the differences between writing for performance media and writing for sequential art, there are many more who can't quite master the craft. The results are a bunch of stiff, stagy, and overliteral interpretations of comics material on film and TV penned by A-list comic book writers, and a lot of vapid, uncompelling comics credited to brand-name, over-the-title Hollywood creative talent (and book authors, for that matter).

The blurring of the lines on the Comic-Con programming schedule between comics, genre-based movies and TV, and *any* continuity-based story offers a preview of the coming mash-up of pop culture genres, style, and delivery formats that is likely to occur in the near term—accelerated by the rise of devices like tablets that enable the seamless blending of media types on a single platform. This kind of programming at Comic-Con acknowledges that the gyre of popular culture is widening out from central points like comics-fantasy-sci-fi to encompass broader swaths of entertainment, even as the genres themselves are deepening with richer characterizations and social commentary.

There are those who theorize that all storytelling in the digital era is gravitating toward this transmedia style, in which books, video, comics, games, and online media all carry different threads of a master story line or explore different facets of a coherent universe. This is definitely a visible trend at Comic-Con, but we should be cautious about speaking in such sweeping terms, especially with properties that are closely associated with a single creative vision. Not every story wants to be told across multiple media, and not every creator is capable of telling a story across multiple media. And while we are currently at a high-water mark for ambitious, continuity-driven, dramatic pop culture entertainment, public taste may swing back toward stand-alone stories that do not inevitably form some larger tapestry of plot and meaning. Sometimes simpler is better.

Such thinking doesn't serve the mood of the moment, in which the pop culture industry is driven by consolidation on the business side and an urgency to maximize the value of intellectual property (IP) assets across all the channels where the corporate owners have a footprint. In the 2010s, it's all about transmedia and cross-over. That's why the personal brands of individual creators and the personae they cultivate on stage at places like Comic-Con weigh so heavily. The participation of creators and talent who have proven their bona fides to the Con cognoscenti signals that a certain mindset and approach stands behind the work. As the world of entertainment options continues to expand and the boundaries between styles continue to blur, the promoters of these properties need to find ways to break through the clutter and signify to potential audiences that "we get it," even if the cultural affinity is not obvious at first glance.

Still, having a panel is a two-edged sword. The detail-oriented Con audience is tough, and if creators don't come across as sincere and convincing, amateur critics will pick them apart and leave their carcasses to rot on Twitter. If you are a creator, it can be the most satisfying thing in the world to have an audience engage seriously with your work and ask challenging questions. On the other hand, if you come to Comic-Con trying to market a weak concept by tickling the fancy of some of the world's pickiest media geeks, you'd better bring your A game.

After Hours: The Twenty-First-Century Comics Publishing Business

Providing better opportunities for creators is one way for small players to compete in creative industries.

After dinner and a flurry of text messages to determine where everyone was going later, Eunice and I headed back to the Hilton Bayfront to meet a group of friends at a "drink-up" meet-and-greet hosted by BOOM! Studios. BOOM! had been pitching the drink-up hard as an annual fan event for the past year or two, and it appeared from the text messages that we were not the only ones in our circle to decide to forgo the Comic Book Legal Defense Fund party (our usual Thursday night stop) for something a bit different.

Every step of the walk from the restaurant in the Gaslamp Quarter where we ate to the Hilton was a plunge deeper into Con land. Nearly everyone on the streets was a convention-goer, fully kitted out in everything from comic-themed T-shirts, hoodies, and buttons to full-on costumes. Everyone appeared to be in some early stage of drunkenness. Trendy restaurants were colonized by tables full of big bearded guys in baggy Wolverine T-shirts and women dressed as Lara Croft. In what looked like a typical singles bar, a small squadron of Imperial storm troopers played *Magic: The Gathering* at the bar with a fellow in a kilt with a large sword strapped to his back. Any ordinary San Diego denizens who were downtown for their night out must have thought they'd wandered into Mardi Gras on the Planet of the Nerds.

We walked past the convention center, where there were still small crowds bustling back and forth to film screenings, club meetings, game tournaments, and other scheduled activities that go on late into the night. A small line for Friday morning's program had already formed outside Hall H.

There was a steady stream of people heading to and from the Hilton, which loomed in the middle distance, silhouetted by the harbor and the bridge. We entered through the reception area and followed the increasing din to the Indigo bar facing the water in the back. Several hundred people were crowded into the space, chatting and networking at high energy.

We got about three steps inside the bar area when a towering figure came bounding toward us out of the crowd. "Rob! Eunice! Great to see you guys!" Before we could reply, we were wrapped in the welcoming embrace of Chip Mosher, at the time BOOM!'s marketing and sales director. We'd met Chip a year or two earlier and had visited him a few times in Seattle and in his hometown of LA, bonding over comics and our shared Generation X frustrations with managing Millennial-age staff in the workplace (the subject of one of my earlier books). Chip's energy meter, which doesn't seem to dip below 7 under any circumstances, was cranked to 11 tonight. This was his event, and he was doing what he does best: making damn sure everyone knew they were in *the* coolest place in the comics universe at that particular moment.

"Let me introduce you guys to a few people," he said, only half-releasing his embrace. He beckoned to a few casually attired young men and introduced them as BOOM!'s editor in chief and art director. We shook hands and smiled. It was too loud for anything but a perfunctory greeting, and the BOOM! staff needed to spend its time wooing freelancers and winning fans.

BOOM! is one of a handful of new entrants into the comics publishing industry since the late 1990s. It was launched in 2005 with a couple of horror comics, and it has since diversified to include

ComiXology cofounders John Roberts (left) and David Steinberger (right) relax at the BOOM! Studios drink-up with Chip Mosher (center) and ComicsPRO's Amanda Emmert.

everything that a smart, strategically positioned comics publisher would want in its catalog. BOOM! has superheroes (including *Irredeemable*, an original creation of respected veteran Mark Waid), humor titles (such as Shannon Wheeler's Eisner Award–winning *I Thought You Would Be Funnier*), a line of books for kids (Ka-BOOM!), media tie-ins (*Planet of the Apes*), the license (recently reclaimed by Disney) to distribute Disney's venerable Donald Duck and Uncle Scrooge titles, and the inevitable pact with Stan Lee to produce some kind of superhero comics that bear his name and brand. The company has published graphic novels, art books, and alternative-type titles. It issues a steady stream of press releases and announcements, cultivates its fan base through social media, and hosts buzzworthy parties like the Comic-Con drink-up. And it was an industry pioneer in digital comics, doing the first simultaneous day-and-date release way back in 2007.

For its trouble, it has managed to gain something like a 2 percent market share, good for about $5 million gross revenue on sales of about 200,000 units.

As someone who studies entrepreneurship in creative industries, I am constantly stunned by the low returns on ingenuity and effort that seem to haunt the comics business. BOOM! Studios is not alone in this situation. Publishers like Dynamite, IDW, and Avatar Press have all come to the (relatively) mainstream periodical comic book publishing business over the past decade with strong, well-packaged, well-produced offerings from some of the top creators in the field, and they are all fighting like dogs over scraps in a tenement yard.

It should be noted that the small publishers are in a fundamentally different business from Marvel and DC, the "Big Two" that have dominated the industry for decades. Marvel and DC, both of which are now slivers of giant media empires, own the rights to almost all the household-name superhero characters you can think of. They derive most of their income from licensing these properties to everyone from toymakers to fast-food restaurants, as well as developing them into movies, TV series, cartoons, video games, theme-park attractions, and Broadway shows. The income they make from selling comic books amounts to a rounding error in the corporate balance sheet.

In recent times, Marvel and DC each take upward of 35 percent of the total market in both dollar and unit share, while a host of smaller publishers track in the single digits. All told, everyone is fighting over a core audience that may number as few as 300,000 regular readers. The smaller publishers, especially those aiming for the same fanboy/direct market audience as DC and Marvel, can't rely on licensing revenue, at least at first; no one has heard of their properties. They need to build readership for their original characters and concepts, or to get lucky by breathing new life into familiar old characters whose licenses they have acquired. That means that they actually have to create compelling characters and produce comic books that jump off the pages of the Previews catalog or the shelves of a comics shop. And that takes talent.

So how do companies that are fighting over single-digit shares of a tiny, dwindling market attract the kind of creative firepower that can help them compete with the big guys? This is where the entire industry benefits from the glow of Hollywood star power and the buzz of the "peak geek" cultural moment.

Lots of people want to do comics, from amateurs to big-name writers and actors. Small mainstream publishers are perfect venues for up-and-coming artists and writers with promising ideas, visiting dignitaries from other corners of the entertainment world, and for free spirits who want a more stable income than either independent publishers or self-publishing (either print or online) can provide. Smaller companies can also offer creative freedom that the Big Two, with their increasingly centralized creative and production processes, cannot. Their presence at the margins adds vitality and variety to the mainstream market, but their survival depends on the continued interest of other media in comics as a proving ground for concepts, talent, and audience appeal.

Licensed properties or copycat concepts that tie in to other media are pure short-term plays aimed at cashing in on a hot trend or an old-favorite franchise; original content is what builds brand equity for the smaller presses in the long run, especially since so many titles are getting the Hollywood treatment. In the quest for new, potentially licensable characters and media-ready story lines, the policies, history, and behavior of the corporate-owned "Big Two" put them at odds with the interests of the creative community. Few creators of original properties are willing to accept the kind of exploitive, work-for-hire terms that predominated in earlier times. No one wants to create the next hot character without the opportunity to participate in future media revenues or to have a say in the creative strategy. In early 2012, DC provided evidence that even legendary status, prior (nonbinding) assurances of creative control, and the respect of peers take a backseat to profits when it announced a series of prequels to the acclaimed *Watchmen* graphic novel (a corporate-owned property) over the vociferous objections of writer Alan Moore. Marvel successfully sued an aging and destitute freelancer for claiming credit for creating the *Ghost Rider* character and selling signed prints at conventions.

Established industry veterans with big fan followings like Moore, Warren Ellis, and Garth Ennis have gravitated to smaller presses so that they can retain creative and legal control of their creations and enjoy freedom from editorial meddling (though many of these big names also work on corporate-owned projects when the money is right). The star power of these creators within the world of comics helps convince fans and direct market retailers to place orders for unproven titles from second-tier publishers. As a result, a number of entrepreneurial "mainstream" (superhero and genre-oriented) publishers have been able to survive in the market despite the awful economics of the industry.

Oregon-based Dark Horse Comics, founded by Mike Richardson in the mid-1980s, was among the first to lure top-name talent with the promise of creator ownership and control, combined with a professional, forward-looking approach to the business and a keen eye for lucrative licenses (*Star Wars, Buffy*). Perennially in the top five for sales, it has offered perhaps the steadiest stream of original characters and concepts in the mainstream market over the past two decades, including Frank Miller's *Sin City*, Mike Mignola's *Hellboy*, and John Arcudi and Doug Mahnke's *The Mask*, all of which have been developed into creatively and artistically successful movies.

Image Comics, launched by a cadre of bestselling artists looking for a better platform than DC or Marvel could offer in the early 1990s, once seemed like a threat to take over the mainstream with its big, loud superhero comics. After some ups and downs and changes in strategy, the company struck pay dirt again in the late 2000s with Robert Kirkman's era-defining zombie epic *The Walking Dead*, now a hit on the AMC network. Unsurprisingly, *Walking Dead* comics and graphic novels top the sales charts. Another Image property, *Chew*, by John Layman and Rob Guillory, is reportedly in development at Showtime. Both *Chew* and *Walking Dead* are creator-owned.

IDW Publishing, the number 4 or 5 publisher depending on the month, also works both sides of the transmedia street, with successful adaptations of *CSI, Star Trek, True Blood*, and *Doctor Who* to go along with its breakout, media-ready original series *Locke and Key* and *30 Days of Night*. It also publishes archival editions of classic comic strips from the 1930s and 1940s as beautifully designed deluxe hardcovers.

Dynamite Entertainment and other smaller publishers like Avatar Press, Atlas, and First try to win readers by either bringing in fan-favorite writers and artists to refurbish venerable concepts with an up-to-the-minute creative sheen or giving them the freedom to launch projects that the bigger shops wouldn't touch. Avatar's *Crossed*, for example, is a zombie apocalypse title created by Garth Ennis and Jacen Burrows for those who find *Walking Dead* insufficiently gory and disturbing. Dynamite offers updated takes on properties dating from the pulp magazine era of the 1920s and 1930s, including *Zorro, Doc Savage, The Green Hornet, Red Sonja, The Lone Ranger,* and *John Carter of Mars.* Garth Ennis's ribald creator-owned series *The Boys,* Dynamite's best seller, fell into its lap after being kicked off DC's Wildstorm label.

The competition barely dents the revenues of the Big Two, but it has led to some changes in the relationship between the content companies and the creative community. The corporate publishers would obviously prefer to own the IP rather than deal with uppity cartoonists who think they have rights to a character just because they came up with the idea, the story, and the design. Publishers mitigate the dissatisfaction this arrangement causes by paying premium rates to "hired-gun" talent to work on corporate-owned books, and by making special arrangements with top-name creators who invent new characters and concepts. Marvel Comics, which tightly controls its corporate characters like Spider-Man and X-Men and has vigorously defended others like Howard the Duck and Blade from claims of ownership by freelance creators, runs a subbranded label called Icon for big-name talents who want to keep their rights in exchange for lower page rates and less promotion. Mark Millar's *Kick Ass,* adapted for the screen in 2010, came out of this process. DC has similar relationships with certain creators. Now all publishers may be under further pressure: Digital self-publishing offers new avenues to market that don't require publishers at all.

But competition for talent runs both ways. Hollywood's insatiable hunger for comics has created a gold-rush mentality in the industry. For ambitious creators, comics are a much better way to get your idea in front of a producer than sliding your dog-eared screenplay under the door of a men's room stall at a trendy Beverly

Hills eatery. Why not find an artist, get your masterwork published by one of the new firms that let creators keep their rights, then work with one of the agents who specialize in bringing these kinds of projects to production companies?

The visual aspect of comics helps you sell your idea. When filmmakers read comics, they see storyboards: illustrations of how shots can be blocked out and the story created visually. That puts comics a step ahead of written treatments and verbal pitches in terms of scoping out potential costs and logistics. A good artist creates a template for the production design and can even use likenesses to suggest possible casting. When production executives see comics, they see properties that already have a track record in other media, assuaging their fears of working with purely original material. They need not know that the comic may have only sold 5,000 copies, most of them to members of the cartoonist's family. If it is professionally published and well packaged, it's worthy of consideration. After all, comics are hot. Just look at all the people who go to Comic-Con.

This dynamic draws talent and money into the low-sales, low-revenue comics industry that seemingly could realize better returns elsewhere in the entertainment/pop culture universe. It has made the business extremely competitive, especially at the highest levels. Despite the flood of new publishers and titles on the shelves, getting work as a professional is harder than ever. The rising level of skill among artists is evident from just flipping through the pages of a modern comic book, which bears little resemblance to the cheap pamphlets that many of us snapped up for a quarter apiece at the newsstand or 7-Eleven back in the 1970s. The aisles of Comic-Con and every smaller show around the country are crammed with young Art Institute graduates toting portfolios of samples to thrust under the noses of editors. Marvel and DC have become especially selective, but it's not easy for anyone.

All that heat helps bring Comic-Con gatherings like the BOOM! Studios drink-up to a boil. Even small publishers have reason to believe that they might be developing the next big media tie-in. Even artists and writers making meager page rates on books selling in the mid-thousands could get escape velocity faster than you can say "Bryan Lee O'Malley" if their quirky-funny-weird-stylish-genre-bending tale of fantasy and adventure strikes the right chord. So drink up and be merry, starving cartoonists, for tomorrow we all may . . . become rich!

CHAPTER ④

FRIDAY:
ESCAPE
VELOCITY

As Friday morning dawned and we began feeling the effects of the past several days of round-the-clock activity, the reality that there were still three more full days of Comic-Con ahead hit us. The event sprawls, not just over space, but over time as well.

On Friday, the crowds would be fortified by a new contingent of folks driving down from LA for the day or the weekend as we headed toward the peak turnout of more than 130,000. We had a few panels we wanted to attend, but we dreaded the likelihood of spending hours in lines. My plan was to spend most of the morning walking the exhibit hall talking to artists, particularly those in the independent, small-press, and alt.comics areas. In the late afternoon, we'd be called in for our volunteer duty as the setup crew for the Eisner Awards. The award ceremony itself would take up the rest of the evening.

We drew back the blinds and looked down at the street. The San Diego trolleys, on a special schedule for the Con, were making stops every couple of minutes to disgorge another few hundred fans to feed the growing mob scene. Clouds of people drifted across Harbor Drive, which separated downtown and the trolley line from the convention center. We sipped our coffee and took turns pointing out costumes.

Downstairs, the lobby of the Marriott was teeming. Professionals and cartoonists hauling portfolios jostled with women in chain-mail bikinis and dealers pushing dollies heaped with white boxes. The check-in line was out the door, and we spied someone at the counter having a meltdown over a lost reservation. Who could blame her? This is the worst-case scenario: to be without a hotel room despite months of planning, when every room within a 50-mile radius is full or marked up to 10 times the rack rate.

We passed by the makeshift snack bar and continued down the escalator to the ground floor, taking the back way to the convention center to avoid the crowds on the street.

By the time we arrived, the exhibit hall was open and already packed. We entered through the Hall A doors, at the end of the convention center nearest the hotel, made our rendezvous plans, and headed our separate ways.

I decided to begin my day at Artists' Alley, the warren of tables where individual cartoonists and special guests of Comic-Con set up shop to meet fans, sell their original artwork and sketches, and sign copies of their books and comics. In accordance with old-time Comic-Con tradition, Artists' Alley tables are free. Now that real estate in the exhibit hall is at such a premium, the artists have been moved to the far edge of the room in Hall G, several hundred very crowded yards from where I found myself.

The middle of the floor, where the big Hollywood and video-game companies had set up their enormous, imposing displays, was just about impassable. It took more than half an hour, admittedly with lots of distractions and detours, to get from one end of the room to the other. The crowd thinned out considerably past aisle 4500, where the megabooths gave way to fantasy illustrators, fashion designers, dealers in original art, and purveyors of collectible books. In Artists' Alley against the far wall, it was merely the equivalent of the busiest day at any ordinary comics convention— which is to say, practically deserted by Comic-Con standards.

I was especially interested in seeing Jordi Bernet, a legendary European artist with a bold storytelling style that harkened back to classic 1940s American comic strips like *Terry and the Pirates*. He rarely made the trip from Spain, and he hadn't been to Comic-Con since the mid-1990s. There was only one other person in line at Bernet's table, a dealer who had brought all 55 issues of *Jonah Hex* to get them signed, thereby increasing their value as collectibles. The dealer looked on with indifference as Bernet robotically affixed his signature to cover after cover. No words were exchanged. No cash either, as far as I could tell.

While I was waiting, I browsed through the sketches for sale, ranging from pencil roughs to fully realized inked drawings and originals of published pages, each one slightly beyond my price range. Eventually, the dealer moved on. I had a brief conversation with Bernet through his son, who translated between my English and his father's Spanish. I believe I remarked on a great sketch in the pile of the old pulp character The Shadow, leading to a brief

Photo by Henrik Andreasen

Artist Jordi Bernet displays a sketch for a fan at his table in Artists' Alley.

conversation about Frank Robbins, an inspiration of Bernet's who had once drawn the *Shadow* comic book. Such are the things that fans and artists talk about at Artists' Alley tables.

In the next aisle, I saw British artist David Lloyd, best known for his work illustrating Alan Moore's anarchist thriller *V for Vendetta*, sitting by himself trying to unload copies of an old graphic novel. As he paged through my sketchbook, he saw the last page, which had a quick drawing that Bernet had done for me while we were chatting. "Is this by Jordi Bernet?" he asked incredulously, putting the accent on the first syllable of Bernet's last name. "Where on earth did you get that?"

I cocked my head to the left, and Lloyd noticed for the first time that Bernet was sitting not five feet over his shoulder. "Comic-Con," he said with a sigh. No further explanation was necessary.

Hall H: Transmedia Overdrive
Taking established properties into a new medium always involves tradeoffs between fidelity to the source material and reaching a mass audience.

Less than five feet over Lloyd's other shoulder from where these two distinguished European artists sat greeting a smattering of fans, on the other side of a wall that separated the main body of the exhibit floor (Halls A–G) from Hall H, two other masters of words and pictures were addressing a slightly larger audience.

Those two would be Peter Jackson and Steven Spielberg, kicking off the day's program in the convention's largest venue with an hour-long panel on their upcoming film adaptation of Europe's most popular comic character, Tintin.

As much as I might have been interested in hearing these two gentlemen discuss their work and share some previews of the film in progress, getting into Hall H on a whim is a nonstarter. Not every event in Hall H draws Camp Breaking Dawn–magnitude fan intensity, but there is always a line, and unless you are at the very front of it, there is no guarantee that you will get in. Hall H is the 6,500-seat bedroom where the relationship between comics and Hollywood is consummated, in public, nine times a day over the long weekend. It draws a crowd.

People point to the popularity of Hall H programming as a sign that Comic-Con is not about comics anymore, but is just a big

Photo by Doug Kline

Filmmaker Steven Spielberg talking TinTin with the Comic-Con faithful in Hall H.

orgy of Hollywood marketing and hype. It's certainly true that the hype is louder and the names are bigger than ever. Star power has undoubtedly played a role in Comic-Con's off-the-charts attendance boom since the late 1990s, and it has contributed to the media-driven narrative that San Diego is *the* place to be for the entertainment industry.

The truth is that comics fandom has been obsessed with movies from the very earliest days. Forrest J. Ackerman, publisher of the seminal genre-film zine *Famous Monsters of Filmland*, was a guest at the first San Diego Con in 1970 and attended regularly until his death in 2008, helping to cross-pollinate interest between comics and horror and science fiction films. Pioneering special effects director Ray Harryhausen, animator Ralph Bakshi, and B-movie king Lloyd Kaufman may be marginal figures in the film industry, but they are honored guests whenever they turn up at Comic-Con. *Star Wars* famously gave fans a preview at Comic-Con in 1976, and many other movies since then have followed suit.

Death Stars, ghouls, and stop-action sea monsters are all good fun, but nothing turns the crank of comics fans more than big-budget movies that faithfully and respectfully bring superheroes to life on screen. The sense of emotional investment in the popular and artistic success of these movies is hard to fathom if you have not experienced the sense of being an outsider, a nerd, or a loser because of your choice in reading matter. A great superhero film provides much more than an afternoon's entertainment for the long-time comics fan; it validates all those hours spent indulging in a disreputable passion by showing the world that there are some amazing, entertaining, and very lucrative ideas packed into those weird little pamphlets. For fans of a certain age, it's hard to top the experience of Christopher Reeve making you—and all your non-comics-reading friends—believe a man can fly.

Those moments of glee were few and far between in the 1970s and 1980s, when special effects technology was not quite good enough to sell the whole men-in-tights thing, screenwriters didn't get the comics mindset very well, and filmmakers tended to treat the whole genre as a "(Zap! Bam! Pow!)" campy joke. As recently as the mid-1990s, costumed characters were considered box office poison. The Batman franchise, launched so promisingly by Tim Burton in 1989, came to a grisly end with *Batman & Robin*, a neutron bomb of a movie that left the idea of the superhero film intact but destroyed all life within it.

Then came the summers of 2000 and 2001, with the twin peaks of *X-Men* and *Spider-Man*: well-realized, faithfully executed comic book adaptations that worked well as movies and did boffo box office. Around this same time, a new generation that had been raised not just with comics, but with the sophisticated comics fan culture of the 1970s and 1980s, started coming to power in Hollywood studios. They *did* get it, and the box office receipts helped them convince their bosses that the public was ready for superheroes to go mainstream. Thus began the torrid stage of the romance between Comic-Con and Hollywood, which continues to this day.

It's not surprising that Hollywood would turn to comics for inspiration. Comics, like film, are a visual medium, and there are decades' worth of great material, largely unknown to the wider public, buried in those long white boxes of back issues. Comics fans have been saying for years that "they oughta make a movie" of nearly every title on the shelves.

It is also not a shocker that Hollywood has taken a shine to Comic-Con. Let's see: 130,000 pop culture fanatics to market to, all in one place, teeming with press. What's not to like? The advent of social media has only accelerated and amplified the effect that studios hope to achieve—word-of-mouth buzz from trusted, authoritative, and authentic voices, urging their millions of Facebook friends, Twitter followers, blog readers, and online gaming partners to check out this amazingly awesome new thing they saw at the coolest event in the freakin' universe, Comic-Con!

Note that this doesn't always work. In 2010, Eunice and I wanted to see the panel featuring the entire cast of the much-buzzed *Scott Pilgrim vs. the World*, based on the million-selling graphic novel series by Bryan Lee O'Malley and beloved by hipsters everywhere—occupying the prime timeslot of Saturday evening on the Hall H schedule. The panel was fantastic; the clips brought roars of laughter and standing ovations; the filmmakers were clearly simpatico with the source material; the celebrity cast, present in its entirety, was funny and unpredictable (diminutive star Michael Cera was wearing a Captain America costume, complete with padded muscles); and everyone in the hall was probably tweeting, Facebooking, and skywriting at the top of their lungs to tell the world how much they couldn't wait to see the movie.

Funny thing: *Scott Pilgrim vs. the World* came out a few weeks later and went straight to the pet cemetery. The Comic-Con buzz generated in Hall H that year was as loud and positive as any I've heard about any media property in the 12 years I've attended the Con, and it still couldn't save this offbeat, genre-crossing movie at the box office.

So far, studios have stuck with the comics formula, despite the hit-or-miss quality of the marketing payoff and the spotty track record of comics properties in both critical and commercial terms, because when movies of this kind hit, they hit big. And they spin off sequels and create the coveted "franchise," a moneymaking machine that brings in bigger audiences with reduced marketing costs each time out.

The result has been a windfall for intellectual property owners (either creators or publishers). For most cartoonists, the money they get just to option a title for development is a big paycheck, even if the film never gets close to being made. Entire comics publishing enterprises now exist to harvest Hollywood dollars, with the comics themselves serving as little more than slick marketing flyers for potential blockbuster franchises. When Disney paid $4 billion for Marvel Comics in 2009, it seemed unlikely that it was all that interested in getting into the comic book business, given that Disney has licensed its own characters to other comics publishers for decades. But Marvel had demonstrated two important strengths: its content was a magnet for tween- and teenage boys, filling a long-time gap in Disney's market reach; and it had demonstrated the unique ability to bring its entire universe of interrelated characters and stories to the screen in a potentially endless franchise featuring the most popular comic book properties in the world. If Disney even comes close to pulling it off, $4 billion will seem like the bargain of the century.

The snag in this money conveyor belt is all those pesky comics fans. Comics fans take a proprietary interest in the characters and the story lines. Having been burned by bad, campy, or ill-conceived renditions of comics in the mass media that made their enthusiasm seem ridiculous to outsiders, they greet each new announced comics-related project by scrutinizing the creative team, the cast, and the production details, closely tracking the development of the script and publicly debating every breadcrumb of evidence across the Internet. Though the volume of their commentaries vastly exceeds their numbers, studio marketing departments can't afford to ignore these early influencers. The difference between good buzz and bad buzz leading up to a release can mean the difference between winning the all-important opening weekend and coming in second.

Comic-Con is the Iowa caucus for comics and genre movies: the early barometer that can make or break a campaign. And like the folks who turn out every four years in Iowa to vet their party's presidential field before the general election, those in the Comic-Con crowd are as unrepresentative of the wider world as they are committed to their particular ideologies. But they are very important, especially because the lights of the media blaze down on San Diego like the Eye of Sauron. Consequently, an amusing asymmetry has emerged in the relationship between the studios and the Comic-Con audience.

Even the biggest film stars who come to San Diego now act as if they are casual comics fans, as steeped in esoteric trivia as the guy in the third row wearing the Ambush Bug costume. I recall the stately Helen Mirren appearing on a panel in 2010 sporting a T-shirt honoring the plainspoken comics memoirist Harvey Pekar, who had died several weeks previously (a very sophisticated choice on the part of her PR staff, I must say). The burden of having to seem geek-tolerant and *totally not* the kind of popular girl that dissed nerds in high school falls especially heavily on the shoulders of the hot young actresses cast in comics-oriented action movies. Luckily, it doesn't take much work for them to win over most comics fans. If every star who professed fandom from the stage at Comic-Con actually bought comics, there wouldn't be a sales problem. But, you know, they're actors. They can pull it off.

Directors of comics-related properties who come to the Con to discuss their works in progress must go a step further. They are obliged to pay obsequious homage to their source material or face the wrath of the crowd. "We loved [comic creator X, famous only within the comics community]'s vision and want to make sure we get as close to that as possible" is a guaranteed applause line in Hall H, and promises of this sort follow filmmakers through the production process as stills from the movie leak out and are splayed out on dissection plates across the comicsphere. The Con audience is famously fickle, not to mention picky and literal about story details in ways far beyond those of ordinary mortals. Poorly designed costumes, scenes that don't look right, or evidence of miscast actors can put a comics-related project behind the eight ball with the only audience that's paying attention years before a film is released.

The problem is, faithfulness to source material is not always the path to box office gold. Many fan-favorite comics are grandiose, bombastic, and slightly ridiculous; it's part of their appeal. Translating these epics to a live-action medium requires a deft touch. Dialogue that sparkles on the page can die in the mouth of a live actor. Manipulations of reality that a comics artist can accomplish with the flick of a brush might take millions of dollars of computer-generated imagery (CGI) to realize on-screen and still ring false. Most of all, the shift in context can be fatal. Like a goth band playing an outdoor concert on a sunny day, the music may sound the same, but the vibe just isn't right.

Watchmen (2009) is perhaps the signal example of filmmaking designed to cater to Comic-Con fundamentalism. Alan Moore and Dave Gibbons's classic 12-issue miniseries came out in 1986 and was later collected into a bestselling graphic novel. It is considered by many to be the literary peak of the superhero genre and a masterpiece of graphic storytelling. Deliberately paced, ornately constructed, and permeated with Reagan/Thatcher-era political paranoia, it was optioned for development almost immediately after its publication, but it languished for a quarter century because no one could figure out how to film it. When the latest project was announced in the mid-2000s, expectations were skyhigh.

Director Zack Snyder, who'd proven his bona fides by bringing Frank Miller's testosterone-fueled, visually impactful, one-dimensional graphic novel *300* to the screen as a testosterone-fueled, visually impactful, one-dimensional film that looked like Miller's drawings had come to life, had a couple of ways to go. He could have reimagined *Watchmen* in cinematic terms by making some changes to the story and narrative to fit the strengths of the film medium. But doing so would have meant tampering with a Sacred

Text and courting the wrath of the Comic-Con faithful. Instead, he took the Hall H pledge: change nothing; be true to the literal word and image; recreate the 1986 graphic novel down to the last detail, sparing no expense or CGI trick.

When *Watchmen* was released to massive hype in the spring of 2009, the wider audience might have wished that he had changed a *few* things to make the story accessible to people who were just in the theater to see a good movie. Snyder made the film so earnestly reverential that he didn't correct for flaws in the original or consider how some of Moore's cold war concerns and 1980s storytelling techniques might fall flat with a postmillennial audience. The visual framing of every shot was adapted almost verbatim from artist Dave Gibbons's pages and realized with state-of-the-art digital effects, but on the big screen, the costumes just looked silly. The result was a movie that pleased no one: not the mass audience, which found it inexplicably pretentious and confusing; not the comics fans, who found it embarrassing; and not Moore himself, whose work has been particularly ill served in film adaptations over the years.

I don't mean to pick on *Watchmen* specifically; Snyder took on a tough challenge and succeeded in some important ways, despite the film's flaws. But it's telling that bad comic book movies are often bad in this same overliteral way. With *Watchmen*, Snyder held a mirror up to the face of the Comic-Con tastemaking crowd and revealed to the world the limitations of the originalist instincts of hard-core comics fans when it comes to making movie blockbusters.

When we talk about the transmedia future, we're talking about getting this balance right. Comics is a medium unto itself. *Watchmen* works supremely well as sequential art, where readers can linger over the details, go back and reread different sections, identify with visual and narrative allusions to the history of comics themselves, and savor the buildup of the long story line. All that goodness can be undone by uprooting the property from its native medium. If you try to film a story that was created for comics—whether one as elaborate as *Watchmen* or as straightforward as *The Fantastic Four*—without thinking deeply about what parts of the experience carry over into the motion picture medium and which don't, you end up with a very low-resolution version of the creative concept. That can end up hurting your brand or property with everyone, not extending it to a new audience.

The same problem can sometimes go the other way, when properties licensed from other media are brought into comics. Comic book adaptations of films, TV shows, and cartoons are common, but they have always had a spotty history. Because nearly every reader starts with a fixed mental picture of the original movie or TV show, the sequential art medium has a hard time matching up to live action—particularly when artists are required to capture the likeness of the actors portraying the characters rather than just drawing original characters who fit the story. Even the most successful movie property in comics, *Star Wars*, fares much better when the creative teams can improvise on the broader themes and tease out dangling plot threads rather than adapting the movies themselves.

Finding the balance for telling satisfying stories across multiple media is the key to the future of comics and pop culture properties as we move from a world of siloed audiences and media types to a global mashup of styles and formats. Sometimes the success or failure of a transmedia project comes down to one brilliant decision (casting Robert Downey Jr. as likably arrogant Tony Stark in *Iron Man*) or one boneheaded one (thinking Frank Miller was the right guy to adapt Will Eisner's *The Spirit* for the big screen), from which all good and bad things about the project then flow. Most of the time, it is more complex.

Hall H is the test lab where these experiments are first exposed to the light of day. It's not a natural environment, and the peculiarities of the setting and the crowd can introduce some distortions into both the creative and the marketing processes.

So far, Hollywood has been willing to tolerate the distortions and indulge the demanding tastes of the Comic-Con audience in exchange for access to the mother lode of franchise-worthy content from the comics universe and the built-in fan base. As long as this relationship continues, it's endless summer for the comics industry. All the problems of sales and distribution vanish in a cloud of movie money, and everyone can keep flooding the market with thousands of titles. Comics, movies, video games, toys, and fashion will continue to fuse into "branded transmedia content," capitalizing on the mind share of familiar names and logos to keep a global audience coming back for more.

Inevitably, however, even long, hot summers give way to the cool and dark of autumn. Big-time disappointments like *Watchmen, Scott Pilgrim,* and *Green Lantern* did not kill the comics-movie buzz as thoroughly as *Batman & Robin* did back in the 1990s, but there may soon come a time when the superhero genre loses its charm for the mass audience. At the ICv2 conference, there were rumblings that the day of reckoning is at hand and that studios might not be so ready to say yes to new projects. In that scenario, what is the value of DC to Warner Brothers, or Marvel to Disney? Where is the path to profits that help BOOM! Studios and IDW and the others repay their investors and keep their creative talent engaged?

"Mainstream comics" have lashed themselves to the mast of the entertainment industry. Their future is now in the hands of studio executives and marketing teams, who see them, and the comics audience, as useful but ultimately disposable pieces in a much bigger game. Waiting in the three-hour line to get into Hall H on the weekend, it's easy to imagine the future of comics with the transmedia winds at their back. It's also chilling to consider what might happen if the gales ever subside.

Artists at the Circus: Are Alt.Comics Part of Pop Culture?
The ongoing mix of art and commerce in the twenty-first century may soon lead to greater market segmentation within the pop culture space.

Despite the encroachments of Hollywood, there remains a part of Comic-Con that is still fundamentally about comics and the people who make them, many of whom have no interest in superheroes, movies, or video games. For decades, this "comics-as-art" strain has coexisted with the superhero mainstream, united by a common medium of expression. "It's all just comics!" has been a rallying cry across the diverse tribes at San Diego for decades. Lately it's taken on an ironic inflection as serious artists fight with their louder, gaudier, and better-resourced cousins for space and recognition, and you can see the contrasts play out during the five days of the Con.

If you are interested in checking out the variety of personal and independent voices working in comics at Comic-Con, you'd best bring a comfortable pair of walking shoes. The distinction between being a working professional cartoonist, a self-published independent, a small press, or an alternative publisher can be purely semantic, as any one of those terms could translate to "one guy (or gal) doing his (or her) own comics." But at Comic-Con, the working cartoonists who take free tables in Artists' Alley are marooned at the far end of Hall G, independents have prime real estate at the front of Hall C, the small press area is in the back by the snack bar, and the alternative publishers like Last Gasp, Fantagraphics, and Drawn and Quarterly occupy a relatively sedate zone between the booths of the collectible comics dealers and the bigger imprints like DC and Marvel.

The scale of these individual publishing enterprises doesn't necessarily tell you anything about their subject matter. Some ground-level creators are doing superhero or genre-type material in very small print runs or on the web, hoping to get noticed by editors higher up on the food chain; some fine artists are using comics as a medium for visual experimentation and have no interest in traditional comic book subject matter at all; others are working in literary genres, principally autobiography or magical realism, taking advantage of the broader palette of sequential art to add a new dimension to their storytelling.

This last tradition is what cordons off "alt.comics" from other independent and small press activity. These folks take their cues from the underground comics of the 1960s, which themselves descended from comics' playful, satiric, or absurdist veins, typified by the work of creators like Basil Wolverton, Harvey Kurtzman, and Walt Kelly. In modern times, the influence of Robert Crumb looms large as the inspiration for at least two generations of confessional, explicit, autobiographical stories, illustrated in a deliberately "smaller-than-life" style to contrast with the bombastic affectations of the "mainstream" superhero books.

The undergrounds livened up the medium by introducing adult themes, but the novelty of comics with sex and drugs soon wore thin, and the distribution channel (head shops) collapsed as the war on drugs intensified through the 1970s. Still, the floodgates of creative experimentation were open, and the Baby Boom generation of readers and creators was ready to push the boundaries. The alternative comics movement in North America grew increasingly self-conscious and art-oriented during the 1980s under the editorial leadership of three pugnacious Baby Boomers who will probably cringe at being mentioned in the same sentence: Denis Kitchen (Kitchen Sink Press), Art Spiegelman (*RAW*), and Gary Groth (Fantagraphics).

Kitchen Sink, from its humble beginnings in 1969, carried the torch of the underground into the 1970s and 1980s, mixing adventurous newcomers like Chester Brown, Joe Matt, Charles Burns, Reed Waller, and Kate Worley with past masters Will Eisner, Milton Caniff, and Al Capp; 1960s-era standouts Jack Jackson, Rand Holmes, Crumb, and Kitchen himself; and up-and-coming talents with a more mainstream bent like Mark Schultz (*Cadillacs and Dinosaurs*), Don Simpson (*Megaton Man*), and James O'Barr (*The Crow*). This blend of old and new helped bring more challenging and personal work to the attention of traditional comics fans without the confrontational edge that fueled others in the movement.

Spiegelman and his wife, Françoise Mouly, launched *RAW*, an audacious oversized magazine in the style of Andy Warhol's *Interview*, in 1980, and for most of the decade, it embodied the avant-garde sensibilities pouring out of the downtown New York art scene. Featuring the primitivist stylings of Gary Panter, early work by Charles Burns, and the grotesque pointillist caricatures of Drew Friedman, *RAW* pushed the aesthetics of comics far beyond anything that had come before. Spiegelman himself carried the ball over the goal line for comics' first and arguably biggest literary triumph when his Holocaust memoir *Maus*, told in graphic novel form using animals to depict Nazis and their Jewish victims, won the Pulitzer Prize in 1986.

Groth, along with then-partner Mike Catron (and eventually copublisher Kim Thompson), acquired an old-time comics fanzine called the *Nostalgia Journal* in 1976 and turned it into *The Comics Journal*, a fire-breathing news and opinion organ that tried to bring higher standards to comics and comics criticism. In the 1980s, Fantagraphics began publishing some of the most important work by a new generation of U.S. and European alternative comics creators, starting with the magnificent *Love and Rockets* by Los Bros Hernandez (Jaime, Gilbert, and Mario), and eventually including top talent like Peter Bagge (*Hate*), Dan Clowes (*Eightball, Ghost World*), Jim Woodring, and many others. Fantagraphics remains a publishing force to this day; it has recently focused on bringing out deluxe editions of archival material (*Peanuts, Krazy Kat*) and critical works rather than periodicals.

Through the 1990s, more and better serious work from this movement began appearing, challenging and eventually demolishing old critical prejudices that presumed that any drawn stories were necessarily aimed at children or illiterates. The stylists who got their start in the 1980s and 1990s now produce graphic novels that get respectful reviews in highbrow publications and rank with some of the most interesting literary works of the new century.

The alt.comics booths at Comic-Con are piled high with beautifully designed editions of thoughtful works of fiction, comment, and personal narrative. Some of the most accomplished creators working in any medium are on hand to sign, sketch, and converse. In 2011, Chester Brown, author of a controversial graphic memoir *Paying for It* (about his personal experiences patronizing prostitutes) that was currently climbing the bestseller charts, was a frequent presence at the Drawn and Quarterly booth, engaging interested parties in discussions about the morality of the sex industry or whatever else was on their minds.

The atmosphere in their section of the exhibit hall is so different from that of its big-media neighbors that it is sometimes hard to believe that you are in the same room. At any other kind of show, these serious artists and authors would be the center of attention. In any other medium, their works would be considered "mainstream," while costumed superheroes would be shelved in the children's section. But at Comic-Con, the bestselling authors and serious artists are "alternative," and they stand watching crowds of adults in spandex costumes bustling off to have their photos taken with Lou "The Hulk" Ferrigno.

The presence of the "alternative" publishers and creators may seem out of place in the circus atmosphere of Comic-Con in the 2010s, but the leading contemporary publishers of literary comics and graphic novels—Top Shelf, Drawn and Quarterly, First Second, NBM, Fantagraphics, and a handful of others—are as important to the artistic future of the comics medium as Hollywood and the video-game industry are to its commercial future.

It should also be noted that the development of comics as a medium for the exploration of serious literary and artistic topics occurred in parallel with the exploitation of comics genres and comics properties in the mass media. Though these are often viewed as interrelated by those outside the industry, including critics and cultural gatekeepers, they are actually two distinct phenomena.

A prime contributor to the confusion between the commercial and artistic successes of comics is the rise of the term *graphic novel*, originally popularized by Will Eisner in 1977 to distinguish his long-form collection of Depression-era stories, *A Contract with God*,

Photo by Henrik Andreasen

Acclaimed graphic novelist Chester Brown promotes his latest work at the booth of his publisher, Drawn and Quarterly.

from other kinds of work that were then being produced in hopes of attracting a mass-market publisher. In the 1990s, as the big comics companies sought to expand their markets through the bookstore channels, any bound collection of work in comics format, from original long-form works to reprinted superhero stories, was designated a "graphic novel" for marketing and categorization purposes. The distinction between comics and graphic novels, which Eisner and his ambitious progeny once hoped might separate artistic and literary efforts from commercial ones, crumbled.

The commercial end of the spectrum benefits from this confusion because the existence of critically recognized, serious work in the sequential art medium, such as the graphic novels of Marjane Satrapi (*Persepolis*) or Robert Crumb (*Genesis*), confers a penumbra of artistic respectability over *all* comics—particularly those sold in bookstores. This is an ironic reversal from earlier times, when artists working in the industry told friends that they drew greeting cards rather than admit that they did comics. Now even the most commercial-minded purveyors of superheroics and zombie tales can claim the impressive title "graphic novelist"— never mind if their work is any good. In this way, the critically acclaimed work of the serious artists serves as air cover for the colonization of popular culture by the more commercial end of the comics industry.

The process also works in reverse, causing a lot of agita among the literary comics crowd. Critics have come a long way in their ability to discuss works in the sequential art medium intelligently, but there is still a lingering perception that the shared visual language of comics equates to a shared sensibility among all cartoonists, regardless of obvious differences in their styles and interests. The creators of graphic novels, drawn books, and sequential art memoirs are thus presumed to have some kind of inherent affinity with the purveyors of *Spawn* and *Spider-Man* just because they are working in the same medium. After all, it's just comics.

There are some who believe that the presence of serious alt.comics creators and publishers at Comic-Con just muddies the waters. Writer/artist Eddie Campbell, who has given quite a bit of thought to the medium of comics and its history in addition to creating deep and personal work, was absent from San Diego because he did not feel that his current material benefited from association with the more pop culture aspects of the show. Literary comics share an aesthetic heritage with other work in the comics medium (which was quite diverse in terms of subject matter prior to the 1970s), but at this point in the medium's development, many people feel that the market should move beyond the "Zap! Bam! Pow! Comics Aren't Just for Kids Anymore" headlines that have topped trend stories on graphic novels in the media for decades. Events like Comic-Con, with their prominent emphasis on superheroes and Hollywood, reinforce old prejudices and do not help promote broader awareness of the potential of the art form beyond the obvious.

Campbell's point is important, but the boundaries are not so clean. Graphic novels offer a continuum of content ranging from pure pop culture (such as superheroes and fantasy) to realistic genre work (mystery, horror, and so on) to traditional literary topics like general fiction, autobiography, and political commentary. Artists often use the visual dimension of graphic storytelling to make allusions to parts of the comic heritage that are very fan-oriented and pop culture–specific, even in the context of more serious work. The reality is that despite enormous progress in broadening the audience, many consumers of graphic novels are grown-up comic book readers. They understand the visual language and connect to the author's intentions because of their insider knowledge, just like mainstream fans of superhero comics.

There is also a lot of crossover among the creative talent, partly because few alt.comics publishers can match the paychecks of the mainstream. Matt Kindt, creator of the delightful graphic novel *Super Spy*, has done work for Marvel and DC; David Mazzucchelli drew *Daredevil* and *Batman* in the 1980s before he produced his

2010 tour de force *Asterios Polyp*. Even the mostly independent Campbell has done the odd job for DC and Vertigo. This does not make these creators less serious by any means, but it does end up creating some cross-pollination of readership.

Though its audience and talent pool may overlap with that of the commercial comics industry to a larger degree than it might want to admit, the alt.comics scene is largely self-contained and pursues its own aesthetic. Most of the time, this crowd gathers at indie-oriented comics shows like The MoCCA Festival, sponsored by New York's Museum of Comic and Cartoon Art, the Small Press Expo (SPX), the Alternative Press Expo (APE), and Portland's Stumptown Comics Show, where its revels are undiluted by the presence of costumed fans and professional wrestlers.

Because the direct market has not exactly been kind to nonmainstream comics over the years, many creators and publishers have tried to develop separate distribution channels to avoid the fist-sized knot of traditional comics stores. Alt titles have found homes in music shops, art galleries, specialty stores, and independent bookstores (though their distribution prospects have lately dimmed in tandem with the general decline of independent retail). Many top talents are published by traditional book imprints like Norton or Random House, and avoid the direct market almost entirely. Some top creators took to the Internet much earlier than the larger players (usually in the form of advertising-supported or syndicated web-comics or comic/blog hybrids rather than as digital downloads). As we will see, a lot of the most successful online comics creators fit more neatly into the "alternative" or "new mainstream" modes than they do into the popular print genres, and these are the folks who have figured out how to make a living completely outside the old publisher/distribution model.

Their transmedia model works differently as well. When alt. comics properties make it to the big screen, as in the case of *Ghost World*, *Persepolis*, and *American Splendor* in recent years, they look and behave more like adaptations of books than like adaptations of comics. It's hard to imagine anything in the alt.comics space becoming a "tentpole franchise" or summer blockbuster material, and it's even harder to imagine the work of, say, Chris Ware or Alison Bechdel being made into a video game.

The continued artistic development and critical reception of alt.comics seems assured. Their access to their audience is not as problematic as that of comics sold exclusively through the direct market, and the barriers to digital adoption are not as profound. In September 2011, the alt.comics publisher Top Shelf started making complete graphic novels available in digital format through various channels at appealing price points, and others are likely to follow suit. Graphic novels figured heavily in the launch strategies of Amazon's and Barnes & Noble's competing tablet products that debuted in late 2011. It stands to reason that literary-oriented graphic novels with appeal beyond the superhero fan base are a killer app for hardware and content vendors selling to the affluent, literate, and tech-savvy early adopters who will decide the first round of their competition.

The publishers who specialize in graphic novels and reprints are also likely to hang on to whatever market remains for high-end, well-designed print books, because the design of graphic publications frequently adds a lot to the content, and the packaging is part of the total creative conception. Their audience is not just the Wednesday comics shop crowd but book buyers: people who do not mind shelling out for a handsome edition that sits proudly on the shelf or the coffee table.

What is uncertain is whether literary comics and graphic novels will continue to remain a part of popular culture just because they share a graphic vocabulary and heritage with mainstream comics. As DC, Marvel, Image, and the others form closer connections with other media and the commercial entertainment industry, alt.comics will continue to push the aesthetic and storytelling boundaries of the medium. Their talent pools and audience may diverge even further as new generations of creators emerge who owe less to the common comics ancestry and more to their immediate influences in art and literature. The continued presence of the alt.comics community at venues like Comic-Con will serve as a test to determine whether the world of popular culture still has a place for the artistic and the experimental.

If it turns out that the big comics publishers can't survive the current market challenges—if digital distribution leads to the demise of the direct market, or if the relationship with Hollywood sours—the future of comics may belong exclusively to the individual voices and the small presses. In that scenario, the entire perception of comics within the culture would shift away from spectacular superheroics and genre work, and be seen increasingly as the province of idiosyncratic artists working in a medium of words and pictures. In this "Ghost World" of high artistic achievement but low cultural salience, the industry, the vocation, and the hobbyist aspects of comics would be much diminished in economic viability, but the respect accorded to top creators and prestigious editions of their work would be at an all-time high. Comics as popular culture would fade away, replaced by a more exclusive and niche-oriented art form.

There is precedent for this kind of rapid marginalization of a mass entertainment medium. In the 1920s, 1930s, and 1940s, jazz was American popular music. When the economics of the postwar period made it hard for the big bands to maintain their audience through touring, smaller groups turned to styles like bebop, which emphasized individual voices and challenging harmonics. This appealed to critics and serious listeners, but it alienated the mass audience that wanted accessible dance music. By the 1960s, jazz listeners consisted primarily of connoisseurs and fellow musicians, and jazz had been supplanted in the popular music vernacular by rock and roll.

A future in which American comics have transcended popular culture, for better or worse, is hard to imagine when walking the Comic-Con exhibit hall in 2011—a place that savors more of Ozzy Ozbourne than Thelonious Monk. But then again, it was probably hard to imagine the intimate jazz clubs and cultural festivals of today from the packed dance floor of the Savoy Ballroom in 1941.

The Future of Nostalgia: How Fans Co-create Their Media Experience

Nostalgia gives fandom its soul and stickiness, but the changing generational tastes of fans feed back into the business in unexpected ways and transform old notions of content creation.

After spending the morning hanging out with creators whose individual visions are pushing comics into the future, I planned to spend the afternoon basking in comics' glorious past. Buried deep in the Comic-Con Events Guide is a programming track dedicated to interviews and discussions with the art form's most illustrious living creators and historical figures, or tributes to ones who are no longer around.

These panels were the centerpiece of Comic-Con in the old days, before the Hollywood-transmedia deluge. Motivated by a desire to recognize the neglected heroes of the early days of comics, fans would get together to talk about, or with, Jack Kirby, Will Eisner, Harvey Kurtzman, and other pioneers. Because the American comic book industry traces its roots only as far back as the 1930s, a great many of the most important figures were active into the 1970s, 1980s, and beyond. Some had moved on to other pursuits and had no idea that anyone took their comic work seriously until they trundled out onto the Comic-Con stage to peals of applause. Attending these panels was the equivalent of going to the Constitution Center in Philadelphia to hear the Founding Fathers themselves debate the fine points of federalism: super cool if you happen to be into that kind of thing (and worse than watching your grandmother clean her dentures if you are not). For longtime attendees, this track of programming *is* Comic-Con; everything else is just noise.

The sentimentality and nostalgia that inspired the early fans are woven into the DNA of the institutions they created, including Comic-Con. Vestiges of the old ways have persisted even as Comic-Con mutated into the pop culture monstrosity it has become in the 2010s. Heidi MacDonald calls these atavistic relics "ancient Pictish rituals," equating them to the mysterious folkways of rural Britain that survived succeeding waves of foreign conquerors. Their antiquity confers authenticity, a commodity that is more valuable at Comic-Con because of its short supply. Panels featuring old-timers are lightly attended, but they are real. They anchor comics fandom and comics conventions in something other than consumerism and spectacle.

These days, the ranks of the Golden Age greats have thinned to nearly bare, but even into the current day it is possible to make a human connection to the very beginnings of the industry. Jerry Robinson, an artist who worked on the first *Batman* stories in the late 1930s (he created the Joker) and remained a vocal advocate for creators' rights throughout his long career, was signing, sketching, and greeting fans in Artists' Alley between panel appearances and interviews at the 2011 convention. (He passed away the following December at age 89.) A few others from this era are still around if you know where to look. But time marches on, and soon we will say goodbye to the last of the founding fathers.

We may also soon be saying goodbye to the first generation of fans who cared about them, and that is arguably an even greater break from the past for comics, Comic-Con, and the widening world of pop culture in which comics play a part. All popular art forms and hobbies have fans, but comics fandom is unique in the way it combines nostalgia, scholarship, amateur creativity, advocacy, community, and performance. Fandom has traced its own arc in parallel with that of the comics industry and the comics art form, and has been influenced by the same dynamics present in the wider culture, including technology and the procession of generations.

In today's social-media-driven, always-connected world, it's trendy to talk about "co-creation of content" and "crowdsourcing your brand" to customers. Comics fandom has embodied this principle for more than 50 years. To be a comics fan, it is rarely enough to simply "like" comics; you need to know them inside and out, and to express opinions that reflect your well-developed tastes. Sometimes this takes the form of creating original works in beloved genres or using familiar characters and scenarios.

Comics fans were early adopters of "fan fiction" (independent and unlicensed stories featuring characters from popular comics, films, and TV shows like *Star Trek*), which has proved to be a bane to litigious-minded corporate IP owners. As software and networks lowered the barriers to publishing and media creation, fan fiction extended to digital media and community sites with wide reach, forcing content owners to either reach an accommodation with fans or confront them more directly with cease-and-desist letters (a strategy that usually comes with disastrous PR blowback).

Fan-produced *Star Wars* films, screened annually at Comic-Con, feature stunning production values and special effects in addition to story lines that build on the mythos. Lucasfilm offers awards, and sometimes jobs, for the winners. Original works like the web series *The Guild* have added a layer of professionalism to the fan-fiction tradition, creating a revolutionary new channel for the creation and distribution of video content. Production companies in the 2010s are paying close attention to this trend, and original web-produced series are likely to play a very big part in the media mix as the decade unfolds.

Today, businesses in a wide variety of industries are investing billions to generate the kind of fan engagement that comics have had since their earliest days. The comics industry anticipated, sometimes by decades, best practices around customer relationship management, at least with readers and fans. As far back as the 1960s, editors engaged in dialogues with readers in the letter pages of the magazines. DC editor Julius Schwartz printed the addresses of his correspondents, encouraging fans to form connections with one another in a postcard-driven social network. These connections laid the groundwork for the fandom that eventually snowballed into comics culture and Comic-Con.

Marvel editor-in-chief Stan Lee established a clear voice for the Marvel brand in his house ads and "Stan's Soap Box" columns, giving birth to the catchphrases that follow him around half a century later ("Face front, true believers!" "Nuff Said!"). These little touches made readers feel special, and they provided differentiated value to the content of Marvel comics that was obvious to anyone who was paying attention at the time. The brand loyalty of "Marvel Zombies" is legendary, and in some cases it persisted well into adulthood.

DC Comics even conducted an early experiment in crowdsourcing in the late 1980s, asking fans to determine the fate of an annoying new version of Batman's sidekick Robin as his life hung in the balance. Bloodthirsty readers gave the new Robin (Jason Todd) the thumbs down, and the creative team dutifully had him killed in an explosion. Companies looking to the wisdom of crowds for product development guidance might want to keep this example in mind.

When the Internet came along, comics publishers were among the first to set up organized sites and chat rooms to engage fans online. Though these often degenerated into pools of rancor and invective, they clearly ignited the passions of the audience and created a sense of intrigue and anticipation around every new story line, every change in creative teams, and any rumors of upcoming developments. The convention panel appearances of Marvel chief creative officer (formerly editor-in-chief) Joe Quesada or his DC counterpart Dan DiDio took on the atmosphere of Pentagon briefings, with closed-mouthed executives and sworn-to-secrecy creative teams sparring with fans and bloggers digging for details.

The intensity of dedicated fans can be a bit overwhelming to ordinary people. Though nerds have broken through to achieve greater recognition and a modicum of respect in the mainstream culture, portrayals such as those on CBS's popular comedy *The Big Bang Theory* are funny because they are kind of true. Marketing professionals like to talk about consumer influencers and opinion leaders. These folks have plenty of opinions, highly refined taste in their fields of interest, and a great love of sharing their views. Because they clearly do not court popularity in the conventional sense, their voices are highly credible—and they know it.

The high level and changing nature of fan engagement since the early 1960s has influenced the development of the medium, both commercially and artistically. Crossover between fans and professionals is common; the letter columns of 1960s DC and Marvel comics are studded with missives from future writers, artists, and editors. Today a lot of the top fan-oriented publications are edited by ex-pros. Companies shape their plot lines and "event" story lines to suit the tastes of fans, and go to great lengths to create intrigue in the fan community around the most picayune details of story and art.

The close attention to the content of comics, their history and development, and the importance of individual styles give comics fandom its coherence and keeps fans engaged, because the conversation never ends. The reverence for the past is conservative in the best and truest sense of the word; it is the glue that binds all the tribes of Comic-Con together after 40 years. But it is also fundamentally backward-looking, and at its worst, it draws current-day comics continuously back to tropes, story lines, and formats that are well past their sell-by date.

The contributions of the early comics fans was the subject of the panel I attended on Friday afternoon. One of the themes of the 2011 Comic-Con was the fiftieth anniversary of fandom (the first amateur-published writing about comics history dates to 1961). A dozen of the most illustrious veterans of those days were invited as special guests, with events and celebrations sprinkled throughout the weekend. I was a few minutes late for the start, but this was not a panel where you had to worry about getting into the venue. It was in one of the smaller meeting rooms, and the room was less than half full when I arrived.

On stage, the panel's moderator, Mark Evanier (himself an early fan-turned-professional and a member of the exclusive San Diego "lifers" club, attending every show since 1970) was encouraging the participants to tell stories about how they went from being people who were interested in old comics to the progenitors of a subculture. The panel was an interesting assortment. Dick Lupoff, an accomplished science fiction author, and his wife, Pat, have bragging rights to not only being the first fans to publish a comics-oriented column in their SF zine *Xero* back in the early 1960s, but being the first fans to dress up in superhero costumes (as Captain and Mary Marvel). Maggie Thompson and her late husband, Don, followed shortly thereafter, and later achieved success with the professionally published *Comic Buyers Guide*. Writers Roy Thomas and Paul Levitz not only made the leap from fans to comics professionals, but climbed to the highest pinnacles of the industry. Thomas succeeded Stan Lee as editor in chief at Marvel in the mid-1970s; Levitz is the immediate past publisher (and previously editor in chief) for DC, stepping down in 2010.

All these folks got their start publishing mimeographed newsletters and amateur comics in the 1960s, in print runs of several hundred at most. Their project was to gain appreciation for the medium of comics and recognition for the talents of their creators. Typical of the pre-Baby Boom "Silent Generation," these early fans brought diligence, attention to detail, and a sense of moral purpose to their efforts. The first zines were infused with a sense of discovery and nostalgia, but also a kind of missionary zeal to make readers understand the true genius of Carl Barks (the uncredited artist who drew the best-loved Disney duck stories) or the epic grandeur inspired by the nearly forgotten heroes of DC's Justice Society of America.

At the time they were writing, comics were seen as disposable entertainment for children at best, and as fiendish corruptors of young morals at worst. No one, not even most people involved in the industry, took much pride in the work. Only a few audacious voices, like that of Will Eisner, had ever claimed that comics could be anything approaching art or literature. A few dedicated fans set out to change that, and half a century later, the entire world has come around to their view. It's a rather remarkable achievement.

The first generation of fans made its case with an optimism and earnestness characteristic of the pre-Vietnam 1960s. Before long, the Baby Boomers arrived, supplementing the nostalgic appreciation of the pioneers with an enthusiasm for the current crop of comics (primarily the groundbreaking work being done by Jack Kirby, Stan Lee, and Steve Ditko at Marvel), a strident agenda of social, political, and aesthetic concerns, and a self-conscious sense of being part of a movement.

Newcomers like Gary Groth, the fiery young publisher of the *Comics Journal* starting in the 1970s, grew increasingly disgusted with the sentimentality and lack of rigorous critical approaches that pervaded old-school fandom. Groth brought a righteous tone of Boomer activism and real-world engagement to comics criticism, even if the *Journal*'s intellectual reach sometimes exceeded its grasp. Still, the sense of higher purpose was empowering and sometimes effective: in the mid-1980s, Groth took on a fellow precocious and pugnacious boomer, Marvel's then editor in chief Jim Shooter, over Marvel's shameful treatment of Jack Kirby when the old master was in failing health. Eventually Marvel blinked and Kirby got a decent settlement for the return of his original art.

Trina Robbins, who started out in the 1960s underground movement, brought the values of 1970s-era feminism to comics scholarship as she began a lifelong project to discover and celebrate the voices of great women creators who contributed to comics history, though it was a Generation Xer, Heidi MacDonald, who formed the first important fan group to recognize women in the comics industry, Friends of Lulu, in the early 1990s. Publisher and cartoonist Denis Kitchen, another veteran of the underground, helped move fandom toward political action, founding the Comic Book Legal Defense Fund (CBLDF) in 1986 to support retailers that were being persecuted by local authorities.

By the mid-1990s, the leading edge of Generation X was approaching age 30 and starting to rediscover the comics of its youth, the 1970s, which Boomers disdained as inferior to those of their own cherished childhood. Comics in the 1970s were hastily produced and cheaply printed, and they reflected the shrill social attitudes of the young Boomer creators who were coming into the industry, which mature Boomers found vaguely embarrassing by the 1990s.

John and Pam Morrow, who ran an advertising agency in North Carolina, launched *The Jack Kirby Collector* in 1994 to cultivate appreciation of the classic comic book artist/writer, whose reputation had suffered at the hands of Boomers who were disappointed with his later work. The Morrows' detailed and professional fanzine soon attracted the interest of the crowd of aging "superfans," some of whom had worked in comics during the 1970s and 1980s, as well as a rising crop of Generation X fans who were creating their own communities through e-mail listservs like Kirby-L and ComicArt-L in the early days of the Internet. Today, the TwoMorrows enterprise offers a huge assortment of magazines, monographs, how-to books, biographies, and indexes of comics, mainly focusing on the 1970s to 1980s era. The TwoMorrows booth at Comic-Con, near the front of the hall in the section dominated by old comics dealers, is a popular hub and meeting spot for this cohort of fans. The obsessive detail and pervasive nostalgia of the TwoMorrows publications represent the logical end point of the fannish scholarship pioneered by the first generation. Unfortunately, the attention to detail sometimes veers into a self-parody of kitschy Generation X trivia-mongering that the rising generation of Millennials finds peculiar and offputting.

As we move deeper into the digital era, twenty-first-century fandom is no longer curated and managed by a clique of mandarins with mimeographs. Today's online comicsphere is immediate, interactive, social, and collaborative, and it stretches across thousands of Facebook groups, blogs, news sites, chat rooms, and Twitter hashtags, brimming with conversation, commentary, rumors, gossip, snark, misinformation, amazing amateur and semiprofessional work, and communities for every conceivable subculture. It is also focused on the here and now of the industry much more than on its illustrious and overexcavated history. Reviews and essays are posted on hundreds of blogs. Opinions are shared in chat rooms and community forums. Hundreds of comics-centric "weblebrities" publish weekly video feeds and podcasts. Some, like "The Nerdist" Chris Hardwick, have parleyed this into a larger media footprint. Plenty of comics creators maintain an online presence and often engage in heated give and take with fans. Many are driven mad. Twitter has kicked things up yet another level by providing a level of personal connection between pros and fans. Comics writer turned award-winning fantasy author Neil Gaiman (@neilhimself) was among the first to break a million followers on the service.

The changing taste and behavior of fans is critical to an industry where fans may be the only ones paying attention, and fan influence has affected the efforts of publishers to reach a wider audience. The affection of the 1960s-era fans for 1940s-era comics resulted in the revival of many of these characters, most famously the old DC superhero team, the Justice Society of America. The narrative contrivance that made this possible, involving the creation of alternative dimensions and timelines, ended up burdening the DC universe with newbie-unfriendly plot complications that ripple down to the present day.

Boomer demands for social relevance, maturity, and "realistic" story lines was manifested in the "grim and gritty" style of the mid-1980s, kicking off auspiciously with Frank Miller's *Batman: The Dark Knight* and Alan Moore and Dave Gibbons's *Watchmen*, but soon leading comics into a very dark dead end. The classic revivalism of Generation X fans led to a boom in "retro comics" in the late 1990s, typified by Kurt Busiek's *Astro City* and Mark Waid and Alex Ross's *Kingdom Come*, which championed traditional themes and styles above the exhausted postmodernism of the previous period. Frank Miller once derisively referred to this trend as "nostalgia with a nose ring."

Today, the ahistorical, media-influenced perspective of Millennials is competing with the legacy of older fans who remain active and vocal. The two different polarities seem to be confusing the hell out of the industry and making it more difficult for it to move forward with confidence. The desire, or perhaps requirement, to cater to old fans with long memories leads publishers to endlessly recycle properties that have no relevance to the current day, while at the same time doing away with decades of history in a desperate attempt to bring in young readers who don't know or care about continuity with the past.

Fandom is both the rudder that helps all pop culture media steer toward the future and the anchor that keeps them bound to the past. Resolving the competing agendas of fans can be a bit like negotiating a trade agreement between warring countries. But the future of comics within pop culture uniquely depends on its ability to balance respect for its heritage with an awareness of the here and now.

After Hours: The Eisner Awards

Recognizing creative talent and highlighting your industry's innovation takes on greater meaning in the "attention economy" of the twenty-first century.

At 5:00, we skipped out of the end of our last panel and headed back to our hotel to rest up a bit before our brief stint as on-duty event staff. Each year, Eunice and I work with Jackie Estrada and her team to help put on the Eisner Awards—the comic industry's version of the Oscars. The awards open to the public at 8:15 p.m. and go on for nearly three hours, but prior to the public event, there is a buffet dinner served to nominees, publishers, guests, and sponsors. The room decorations, the registration area, and the stage all need to be set up in advance of that. That task falls to a core group of five or six veteran badged event staff members, including ourselves, and a small army of volunteers.

By 6:00, we'd made our way to the Hilton Bayfront hotel, on the other side of the convention center from the Marriott. Jackie and her assistant were already there with their clipboard and box of materials. Eunice grabbed the stack of labels and table tents indicating which of the nearly 40 tables at the front of the room had been reserved for each group of sponsors and nominees.

Vicky Gunter, Jackie's no-nonsense lieutenant in charge of getting the tables ready, gave instructions to the crew of volunteers. The placement of decorations, name tags, and gift bags is handled with the protocol of a diplomatic summit. Once the setup was complete, Eunice and Vicky stepped outside into the lobby to man the registration table. VIP access is strictly controlled and reserved for invitees and paid sponsors only. Jackie goes to great lengths to determine exactly who is coming and how many guests each is bringing, but each year there are some inevitable misunderstandings, and some Very Important Person storms off with feathers ruffled when she discovers that there is no accommodation for her eight-person entourage of unannounced guests. On one memorable occasion, Eunice turned away the editor in chief of Marvel Comics because he was not on the list (he later got in as the guest of one of his writers).

At 8:15, the doors open to regular attendees, who sit in the back of the room. There is capacity for six or seven hundred, but the event generally draws about a third of that. Over the years, Jackie and the Comic-Con staff have tried to make the ceremony more fan-friendly, adding celebrity guests and presenters, music, stand-up comics, and voice actors as emcees and, for the first time in 2011, using a professional event production company to tighten up the timings and music cues. Despite everyone's best efforts, the Eisners rarely wrap up before 11 p.m.

I returned to the staff table as the setup was just about complete. An unassuming-looking bearded fellow was seated alone at the table, flipping through a program. He was not part of the setup crew and his badge was not visible, so I introduced myself and politely asked him what he was doing there.

"It's OK, I'm convention staff," he said.

"What do you do?"

"I'm John Rogers. I'm the president of Comic-Con." That sounded fairly important.

"Really? I had no idea. We've been coming here 13 years and have been helping with the Eisners for about 8. It's amazing we've never seen you."

"That's good," he said. "Usually the only time you see someone like me is if something goes wrong." He said the organizers like himself, longtime Comic-Con executive director Fae Desmond, and the rest of the management try to stay in the background during the show, letting the spotlight fall on the attendees, celebrities, and festivities.

One can hardly blame them. Coordinating all the moving parts for a show as gargantuan and all-consuming as Comic-Con would be a full-time job for a company of military logistics specialists. Yet Desmond manages only a small full-time staff and Rogers himself holds down an outside job as a network security specialist. I can see how they must have little time to eat, sleep, and bathe, much less court any kind of attention, when things are in motion. Still, for all the enormous number of things that could possibly go wrong in the weeks and months beforehand, let alone the five-day window when Hurricane Comic-Con actually hits San Diego, there have been remarkably few blemishes on any front over the show's 41-year history. Love Comic-Con or hate it, you have to respect the mad skills of the folks who run what is, remarkably, a nonprofit operation.

As we were talking, Jackie Estrada, who had left to change into her evening attire, swept into the room in a glittering dress, accompanied by her husband, Batton, and trailed by several frantic staff people waving papers. On the podium, emcee Bill Morrison (*Futurama, The Simpsons*) and his wife, Kayre, were going over a few last-minute details on staging and delivery. A few guests began filtering in and filling their plates at the buffet line. Almost everyone was at least a little bit dressed up, a small victory in the long twilight struggle against the "Comic-Con look"—large bearded men in baggy shorts and sneakers, popularized by director Kevin Smith—that Jackie and Batton have been waging in an attempt to class up the Eisner ceremony.

Details like that are critical. Nearly everything surrounding the Eisner Awards involves some degree of intrigue. Though they are the oldest surviving comics industry award, and carry the name and blessing of Will Eisner, one of the most important figures in comics history, they struggle for prestige and visibility even within the universe of comics fandom. A competing set of awards, the Harveys (named for *Mad* magazine creator Harvey Kurtzman), are handed out later in the summer at the Baltimore Comic Con in many of the same categories. There are also the Ignatz Awards (mostly for independent comics), the Shusters (for Canadian creators, named for Canadian-born *Superman* artist Joe Shuster), the Shel Dorf Awards (named, ironically, for the founder of San Diego Comic-Con, but presented at the Detroit Fan Fair), and the winners of various reader polls.

Every so often, an unexpected title will get nominated or win, but there is rarely much controversy over nominations because so little is really at stake. There is no evidence that winning an Eisner or any other award makes any difference to sales or to the rates commanded by creative talent; it probably won't help you get your title turned into a movie if there hasn't already been some interest from studios. It is even sometimes a struggle to get publishers to include the award logo on the covers of winning publications.

The honor of association with Will Eisner remains the award's biggest asset. Each year up until his death in 2005 at age 89, Eisner himself would stand on stage through the entire ceremony, presenting the statues to the winners. As one recipient remarked in his acceptance speech, "How cool is this? You don't get an Oscar Award from a guy named Oscar!" Eisner himself even won occasionally, which made for some amusing moments. Now that the master is gone, the Eisner Awards must find ways to up the ante in terms of relevance, especially in the pop culture media beyond the world of comics fans and bloggers. That is Estrada's single-minded focus as she shepherds the awards from nomination to judging to the big Friday night ceremony.

In recent years, Estrada has brought in a grab bag of celebrities, including Samuel L. Jackson, the cast of the film *Scott Pilgrim vs. the World*, Tom Lennon and Ben Garant of the Comedy Central series *Reno 911*, superstar comics creator and film director Frank Miller, Go-Gos guitarist Jane Weidlin, and others to liven things up. A high-water mark of sorts was achieved in 2008, when British comedy host Jonathan Ross left his copresenter, Comic-Con deity Neil Gaiman, speechless after a rapid-fire burst of hilarious innuendo capped with a full-on kiss on the lips.

The timing of the gala has given Estrada yet another battle to fight. The tradition of handing out the Eisners on Friday nights goes back a long way in Comic-Con history, but Friday has become party central, and in the megamedia era, that means that all the big players tend to host their exclusive, fancy blowouts at the same time. Even some creators who don't have golden tickets to these shindigs regard the three-plus-hour awards ceremony as a chore. Much of the U.K. contingent, usually including at least a few nominees, goes for an epic pub crawl on Fridays and can scarcely be "arsed" to make an appearance to claim their hardware.

Gaining wider attention for events like the Eisner Awards is important to the future of comics because they provide institutional legitimacy to an art form that is still on the margins. The Eisners are one of the few venues that do not distinguish between "mainstream" superhero comics and the "alternatives"—a dynamic that helps traditional comics by associating them with books that are already recognized as high quality in the wider world. There

Photo by Jackie Estrada

Brazilian artists Gabriel Bá and Fabio Moon accept their Eisner Awards.

are categories for everything under the sun, including more than a dozen creative categories (best penciller, best inker, best colorist, best letterer, and so on) and some very specific content categories (best U.S. edition of foreign material—Asia, Best Limited Series, Best Collection of Archival Material) where even being nominated can draw attention to overlooked work.

The efforts have paid off to a certain extent. It may be a while before the Eisner ceremony is broadcast live, but in a relatively short time, the awards have gone from a homemade, industry-insider banquet to a gala worthy of coverage by the likes of *Publisher's Weekly*, *USA Today*, *Entertainment Weekly*, and other big-time outlets. Every time an Eisner winner is announced on the on-screen crawl on G4

Network, another clump of pop culture fans gets exposed to this forgotten corner of the entertainment world, or is reintroduced to the source of content that they enjoy in other media. These are the steps by which a marginal industry claws its way back to the center of the wider cultural conversation.

CHAPTER 5

SATURDAY:
PEAK GEEK

At the end of the Eisner Award ceremony, usually around 11:00, the survivors spill out into the corridor outside the Indigo Ballroom, where cocktails are served and a jazz combo plays tastefully in the background. Eventually this boils down to a hard core of 25 to 50 people, typically industry veterans and longtime attendees who see this scene as the last remaining essence of the Comic-Con culture of the 1970s and 1980s. When the bar closes around 1 a.m., the revelries move elsewhere and can go on far into the night.

That means that Saturday gets off to a slow start for a lot of people, including Eunice and me. We took our time, having breakfast in our room while watching the endless crowds down in the street.

Traditionally, Saturday was the day when everyone drove down from LA, doubling the size of the crowds and making for booming business for the exhibitors. Now, every minute of Comic-Con is sold out, and it is hard to say that there's any time when the floor is not busy, but the mystique of the Saturday surge persists.

The biggest Hall H events are usually set for Saturday. This year, things kicked off with *TWIXT*, a new project from Francis Ford Coppola and Dan Deacon (both there in person), followed by a series of movie/media events including *Relativity*, *Knights of Badassdom*, *Snow White and the Huntsman*, and *Dorothy of Oz*, capped by an evening with Comic-Con darling Kevin Smith. I think Eunice wanted to go see *Futurama* and *The Simpsons* in Ballroom 20 (capacity: 3,500), requiring a line commitment of not less than three hours. None of that appealed to me, fortunately. The crowds in the big rooms were just too much to handle.

I had a few panels circled as possibilities: stuff like "Is the Comic Book Doomed?" and "Assassin's Creed: The Creation of a Universe," both of which were relevant to this book. For various reasons, I didn't make it to either one. I did end up seeing Garth Ennis, the Irish-born purveyor of profane action titles with terse, manly names like *Preacher, Hitman, Crossed*, and *The Boys*, thinking there might be something to say about this particular genre of comics. There probably is, but not in this context.

A little bit past 10, we headed down to the convention center, taking the shortcut around the back of the Marriott to avoid the worst of the crowds. Eunice peeled off immediately to stand in her *Futurama* line upstairs. I headed up the central aisle of the exhibit hall, past the indie section and the DC booth, to renew my membership in the Comic Book Legal Defense Fund and say hello to a couple of friends in the small press area.

As I passed the center row, I caught the eye of Joe Ferrara, a great big bearded Italian teddy bear in a Hawaiian shirt and one of

Photo by Jackie Estrada

Retailer and direct market advocate Joe Ferrara and his wife, Dottie.

the great stand-up guys in the industry. Joe is the longtime owner of a store called Atlantis Fantasyworld in Santa Cruz, California (the store had a cameo in the 1988 teen vampire classic *The Lost Boys*), and the head of the committee that selects the Eisner Spirit of Retail award to recognize great comics shops. I had seen him briefly the previous night at the Eisner Awards, but we didn't have time to chat. He made up for that with a boisterous hug and clap on the back, after which I tried to keep up in his wake as he charged across the hall to his next destination.

Joe is a fierce advocate for retailers, not only trying to lift the standards of the stores by educating owners and staff on how to make their environments more inviting, but also leaning on publishers and distributors to keep the end customer in mind. It's a tough, important job, and he's been at it for more than 20 years.

Direct market retailers take a lot of the blame for the declining fortunes of comic books, for reasons discussed earlier. The squalor and clubbiness of bad comics shops is proverbial; the worst shops not only discourage casual readers, but hurt the reputation of the entire industry. At the same time, great stores can do a world of good: upselling and cross-selling opportunities in comics are literally everywhere if you can give customers the right level of service.

I live in Seattle, home to four of the most innovative service-oriented retailers in American business: Nordstrom, REI, Starbucks, and Amazon. And yet I get the best customer experience I receive anywhere at my local comics store, The Comics Dungeon. The employees know me and my wife by name, they know what we like, they make consistently great recommendations, and my trust in them is high enough that I think nothing of spending $25 or $30 on a graphic novel I've never heard of just based on the manager's say-so ("Try *Petrograd*—it's a biography of Rasputin drawn in the style of Will Eisner. I put it in your box for you to have a look."). The store maintains an up-to-the-minute website, a Facebook and Twitter presence, an employee blog, and a weekly mailing list. The owner, a former Microsoft employee, was an early adopter of Groupon and the ComiXology digital storefront.

Despite the best efforts of smart retailers like this all around the country, it remains a very tough business. Margins are tight, and because most comics are nonreturnable, ordering errors can be catastrophic. Problems with the distributor are inevitable, but because Diamond has the market to itself, retailers don't have much leverage. The pragmatic approach is to just order the books you know you can sell, which puts the retailers' priorities out of alignment with those of publishers trying to expand the audience. When customer preorders of a title start falling short, the smart bet is to keep cutting back. That can turn a sales dip into a death spiral, making it nearly impossible for titles to win new readers.

It's clear that comics would benefit from a reinvention of the retail environment. Stores are the social center of the hobby, and the best ones understand that they are not just selling comics; they are selling the experience of buying comics. Many comics stores host gaming tournaments, film and anime screenings, art shows, creator appearances, art workshops, and other events designed to bring fans together. Some are attached to coffee shops, galleries, restaurants, or other retailers with crossover potential (music, fashion, art supplies, and the like). These added features have helped make stores destinations for fans rather than just pickup points for books. According to Scott Tomlin, owner of Comics Dungeon, digital distribution can't, by itself, meet the broader needs of fans or provide the upselling and impulse-purchase advantages of a physical retail location. "Going to a website about beer is not the same as going to a bar," he observed.

As the gender balance of comics fans has tilted more female in recent years, some stores have experimented with girl-geek and singles-night events. Many stores actively recruit female staff to diffuse the boys' club atmosphere. The September 2011 announcement that Toronto, Ontario–based retailer The Beguiling was opening a new location called Little Island Comics, catering primarily to kids, was greeted with a collective "it's about time!" by the rest of the community. But the fact that a comics store aimed at kids is somehow an innovation should tell you a lot about the state of the direct market.

Some forward-thinking retailers who see the digital writing on the wall are even thinking of ways to combine the service and atmosphere of (good) brick-and-mortar retail with the coming move to digital distribution, with stores serving as "fueling stations" for connected devices. Such stores would combine attractive point-of-purchase displays that encourage impulse buying of printed graphic novels and comics and the trusted recommendations and word-of-mouth upselling/cross-selling with a café/lounge area where customers could sample and download digital titles on their tablets or smartphones.

The problem is that the cash-constrained environment of the direct market makes it nearly impossible for most established retailers to make investments in upgrading their facilities or turning their stores into inviting showplaces for new customers. A lot of comics retailers are located in strip malls or other locations where commercial real estate is cheap, owned by landlords who are not inclined toward making big improvements. And even the right strategy does not guarantee success, especially when other economic factors are at work. One award-winning retailer that had garnered national praise for its store design, merchandising mix, and service, Arizona's Atomic Comics, announced that it was going out of business shortly after the 2011 Comic-Con ended, triggering a lot of self-reflection within the industry.

If independently owned retail stores are no longer viable, it is possible that larger retail franchises might see value in incorporating comics (and the fan-magnet comics culture) into their stores, especially if there is the potential for crossover with their established lines. The national video-game retailer GameStop seems like a natural for this approach, although its brick-and-mortar operations could soon be endangered by the same forces of digital disintermediation as people download games directly through their consoles. One could also see a fit with stores like Best Buy or other home electronics and media outlets. Retail locations of the technology companies that supply the digital comics platforms (for example, tablets and smartphones), such as Apple, Microsoft, and Google, could easily feature comics—both physical and digital—as the "software" to drive hardware sales.

In all these cases, the corporate retailers would be smart to employ direct market veterans who have the knowledge, reputations, and relationships to bring customers with them. The people who have made their careers working in retail environments that serve pop culture enthusiasts—whether they be comics stores, specialized video rental shops, game stores, or music emporia—occupy an uncomfortable no-man's-land between service workers and knowledge workers, and the digital economy of the twenty-first century has not found a good way to measure, capture, or reward the value they add to the retail industry. Ideally, their expertise relative to generic, minimum-wage service clerks should afford them the opportunity to remain professionally independent; realistically, that may not be possible without a large-scale reversal of consumer priorities and behaviors. Solutions involving consolidation and co-optation probably don't sound great to many retailers, but they may be the only way to conserve the accumulated social capital of the direct market in the digital era, and thus the only way to maintain the social vitality of the comics hobby.

Joe Ferrara may not have all the answers to how retailers get from today's reality to tomorrow's vision, but he is adamant that the industry as a whole has a stake in the outcome. He traditionally closes his segment of the Eisner Spirit of Retail Awards by exhorting the audience of creators and publishers to "keep making the comics we love, and we'll keep selling them." This year, in the face of so many impending changes, his words seemed more urgent and heartfelt than ever.

Gaming the System: Comics, Video Games, and the Mass Marketing of Geek Culture

Even in a fragmented media environment, there is still a role for mass media in uniting niche audiences around a common self-image.

The back of sections F and G of the exhibit hall belong to the video-game companies: Activision, Electronic Arts, Ubisoft, CapCom, Sony PlayStation, and Microsoft Xbox. Their towering displays are lit up with rows of flat-panel monitors and speakers blasting out music and sound effects. Crowds are packed five and six deep around the demo stations, while teams of well-tanned California girls scramble to hand out swag and freebies.

Early in my career, I wrote the story line for an elaborate video game, and the development company flew me down to E3 (Electronic Entertainment Expo), the gigantic video-game show held annually in Los Angeles. It was one of the few things in my experience that compares to Comic-Con in terms of the sheer noise and scale of the hype. In this part of the floor, it was easy to confuse the two events.

E3 and Comic-Con occupy an overlapping space in the pop culture cosmos, but the similarities are only skin deep. Comic-Con, despite its recent embrace of the wider entertainment world, including video games, retains a trace of its nerdish, nostalgic heritage deep in its soul. E3 is all about the here and now.

The video-game industry is a remorseless, blockbuster-driven business where the budgets of the biggest games can rival those of a Hollywood feature. The results are incredible. In games like Skyrim, Gears of War, Halo, and Red Dead: Redemption, the graphics and stories are beyond cinematic. The maturation of computer hardware has enabled game developers to create entire universes, open to non-linear exploration by individual players or virtual teams. The games have character development, story arcs, plot twists, dialogue, and elaborate backstories that require weeks of intense play to discover.

These stories, like those in mainstream comics, are primarily rooted in genre fiction: fantasy, action, sci-fi, crime, and super-heroes. But while comics require the active participation of the reader to translate the words and pictures on the page into a mental landscape of sound and action, video games deliver the complete immersive experience right out of the box: just add couch and controller. The added dimensions of action and challenge—solving the puzzles, killing the bad guys (sometimes by splattering their skulls with an axe or some other gratifyingly gruesome act of violence), climbing the high-score lists, and being able to compete against real or virtual opponents—give video games a seductive power that comics can't match.

The rise of video games provides a clean single-cause explanation for the decline of comics sales in the 1990s. Games compete for the same finite share of dollars, hours, and brain cells among a common audience of (mostly, but by no means exclusively) male postadolescents. At $40 to $60 for games that provide days and weeks of entertainment value, they are a bargain compared to comics priced at $2.99 or more for 18 to 24 pages that can be read, bagged, and filed in less than half an hour.

Unlike movies, which have not been very successful in developing comic book–type properties that are not based on actual comic books, many of the top-selling and critically acclaimed video games have created original content strong enough to support freestanding franchises. Halo, Mass Effect, Dead Space, Grand Theft Auto, and Assassins Creed all feature ambitious stories that have spawned multiple game titles and have, in some cases, inspired their own comic book adaptations.

The biggest success story going in the opposite direction is *Batman: Arkham Asylum*, developed by Rocksteady Studios and published jointly by Eidos Interactive, Warner Brothers Interactive (part of the parent company of DC Comics, publisher of *Batman*), and Square Enix. The scenario, based on the bestselling graphic novel by Grant Morrison and Dave McKean, was written by Paul Dini, one of the primary creative forces behind the highly regarded *Batman: The Animated Series* cartoons that ran in the 1990s. The cast of voice actors from that series, including Kevin Conroy (Batman), Mark Hamill (the Joker), and Arleen Sorkin (Harley Quinn) reprise their roles in the game.

In addition to being one of the most faithful interpretations of the Batman concept in any medium, *Batman: Arkham Asylum* is one of the highest-rated titles of all time on the basis of game play, as determined by gamers who may or may not have any use for comics or animation. Altogether, the game has sold more than 5 million copies worldwide (no doubt benefiting in part from the massive box office splash of *Batman: The Dark Knight*, which was released around the same time in 2009). From both a commercial and a creative perspective, it is hard to imagine a more effectively executed licensed transmedia strategy.

In 2011, Warner Brothers was hoping that lightning would strike again with the much-anticipated sequel, *Batman: Arkham City*. Promotional material was in evidence all around the convention area, including a gigantic banner draped over a neighboring high-rise. The Warner Brothers booth was packed solid with people curious to get a look at previews and demos for the game, which shipped in October 2011 to enormous sales and rave reviews.

Just down the aisle, another gigantic crowd had formed around the multilevel booth of the G4 network, which was broadcasting

Photo by Doug Kline

The "geek-friendly" G4 Network broadcasts live from its multilevel booth at Comic-Con.

its annual four-hour live Comic-Con special. Cameras on the upper deck were trained on hosts Kevin Pereira and Candace Bailey as they interviewed guests and reported various doings of their correspondents around the convention floor.

G4, a division of NBCUniversal, occupies an interesting niche in the expanding pop culture universe. Originally conceived as a cable channel devoted to video games and technology, it quickly found that it had to broaden its view of "geek culture" to become more viable. The network reaches only 59 million homes via cable and satellite, and its ratings are microscopic, but it makes aggressive use of online channels, including podcasts and the web, and continuously tries to cross-pollinate its fragmented audiences by knitting together just about every aspect of the contemporary twenty-something male slacker experience, including comics, Japanese anime, genre-oriented movies and TV, alternative sports, music, consumer electronics, porn, getting stoned, screwing around, and getting busted.

A few years ago, G4 threatened to break out with the increasing visibility of on-air personality Olivia Munn. When she departed to become a big star elsewhere, the network tried its hand at more mainstream programming, like the Japanese obstacle game show *Ninja Warrior*, just as the rest of the media began to capitalize on a rising tide of interest in nerd culture in the wake of successful network shows like *The Big Bang Theory*.

Attack of the Show (*AOTS*), G4's flagship program, still offers a nightly survey of all things geek during its comically awkward hourlong broadcast. In doing so, it blithely traipses across ancient tribal barriers dividing nerds from jocks, popular kids from stoners, and brains from airheads. The alt.jocks of *Ninja Warrior* fit just as neatly into this postmodern unified theory of geekdom as video gamers or comics fans. We may have our different interests, but we can all share a laugh at a viral video of a skateboarder flying off a roof and landing on his ass.

Despite its antics and its marginal relevance as a commercial broadcast enterprise, G4 was among the first to give airtime to authentic and respectful fan perspectives. Its product reviews are honest, down-to-earth, and well informed, speaking to the genuine tastes and interests of the audience. Comics reviewer Blair Butler (a comedian by trade), for example, has deep knowledge of and genuine affection for the medium, and covers her beat with the assiduousness and sincerity of a financial reporter on CNBC. G4's success in this niche has now drawn other established youth brands like MTV, eager to capitalize on the current vogue for geek chic.

People who watch *AOTS* or *X-Play* (G4's other big "news show," focused exclusively on video games) probably get most of their information online anyway, so it's not like you need G4 as a news source. Websites like Newsarama and Bleeding Cool have been around for longer and provide a greater range and depth of pop culture coverage. But even in the post-TV media era, there is something legitimizing about seeing your interests and your subculture discussed seriously on the tube, without the protective layer of condescension that most mass media apply to lubricate their coverage of comics, toys, genre entertainment, and gaming. G4 treats creative talent in the comics and video-game industries as celebrities on a par with superstar actors and musicians. The network covers Comic-Con mostly as a news story, not as a "hey-look-at-the-freaks" feature. The hosts may be observing some of the goings-on with an ironically cocked eyebrow, but most of the time, the eyebrow is cocked *with* the fans, not *at* them. Among the new young audience for all things geek, that makes all the difference.

To the extent that G4 is a trusted brand within the Comic-Con/ geek culture world, it confers credibility across boundaries and exposes fans of one media type or activity to other instances of their favorite content that they might not be aware of—for example, alerting gamers who like *Batman: Arkham Asylum* to the details of DC's New 52 relaunch, which might bring a few of them into comics stores. It also promotes a more generalized consciousness across the spectrum of media fandom by taking for granted that, say, everyone in the show's audience knows who Stan Lee is and cares about what he's doing next.

Finally, G4 and related geek-aware media confer a sense of coolness around hobbies that were anything but just half a generation ago. Kids today don't feel the same pressure to conceal or deny their interests in comics, *Star Trek*, toys, and fantasy literature once they reach an age where those passions are no longer considered sufficiently trendy by their peer group; there is now social sanction for them in the media. Some may still face bullying for their nerdish ways, but geek media offer a giant "it gets better" message from a slightly older generation that is obviously proud and comfortable with its enthusiasms—and in some cases, creatively and financially successful as well.

In this way, media outlets like G4 are manufacturing a consensus around the transmedia future of pop culture, where the sense of fan community matters more than the content. Fans (of anything) are cool because they have passion for their interests; creators (of anything) are cool because they're the mad geniuses who make the stuff we love; big corporations are cool because they're the ones who spend money to produce our video games and 3D action movies and eight-disc BluRay collectors' sets with bonus features. It's a Millennial, we-all-get-trophies kind of fandom, 180 degrees removed from the activist engagement of the Boomer generation or the snarky exclusivity of Generation Xers, where the high entry costs are what make the subcultures special.

It's also the kind of fandom that goes hand in glove with the convergence of content and media—tailor-made for an era of corporate consolidation, consumerization, intellectual property, and brand management strategies. The G4 mindset is breaking down the barriers, but a world without boundaries means a world without edges. The popularity of nerd-oriented media—clearly in ascendance as we head into 2012—is both an example of how deeply comics culture is pervading the rest of the entertainment ecosystem and a cautionary indicator of potential overexposure and backlash.

The Golden Age: Life in the Dealer's Room

Generational change in the consumer market can have long-term effects, and those can ripple back through the entire industry ecosystem.

As we start to contemplate a future of comics without comic books— and a future of media without media (records, CDs, DVDs, books, and other material repositories of information)—it's important to recognize the role that the objects themselves play in the appeal of the content. Comic books are more than containers of story and art that can be transmuted seamlessly to any new method of delivery. The demise of physical methods of distribution represents a profound change in the atmospherics of media consumption. Despite everything we think we know about the superior convenience of digital, the consequences of this change from a commercial perspective are highly uncertain.

Consider the comic book collectors' market. This is a big part of the culture of the hobby, and the existence of back-issue dealers adds intangible (and sometimes tangible) appeal to the desire to acquire and consume comics. At Comic-Con, old comics sellers used to define the exhibit hall, which was once known as the "dealers' room." These days, most of the dealers are clustered in the "Golden and Silver Age Pavilion" between aisles 200 and 1,000 toward the front of the hall, just adjacent to the alt.comics and book publishers.

The first thing you notice about the dealers at Comic-Con is the familiar faces. These same businesses, and often the same individuals, have been coming back year after year since the 1970s, and have been buying and selling the same books from and to the same aging, dwindling cluster of customers. If you are looking for titles published after 1980, you will not find much to choose from in this part of the room. Every so often, you will see a dealer advertising "new collection just in!" Everything else, you could safely assume, is inventory that may have been sitting in those long white boxes for years or decades.

Dealers' row is still an interesting neighborhood. It's a great place to get into random nerdy conversations about the most obscure and fun bits of comics trivia. In the midst of the chaos of Comic-Con, there is a certain Zen to flipping through long boxes in search of a particularly shiny needle in a particularly gigantic haystack. The physicality of these artifacts is attractive; it creates scarcity that is impossible in the digital economy of abundance.

Unfortunately, this is one part of comics culture that is incompatible with the changes that are sweeping over the industry and, especially, the new audience. With few exceptions, the value assigned to old comics is a by-product of the tastes and habits of an older generation of fans. The intrinsic aspects of the art and content that make certain issues more desirable than others depend on a body of knowledge and a condition of scarcity to drive demand. Most of all, they depend on the pull of nostalgia: "I loved that comic when I was a kid, and now I need to own a mint-condition copy, even if it costs me $500!"

As comics retreated from the mass market after the 1970s, the number of young readers began to shrink. Now, decades later, that shrinkage is rippling through the pool of adults who have a nostalgic affection for the comics of their youth. Baby Boomers, who fueled the expansion of the hobby over the past 40 years, are moving into a life stage (and an economy) where they are more likely to be selling collectibles than buying them, and it's hard to see who is taking their place.

My generation, currently in our forties, is the last gasp of the old order. We grew up as the whole "collectibles" mentality was becoming institutionalized. As kids, we took it for granted that all old comics were worth money—a notion reinforced by media stories about "comic gold in your attic" and "Did you throw away your kid's college fund when you trashed those old comic books?" that ran every time a copy of Marvel Comics #1 changed hands for a new astronomical sum. We saved the comics we bought on the stands and kept them in great condition; we went to conventions and old comics stores armed with lists of "key books" that featured favorite artists, story lines, or characters. We shelled out $20 every spring for the new edition of Robert Overstreet's *Comic Book Price Guide*, which relied for its market research on a survey of dealers who stood to benefit from increasing prices, to help us appraise the value of our holdings. Our misplaced enthusiasm led to the speculative bubble of the mid-1990s, where the Generation X appetite for "hot" artists caused publishers and retailers to flood the market with worthless titles and gimmicks (3D issues, multiple covers, variant editions). The resulting collapse nearly killed the industry.

The transactional approach of Generation X fans toward collecting resulted in some innovations that drained most of the fun out of the hobby. In the past 15 years, eBay has turned every computer into an endless collectibles mall that never closes, and the brutal transparency of auctions has laid bare the myth that the values of most ordinary comics automatically appreciate year after year. A firm called Certified Guarantee Company (CGC) entered the hobby in 2000 with a service that promises to take the guesswork out of the esoteric art of grading the condition of comics (a prime determinant of their value). Certified comics sell for more—sometimes multiples of previously established values, depending on how high the issue rates on CGC's 10-point grade. The trade-off is that the certified comic is entombed in a sealed plastic case and transformed from an interactive work of art and story to a fetish object.

If you get rid of the social and "thrill of the chase" aspects of collecting, and you make it impossible to inspect and appreciate the item you've just bought, all that's left is commerce. And commerce has boomed. As a result of the auction culture and the "validation" of CGC grading criteria, the elite handful of highly prized books in prime condition has set record after record. The winners of these auctions claim their amber-sealed paperweights, store them in climate-controlled vaults, and put them up for auction a year or two later.

In the case of genuinely rare, well-preserved books with broad cultural significance, such as *Action #1* (the 1938 debut of Superman), staggering prices may be justified. But for most of the hundreds of thousands of vintage comics published in the last 75 years, desirability is based on factors known only to a small and shrinking field of collectors, and value is codified in a price guide that reflects these collectors' interests and biases. Within this closed community, books sell and resell for higher and higher prices, creating the appearance of market momentum and occasionally attracting "stupid money" from outside the hobby looking for a fast return. History shows that market conditions of this kind rarely end well.

A recent example shows that even the deepest of insiders can get tripped up in the Ponzi scheme that is today's collectibles market. Steve Geppi is president and founder of Diamond, the only surviving major comics distributor, a highly sophisticated, longtime comics collector, and reputedly a very wealthy guy. In 2006, he agreed to pay $1 million for a trove of original Archie Comics artwork from the 1940s and 1950s from the estate of artist Bob Montana. Montana originals were scarce in the market and much prized by collectors like Geppi and his friends, although Archie art tends to look the same to anyone who is not a specialist in this rather specialized field. Geppi's plan was to sell off a portion of the collection to pay for the pieces he himself wanted to keep. He hired Jerry Weist, another esteemed longtime collectibles guy who literally wrote the book on collecting original comic book art, to assess the value of a number of pieces. To Weist's trained eye, the art was worth a fortune—well in excess of Geppi's offer.

But these two smart guys outsmarted themselves. Geppi quickly glutted the market trying to unload the extra pieces, and even the best works realized only a fraction of the assessed value. He and Weist assumed that there were enough people with enough money who knew enough about old Archie comics to value the original artwork as much as they did. Wrong, wrong, and wrong. And remember, this is for original art, where each piece is unique and handmade—not for a copy of an old magazine that might have been part of a half-million print run. If I were any kind of collectibles dealer, I would find that story chilling.

While the rise of CGC and auctions turned one type of comics collecting into a branch of the financial derivatives trade, the present era has proved a boon for anyone who's just interested in comics for what's inside them. Reprints are everywhere, in every format from the cheapest to the most deluxe. Moreover, the advent of digital media, social computing, and peer-to-peer file sharing has created a boisterous trade in scans of old issues, downloadable free on public networks. Who except speculators or folks old enough to have a genuine sentimental attachment would want to pay a fortune for the moldy old originals when you can read the story in everything from a cheap trade paperback collection to a deluxe hardcover Omnibus Archive Masterworks edition, or just download scans of the entire series free on BitTorrent?

Dealers and old-time collectors may understand this on an intellectual level, but it's hard to teach an old nostalgist new tricks. The circle of dealers and collectors is small and self-contained. It's been operating on the same patterns and shared assumptions for decades. For traditionalists, the convenience of digital comics is about as persuasive as the argument that screw-top caps are better for keeping wine fresh than natural corks: maybe so, but so what? For some people, the experience of tracking down and owning the object is as much a part of the appeal as the content—and the evidence indicates that this is true for a lot of the remaining market for comics and related media.

Chuck Rozanski, a longtime dealer and owner of one of the country's largest collectors' comics inventory (Denver's Mile High Comics), agrees. He says not to be fooled by the lack of action at big conventions: demand for back issues is strong, even given the overall state of the economy, but most of the commerce takes place online and through back channels. Large collections are now passing to new generations through inheritance, bringing new blood into the hobby as heirs get bitten by the bug to upgrade or fill in gaps. Rozanski is backing up his view of the market with a significant personal investment. In 2011, Mile High purchased a giant warehouse in Denver, open to the public one day per month, to store an inventory of more than 2 million back issues. He is betting on scale, and it's probably a good bet. Whatever happens across the collectors' market in general, there will always be room for a couple of superdealers with comprehensive inventories and trusted reputations.

If the decline of the back-issue market affected only the dwindling number of collectors of vintage comics, it would be a loss for those of us who still enjoy the smell of old paper, but it would not mean much to the wider world. However, the overlap among collectors, fans, and professionals within the comics culture is profound. The tastes of current-day comics fans are shaped by the reputation enjoyed by past works—partly reflected through their value in the collectors market. Some retailers who sell new comics also rely partly on back-issue sales to collectors for added revenue or as an outlet for unsold, nonreturnable comics from past years, and they can ill afford to lose another source of income.

The back-issue market creates confusion for publishers: are they selling original content, which can be moved easily to a digital format, or are they selling future collectibles, which must take physical form? Publishers of newspapers and periodicals are having all kinds of trouble making the transition to the online world, but as far as I know, there is not a small army of collectors of *The Economist* or *GQ* back issues demanding that the magazines continue to publish paper copies for them to save in plastic bags and acid-free boxes.

It's also a financial issue. The idea that "[fans think] old comics are worth money" pervades the publishing industry and influences decisions on everything from pricing to print runs to editorial/creative matters. Why do you think DC relaunched 52 new series with first issues, rather than just rebranding the running titles? At least in part because #1 issues sell better to collectors, and publishers know that a lot of people will buy copies just to have them.

Even after the 1990s speculative bust, publishers and retailers still make money from collectors who buy multiple copies of the same issue, or who buy up all the different limited editions and gim-micky variants (some new comics are available with six to ten dif-ferent covers, some of which are kept deliberately scarce) because of the perceived desirability of these rare items. If you are selling only 5,000 copies per month, even a few dozen obsessive collectors buying multiple copies can make a difference. That strategy won't work with digital, where scarcity does not exist. A future in which no one expects old comics to be worth anything looks very different from the past and present.

Most collectors don't prefer the old ways merely for aesthetic rea-sons or because they are sitting on hordes of back issues whose value may decline precipitously. They are very aware of what is being lost in the transition: a community that has been intrinsic to comics fandom since the earliest days. To folks my age and older, tracking down issues one at a time is more fun than clicking on a link. Hold-ing the copy in your hands, with all the old ads and letters pages, is more satisfying than flicking the screen of an iPad. Haggling with a dealer who knows exactly why you want that particular issue ("ah, the secret origin of the Unknown Soldier . . . you don't see that one in VF+ very often!") has no analog in the digital world.

For these reasons, the dealers' room will linger on at Comic-Con and elsewhere long after the economic basis for its existence is exhausted. It is a reminder of a golden age: not the golden age of comics, but the golden age of *collecting* comics. Future generations—perhaps the one being born right now—will eventually grow bored and burned out with the hectic, hell-bent-for-convenience lifestyle of today's Millennials, and may rediscover the simple pleasure of opening an old comic book that their grandfather once enjoyed. When that happens, you can be sure that comics fans of the future will find a way to be nostalgic for an earlier form of nostalgia.

Casual Fans: Mic and Emily's Day

New types of transmedia phenomena can bring in devoted fans with lower entry costs than subcultures dedicated to a single format or genre. While flipping through the dollar boxes in the dealers' area, I ran into my niece Emily and her husband, Mic (pronounced "Mike"), who had made the trip to San Diego from Las Vegas. Eunice and I had managed to hook them up with one-day badges, as we had done the previous year.

Mic and Emily are in their early thirties, and they are fans of comics culture in the broadest sense. They'd be G4 viewers, but they have better things to do with their money than shell out for the higher-level cable package that gets the channel. Emily likes the toys and animated characters she remembers from her youth in the 1980s: *He-Man* and *She-Ra*, *Transformer*, and all things *Star Wars*. She reads a few comics (Marvel's Deadpool is her favorite character) and watches lots of cartoons, science fiction and fantasy shows, and anything with a general connection to the wider nerd universe.

Mic is a hard-core video gamer who traces his enthusiasm back to the days of *Asteroids* and *Battlezone*. He is an aficionado of pinball, collecting old games from as far back as the 1930s and restoring them to working condition. Nearly a dozen are crammed into their snug townhome in Henderson, Nevada (just outside of Las Vegas), along with a stand-up arcade video console souped up to play more than 2,000 different games (says Mic: "It may not look like much, but I made a couple of special modifications myself.").

Mic shares Emily's interest in animation and science fiction: they spent their first date watching episodes of Jhonen Vasquez's twisted cartoon *Invader Zim* on DVD and knew immediately that they were soulmates. They got married in May 2011 in a public park outside Las Vegas, with the entire wedding party (and many guests) outfit-

Photo by Eunice Verstegen

Attendees Mic Messersmith and Emily Wydeven catch their breath after a few hours in the Exhibit Hall.

ted in steampunk (Victorian-era) waistcoats, ruffled skirts, pocket watches, and ornate mechanical accessories. More on that in a bit.

The things that engage their fandom may not overlap completely with my interests or Eunice's, but they avidly and proudly affirm their identity as fans: card-carrying members of the nerd brigade, front-facing true believers. Comics conventions, vintage arcades, and theme exhibits like the Star Trek Experience or the Science Fiction Museum in Seattle all hold interest for them, even if it's only for the vibe of being surrounded by people who share a passion for sharing their passions.

They came to visit us for the Emerald City Comic-Con in Seattle, a modest-sized show of less than 20,000, which they loved. San Diego is in many ways more frustrating, more complicated, more expensive, and less fulfilling. And yet, there are cons, and then there is Comic-Con. As Mic explained, "When we told people we were going to Emerald City, they said, 'Have a good time.' When we said we're going to Comic-Con, they were like, 'Whoa . . . !'"

That said, Mic is not a huge comics fan, and he knew well the hassles he was signing up for by coming to San Diego. He was nearly ready to let Emily spend the day at Comic-Con on her own until I texted him a photograph from the exhibit hall of a pinball machine based on the movie *TRON* set up at one of the booths, offering a grand prize for the weekend's top score. *TRON* and pinball compete for top spot on Mic's geek list. Bull, meet red cape.

Mic and Emily had driven five hours the previous day from Las Vegas to Mic's parents' house in Riverside, then awoke with the dawn to drive another hour south to a park-and-ride, where they caught a trolley to the convention center. Parking was so tight that security guards had to turn convention attendees away from the parking lots of shopping malls many miles from downtown. The tram that Mic and Emily took at 8 a.m. was already crammed with convention-goers, many in full costume, ready to line up for the 9:30 opening of the exhibit hall.

By the time I ran into Mic and Emily, they had been cruising the floor for a good several hours, and the gobstruck look of awe that most people have when they first set foot in the exhibit hall had been partially replaced by one of exhaustion. Saturday at Comic-Con will wear you out. The big booths are more crowded than Hindu temples on festival days (and every bit as colorful). You need a pith helmet and a machete to make your way through the aisles. Traffic stops as Catwoman strikes a pose with a disconcertingly proportioned Power Girl and 30 fanboys whip out their iPhones to share the good times on their Facebook pages. Lines of hundreds of people form instantly and seemingly at random—look, over there, it's Doctor Who! No, wait, there's an exclusive *Star Wars* toy that's only available to the first 500 buyers!—and are pushed to the side by roving bands of security people. Artists are too busy to look up from their drawing pads to say more than a few unintelligible words. Blasts of music and random announcements float up from the booths and hover over the convention floor, adding to the general din of the rabble.

Both Mic and Emily are big fans of Seth MacFarlane's animated shows (*Family Guy, American Dad*), but they knew better than to even attempt entry to the panels featuring MacFarlane and the casts taking place in Ballroom 20 upstairs (capacity: 3,500). If you weren't in line first thing in the morning, you weren't getting in. Still, there's plenty to do just walking around.

Mic ended up spending a long time at the *TRON* pinball machine, although he was not able to claim the high score. He then spent much of his afternoon in mind-lock with fellow gaming enthusiasts, particularly the smaller developers pushing small-scale but highly playable "casual games."

"The folks at the booths of the big game makers are marketing people," he said dismissively. "They're just reading a script and only want to talk about whatever they are trying to sell you that day. The indie guys are for real; they have passion for what they're doing." He also added that you couldn't get close to a booth like those of Electronic Arts or Ubisoft, much less get your hands on the games they were demonstrating.

Emily shopped at the toy and T-shirt booths nearby, hunting down an elusive collectible Hordak figure (from the 1980s animated show *She-Ra: Princess of Power*) that she'd been missing for more than 20 years. She eventually found it at the table of an independent comics publisher who was giving away free action figures to anyone who bought a book or collection. This big score—at a bargain, no less—pleased her immensely and was the highlight of her day.

After a brief chat, they moved on toward the far end of the hall. They later told me that they were checking out the numerous booths selling steampunk fashions, art, comics, toys, and accessories. They had lots to choose from. Steampunk is well represented at Comic-Con.

For those not familiar with the core concept, steampunk posits an alternative history in which the Victorian culture of the late nineteenth century developed mechanical, steam-driven technologies, including computers ("difference engines"), zeppelins and airships, horseless carriages based on ornate clockwork machinery, and other contrivances. These have a striking aesthetic that is far different from their real, modern-age electronic counterparts: elaborate, mysterious, and romantic, recalling a bygone era of industrial design. More than a genre, more than a design sensibility, the steampunk movement finds expression in prose books (notably William Gibson and Bruce Sterling's *The Difference Engine*), comics (Phil and Kaja Foglio's *Girl Genius* and Paul Guinan and Anina Bennett's *Boilerplate*, among others), film (*League of Extraordinary Gentlemen*, based on the graphic novel by Alan Moore and Kevin O'Neill, and the recent remakes of Sherlock Holmes starring Robert Downey Jr.), plus fantasy art, video games, jewelry design, fashion, music, and numerous online communities and websites.

Though steampunk is not comics-related per se, steampunk fans are as vigorously committed to their specific aesthetics and interests as any of the other tribes of Comic-Con, and that goes a long way. The phantasmagoric architecture of steampunk has rigor and integrity. It's hard-edged and cool underneath the frilly ruffles and topcoats, which earns its adherents more respect than the despised

Twilighters, with their moon-eyed maidens, sparkly vampires, and soft-core source texts. The steampunk community likes Comic-Con because it's a good place to dress up in full regalia: the neo-Victorians fit in perfectly in an exhibit hall packed with every conceivable style of clothing, uniform, and costume. The style is also not in any way exclusive to a love of comics, movies, or anything else on offer at the Con. Many steampunks, including Mic and Emily, have broad pop culture tastes.

Steampunk is an interesting example of a subculture that was transmedia almost from its inception. I don't know its exact point of origin, but it seems that all manifestations of the style have an equal claim to authenticity and fan affection, regardless of medium, as long as they are well executed. Fans are not tied to a specific property, creator, or publisher. Elements of steampunk are portable into related genres (science fiction, superheroes, horror, fantasy, and so on) and cross over into other popular styles and subcultures (goth, emo, apocalyptic postindustrial, punk/postpunk). There does not seem to be the same problem of translating the thematic richness of the ideas intact movies, comics, video games, and fashion.

The possibilities inherent in steampunk are attractive enough to engage the interest of casual fans like Mic and Emily at multiple levels—but mostly because the costumes and accessories look so cool and classy. How many people read the previous passage about the steampunk wedding and thought, "Wow, what a fun idea"?

As comics and pop culture try to navigate the minefield of fan obsession and nostalgia that fetters legacy properties to the medium in which they originated, phenomena like steampunk point a way forward. The entry costs to the subculture—dressing a little bit different from the majority, maybe learning a little bit of history—are high enough to create a sense of specialness around the fans who want to buy in without creating formidable barriers to creators or the audience. The style, combining visual and narrative elements, is perfect for all kinds of mixed media, from comics to movies to digital, without creating turf wars. As a result, there's a steady stream of steampunk-oriented content of all kinds, from the humblest self-published work and do-it-yourself fashion accessories to multimillion-dollar special effects films like Martin Scorsese's *Hugo*.

In the transmedia future, more styles and subcultures will be born without a clear attachment to one mode of representation. Comics, movies, fashion, and games will be conceived simultaneously (or follow one another so quickly that it doesn't matter which came first) as instances of a unified concept or a single story. These may emerge as the result of grassroots fan-driven enthusiasm or managed branding campaigns undertaken by big content companies. This might sound too contrived and complicated; however, by providing a 360-degree experience for fans, they will have broader market potential and will provide a more certain revenue stream for creators.

After Hours: Trickster and the Backlash

Every successful media phenomenon will create a backlash. Learn to expect, tolerate, and work with your critics to improve the culture around your industry or product for everyone.

A few weeks before the start of Comic-Con 2011, a press release started making the rounds of comics blogs and news sites, talking about an event called Trickster, a "supplement" to the Comic-Con experience designed to focus on personal visions of art and storytelling. Trickster would offer workshops, chalk-talk creative sessions, a more relaxed exhibit space, and the chance to party late into the night with bands, cocktails, snacks, and entertainment.

In effect, organizers Scott Morse and Ted Mathot were staging a counter-Con at the San Diego Wine and Culinary Center, directly across the street from the convention center. A host of top-drawer creative talent from the comics industry announced their participation, led by *Hellboy* creator Mike Mignola, fan favorites David Mack, Paul Pope, and Mike Allred, and dozens of others with street-cred as independent or idiosyncratic voices.

To some fans, this promised a much-needed correction to the media monstrosity that Comic-Con had become. For years, people had been complaining that the Hollywood invasion had diluted the Con's core focus and mission of promoting comics as a unique art form, not just a minor-league farm system to develop content and talent for other entertainment media. Comics fans and creators felt disrespected and marginalized at their own event. The crowds, the hassles, the registration and hotel booking nightmares, and the spiraling expenses just added insult to injury.

Some opted out altogether, preferring regional and art-focused shows to the noise of Comic-Con. But for most people in the industry and many serious fans, attendance at San Diego is mandatory— for networking and getting jobs, for seeing and being seen, or just for avoiding the horrible feeling of missing something important.

Trickster offered an obvious and elegant solution—an event that restored pride of place to comics and comics arts while providing the necessary proximity to San Diego Comic-Con and its whole constellation of industry, networking, and social events. Trickster billed itself as Slamdance to Comic-Con's Sundance, an apt analogy in many ways.

Reactions to Trickster within the Comic-Con establishment were mostly muted, but underneath, an argument festered as to whether the relationship between the Con and Trickster was symbiotic or parasitic. The Con enjoys an embarrassment of riches in terms of attendance, exhibitor participation, guests, media coverage, and prestige; a small-scale happening like Trickster does not rate as competition in any real way. Also, organizers understand that the only place for the Con to grow in the future is outside the four walls of the convention center (and perhaps outside of San Diego, although that is a different conversation). In 2011, Con-related events were already scheduled in hotels and venues all around the Gaslamp Quarter. One more event, even if it was organized outside the umbrella of Comic-Con International, didn't really make much difference, and might even be helpful in creating a diversity of experience.

At the same time, some felt that the creators who hopped on the Trickster bandwagon were just being opportunistic, riding a trendy wave of resentment against the Con while continuing to benefit from it. Nearly all of the participants in the Trickster programming schedule also had a presence in the Comic-Con exhibit hall; many had been invited guests of the Con at one point or another. Now they were biting the hand that fed them in an attempt to pander to hipsters who posed as "too cool for Comic-Con." I was treated to this perspective on Trickster every time I stopped by the Exhibit A booth.

I had checked out Trickster briefly on Friday afternoon on my way to another event. Not much was going on at the time. The bookstore was open, but it was lightly stocked and lightly attended. If a program was taking place, it was somewhere in the back, because the front room was empty. A few people milled around looking at artwork. It didn't seem at all like a big deal.

On Saturday night, we decided to give it another shot. We were coming back from an event at the convention center and saw a crowd of several hundred gathered on the lawn between the front of the culinary center and the train tracks.

It was a beautiful evening, and the party was in full swing. A bar set up just inside the doorway was doing a booming business selling beer and wine. Next door, the comic-themed band Kirby Krackle provided a sonic backdrop. The interior spaces were full, but not oppressively crowded; outside, people sat at tables, milled around, or sprawled on the grass.

The mostly young crowd was having a blast. Fans mingled with professionals; aspiring artists chatted with editors; singles flirted; a few people were getting loose and boisterous. The scene was neither nerdy nor pretentious. The bombastic unreality of Comic-Con was almost entirely absent. No one was in costume, with the exception of one lonely fellow sporting a red Superman cape, and no one paid much attention to the various A-list celebrities and creators who passed through.

You wouldn't know it from watching media reports of comics conventions, with their emphasis on the most freakish and geekish spectacles, but this casual scene is a good representation of the audience for contemporary comics. People I spoke to in the Trickster crowd had broad taste in what they read and liked. Some were into literary and alt.comics, but most liked at least some superheroes. Comics are part of their media diet, but their interests are not limited to pop culture obsessions. They have lives, jobs, lovers, and decent haircuts. They will read graphic novels on the subway without feeling embarrassed and check out Newsarama or Comic Book Resources on their iPhones during boring meetings at work.

Scenes like this make it hard to understand why the comics industry is having so much trouble connecting with a mass audience. The audience is there. The interest in the product is there. The

Photo by Doug Kline

Kyle Stephens of the "nerd rock" band Kirby Krackle performs at Trickster.

disposable income is (mostly) there. The stigma is gone: comics are cool. And for every one of the creative and curious young people whose interest in comics was strong enough to bring them to San Diego for Comic-Con, there are hundreds or thousands more just like them who don't know what they're missing.

So the questions remain: how to engage? How to turn interest and attention into revenue? How to bring the breadth and vitality that exist in today's comics scene to a wider global audience? And how to get past the short-term pitfalls and uncertainties of digital distribution before it's too late for the industry?

As Comic-Con headed into its final stretch, we ambled back to our hotel in the small hours of the morning. The day ahead would provide some insights into the answers.

CHAPTER ⟨6⟩

SUNDAY:
TO INFINITY
AND BEYOND

After Saturday night, Comic-Con usually feels like it's over. But it's not; there's a full day to go. Some people only come on Sunday, the day that has traditionally offered the most kid-friendly programming. For those people, everything must seem new and fresh and full of energy.

Just about everyone else is a dead-eyed zombie. Exhausted artists hurry through their list of commissioned sketches. Dealers start slashing prices, desperate to unload inventory and reduce the load they need to take back. Attendees stagger through the aisles on cramped, aching legs, trying to check one more item off their to-do lists.

Photo by Eunice Verstegen

Artist, agent, and publisher Denis Kitchen (right) looks none the worse for wear on Sunday afternoon.

I was on my way back from Artists' Alley when I ran into agent/publisher/artist/author/man-about-town Denis Kitchen, who had arranged a very big favor for Eunice and me: invitations to an exclusive after-Con event called the Dead Dog Party, a traditional gathering of Comic-Con veterans and pros. Access to the event is tightly controlled: you need to present your invitation card, and it's good only for yourself—no guests. He handed over the precious cargo, which I quickly shoved into a secure pocket of my jacket.

Denis was in a punchy mood as he showed me some of the odd-ball collectibles he'd gathered on his brief trip around the exhibit hall. Crowds surged and swirled around us. As a veteran of more than 40 years in the industry, Denis had perfected the ability to tune out the noise of the Con and react to the absurdities of it with dry wit, despite having spent the past four days in back-to-back meetings from breakfast until the small hours of the night. Industry professionals who come to Comic-Con are not here for the fun, games, and costumes, and they rarely have time for shopping. Every waking hour is spent lining up new projects, refreshing old connections, finalizing details, making introductions, and following up on leads. Beneath all the craziness, Comic-Con is, at least in part, a trade show. It is a hell of a place to do business, but lots of business does get done.

The transfer of invitations complete, we plunged back into the maelstrom, eager to track down last-minute gifts, scrounge for last-day bargains, and exchange greetings with any friends we might encounter in these last few random hours.

Storming the Gates: Comics in Schools, Libraries, and Museums

As the walls between high culture and mass culture continue to dissolve, the relationships between cultural institutions and commercial media are changing.

On Sunday, Comic-Con focuses on kids and families, and programs designed to appeal to educators and librarians are offered throughout the Con. One of the most popular panels with educators is one called "The Secret Origins of Good Readers," usually held on Sunday morning and hosted by Dr. Robyn Hill of National University and Mimi Cruz, owner of the award-winning Night Flight Comics stores in Salt Lake City. In addition to being passionate advocates on this subject, Robyn and Mimi are fellow Eisner Award staff members and old pals. We ran into them at the Exhibit A booth on Sunday morning as they were preparing for their panel.

The Secret Origins panel and the accompanying handbook developed by Cruz and Hill in 2004 help educators use comics to encourage reluctant readers and kindle a passion for reading in kids. When they first started doing their panel in the early 2000s, the idea that comics had value as teaching tools was at the fringes of educational theory. The only place for comics in the classroom was their traditional spot: wedged between the pages of a textbook to fool the prying eyes of teachers. At least in the United States, comics still carried a stigma among educators that dated from the dark days of the 1950s, when behavioral psychologist Dr. Frederic Wertham attacked the entire medium as an incubator of juvenile delinquency. At conventions, Robyn carries a vintage copy of Wertham's anticomics screed, *Seduction of the Innocent*, which she encourages cartoonists to deface with drawings and signatures—perhaps as a way to break the curse the old prude cast over American comics for nearly half a century.

The mojo seems to be working. For the past 15 years, the artful stylings of graphic novelists and comics-based storytellers have overcome the cultural stigma imposed by Wertham and his ilk; today, comics are marching relentlessly into both the schoolhouse and the library. The design and fast-moving stories found in comics appeal to the Millennial learning style, and the residual outlaw reputation of comics endears them to youngsters from backgrounds where books and literacy are not socially encouraged. Bill McGrath, another frequent member of the Secret Origins panel, successfully uses comics to teach reading skills to kids in the juvenile justice system.

Hill, Cruz, and McGrath tend to focus on using "off-the-shelf," commercially available comics in an educational setting, but Hill notes that this sometimes creates controversy, especially among parents. Recently, some textbook companies have been developing custom materials in sequential art format, designed by educators for use in a classroom environment. Then there are graphic novels created either with an educational purpose in mind or with some clear instructional value, such as the science-oriented work of Jim Ottaviani or the humorous *Cartoon History of the Universe* books by Larry Gonick.

As the generation that grew up with comics in the classroom makes its way into the workforce, we are likely to see an increasing demand for comics-style training materials. Fortunately, a template for this already exists: among his many other accomplishments, Will Eisner pioneered instructional comics, creating the long-running illustrated technical journal *PS: Preventative Maintenance Monthly* under contract with the U.S. Army in the 1950s.

The range of subject matter need not be limited to vocational and technical material. In 2008, bestselling business writer Daniel Pink wrote a guide for young job seekers called *The Adventures of Johnny Bunko: The Last Career Guide You'll Ever Need*, with artwork by Rob Ten Pas. Chicago-based publisher Round Table Press has been adapting business classics as graphic novels. Individual companies are increasingly commissioning workforce training and marketing materials in comic format for internal use. My communications firm, MediaPlant, has recently been doing a series of competitive sales guides, training manuals, and webcomics for Microsoft using this creative approach, working with a Portland-based studio.

Librarians, both academic and public, have noted the escalating circulation figures for graphic novels and are eager to tap into anything that gets books into people's hands. Many bigger comics con-

Will Eisner pioneered instructional comics in the 1950s with strips like this one, educating U.S. service personnel on ways to maintain their equipment.

ventions, including Comic-Con, have special programming tracks devoted to librarians. Publishers of graphic novels are welcome at publishing trade shows and meetings of the American Library Association (ALA). Comics have been shelved at the Library of Congress. There is even a comic strip for librarians, *Unshelved*, by Gene Ambaum and Bill Barnes, which has grown into a full Web-based community with merchandise, news, and book reviews in comics format.

The critical success of graphic novels is one important factor that helped to change institutional opinions about comics. Art Spiegelman, the one-time underground cartoonist, avant-garde bomb thrower, and inventor of the demented Wacky Pack trading cards that corrupted young minds like mine in the early 1970s, bears a lot of the responsibility for this transformation. With his master-work *Maus* (1986), not only did he bring the most serious possible adult subject matter into the sequential art medium, but he did so through the most inviting and accessible motif in the comic book vocabulary, the "funny animal" story. Because Spiegelman was a more self-consciously artistic figure and operated in the highbrow world of the New York downtown scene, it was easier for academic critics to treat *Maus* as a "real" work of literature, especially once they got air cover from the Pulitzer committee. It was a work worthy of study, one that clearly belonged in libraries and belonged in schools. It also helped that *Maus* was a book, with a spine and an ISBN, published by a real publisher.

Acclaimed graphic novels that followed *Maus* but still hewed to the superhero genre, such as Frank Miller's *The Dark Knight Returns* and Alan Moore and Dave Gibbons's *Watchmen*, had to overcome skepticism but eventually established the precedent that comics with superheroes could carry a thematic payload that made them good grist for the academic mill. At the same time, creators expanded the range of nonfiction comics with works of graphic journalism (exemplified by 1996's *Palestine* by Joe Sacco), history (such as Rick Geary's matter-of-fact true crime series, *A Treasury of Victorian Murder*), and even literary criticism (*The Beats: A Graphic History*, a 2010 collection of drawn essays chronicling the writers of the 1950s Beat Generation).

The battle for acceptance dragged on through the 1990s as market confusion about graphic novels (a term used indiscriminately for original long-form works and collected editions of previously published comic books) overshadowed the growing divide between mainstream and literary-oriented efforts. Schools and libraries that did not cultivate a deeper knowledge of the comics landscape discovered that there were important differences between a brilliant, accessible, all-audience masterpiece like Marjane Satrapi's *Persepolis* (about her life growing up under the Islamic government in Iran) and, say, the DC collection *Identity Crisis*, a disturbing, adult-themed superhero saga written by author Brad Meltzer. Today, more and better resources exist to help librarians build collections that are appropriate for the needs of their communities or institutions.

As interesting as the migration of comics into the corridors of highbrow respectability is the newfound shameless affection of many of today's leading literary lights for comic book culture. Michael Chabon, Jonathan Lethem, Junot Diaz, David Hajdu, and Rick Moody are as "establishment" as the literary establishment gets in the 2000s, and many of them are out-and-proud comics fans whose best works directly embrace the art form and its history with little trace of irony.

This appears to be a generational phenomenon, part of the same Generation X project to refurbish the reputation of the 1970s as the *TwoMorrows* fanzines or graphic novels like Ellen Forney's *Monkey Food* (collecting her late 1990s retro strip, "I Was Seven in '75"). There is a saying in comics fandom that "the golden age of comics is whatever year you were eight years old," and for today's forty-something literary lions, that's the mid-1970s: the last days of the pre-direct market era, when comics bought on the newsstand played a meaningful role in an American kid's life. It's easy to see that kind of motivation behind Jonathan Lethem's rose-tinged remembrance of *Omega the Unknown*, an obscure Marvel title from the mid-1970s that was featured in his acclaimed novel *The Fortress of Solitude*.

What is even more remarkable is that Lethem ended up writing an updated *Omega the Unknown* miniseries for Marvel in 2007—an act that would have led to the revocation of his membership card in the highbrow literary circle not long ago.

Michael Chabon, whose Pulitzer Prize–winning bestseller, *The Amazing Adventures of Kavalier and Clay*, is a deep exploration of the social iconography of the golden age of American comics in the 1930s and 1940s, is one of the most unabashed champions of comics culture among the literati. Chabon has been to Comic-Con many times, both as a guest and as an attendee. One of the most memorable panels I have attended in more than a dozen years of going to Comic-Con was a conversation between Chabon and Will Eisner in 2002 on the real-life antics of the Kavalier and Clay generation. To close the circle, the Dark Horse series *The Escapist*, based on the character created in Chabon's book and overseen by the author, featured Will Eisner's last work (a return to his iconic character The Spirit) and won an Eisner Award at the emotional first awards ceremony following Eisner's death in 2005.

How deeply have comics planted their flag on the grounds of serious literature? You can't get any closer to the heart of the American literary establishment than *The New Yorker* magazine, and the art editor of *The New Yorker* is none other than Françoise Mouly, copublisher of *RAW* back in the 1980s and wife of *Maus* man Art Spiegelman. Under her editorship, Chris Ware, Craig Thompson, Chester Brown, Daniel Clowes, and others in the favored circle of the alt.comics mafia have all done covers or interior features for the institutional bastion of American letters. *The New Yorker* is not alone in harnessing the talent and mystique of successful graphic novelists to sell magazines. Each issue of the trendy ideas journal *The Believer* features a cover by Charles Burns, the postmodern comics master and graphic novelist whose early work graced the pages of *Dope Comix* and *Death Rattle*. Comic artists with art world cred have also done album covers, posters, ads, book jackets, and other work with wide cultural exposure.

The book-comics mutual admiration society is not just fashionable slumming by a bunch of New York literary-salon types: the bestseller lists are crowded with authors who have dabbled with, or got their starts in, comics: George R. R. Martin, Stephen King, Joe Lansdale, Brad Meltzer, Greg Rucka, and Clive Barker all have their feet planted firmly on both sides of the line.

Arguably the most popular and charismatic figure to straddle both worlds is Neil Gaiman, who emerged from comics with a stellar reputation as the creator of *Sandman* for DC/Vertigo and has produced an almost unbroken string of commercially and artistically successful fantasy and horror tales in book, film, television, and comics format for the better part of two decades. His regular appearances at Comic-Con (every few years in recent times), in which he makes himself available round the clock at panels, readings, fan events, awards shows, movie premieres, and parties, are notable for the excitement and attention they generate, even in the supersaturated environment of the rest of the Con. Gaiman is a true avatar of the transmedia era, someone who has built a distinct personal brand that spans the entire gamut of popular culture, purely on the basis of his creative talent and voice.

All this literary adulation is helpful for storming the gates of libraries and universities, but that is not the only front where comics are advancing on high culture. Comics are as much about pictures as they are about words. In the art world, they are making strides in gaining respect within the visual arts establishment commensurate with their rising reputation as books and literature.

Aesthetically speaking, comics started out behind the eight ball as the object of the ironic stylings of pop artists like Roy Lichtenstein. Ask hardworking veteran comic book artists like John Romita (who later went on to draw *Spider-Man*) what they think of the re-creations by "fine artists" like Lichtenstein of panels that they drew in romance comics for $15 a page now fetching millions at auction and hanging in the galleries of the Museum of Modern Art (MoMA) in New York. Another great from that era, Carmine Infantino, had one of the most distinctive design sensibilities of the 1960s, but it is known to the wider public only as the basis for the campy *Batman* TV show. Harvey Kurtzman's visual comedy style, established in his signature creation, *Mad*, not only set the standard for satire in comics but influenced generations of American comedy in film, TV, and stand-up. His contributions remained under-recognized for decades, in part because of the medium in which he worked.

Within the community of comics fans, original art—the actual comic book pages drawn by the artist(s) on oversized Bristol board, rendered in pen and ink—has been a collectible since the 1960s, when some editors sent pages to fans as a reward for sending a particularly insightful letter of comment, and some staff members helped themselves to originals that were gathering dust in their employers' storerooms. By the mid-1970s, most artists had worked out arrangements to have their originals returned by the publishers so that they could sell them and make a little extra money over their page rate. Every convention features at least a few tables of art dealers with big portfolios of originals selling at prices from less than $100 to many thousands of dollars, depending on the artist, the title, and the quality of the page.

Comics collectors' criteria for evaluating and pricing original art are sometimes at odds with standards prevalent in the wider art market. Comics collectors tend to prefer superheroes, story lines, and poses that are considered iconic within the hobby. Bold pages and covers by classic-era artists like Neal Adams, John Buscema, and Gil Kane, who specialized in dramatic action scenes, are high priced and collectible despite the artists not being especially well known or well regarded outside of comics. Artists with a more subtle touch or a more experimental style are rarely as popular.

This dynamic has encouraged many contemporary comics artists to lay out their pages with lots of dramatic poses and action shots so as to pump up the aftermarket value of their originals. Because comics are a visual medium, artists have quite a bit of say in the creative process. Their preference for action shots over character development and pacing has resulted in a "decompressed" style of storytelling for many superhero comics, where less happens in a given 18- to 22-page episode than was the case 20 years ago. In effect, this means that readers are getting less story for their money even as the price of single issues has increased tenfold over the same period. This has not helped comics find new audiences in the face of competition from story-rich entertainment options in other media.

That said, the artistic skill and innovation that are on display within comics pages have been on the rise for decades. Underground comics and their successors like *RAW* embraced a more fine-art sensibility from the start, and artists from that movement, like Robert Crumb, Robert Williams, Art Spiegelman, Gary Panter, and Charles Burns, have all had much greater success at being taken seriously in the art world from the get-go. The same is true of stylistic innovators like Bill Sienkiewicz, Dave McKean, and David Mack, who pioneered the use of digital and mixed-media techniques in the comics idiom to produce striking, distinctive, museum-quality artistic works. Many of these figures, and/or their agents and galleries, can be found in the exhibit hall of Comic-Con hawking their wares alongside the purveyors of light sabers and zombie-themed handbags.

In the past 10 years, curated museum shows like the groundbreaking Masters of American Comics exhibit that opened at the Los Angeles Museum of Contemporary Art and the Hammer Museum in 2006 have begun to put the skills of comics masters like Jack Kirby, Will Eisner, and Harvey Kurtzman in a fine art context. Aesthetic theorists like R. C. Harvey, Scott McCloud, and, again, Eisner himself have helped lead the critical discourse to a higher plane. High-toned New York galleries are now exhibiting original comics art and comics-themed work at art-world prices, and acknowledged masterpieces are selling for six figures or more at Sotheby's. The classic comics artists are the subjects of beautifully designed art books and library editions of their collected works, studied and admired for their formal qualities and their exquisite craft.

In both their words and their pictures, comics have ascended from the subbasement of American culture to the pinnacle of acceptance and critical regard over the past 35 years. The question for the future is whether their popularity with elite connoisseurs and guardians of taste can coexist with their earthy roots as a pop culture medium. Is the term *comics* big enough to span a continuum that extends from *Spawn* and *The Incredible Hulk* to *Maus* and *Black Hole*, or is the fate of the comics business now completely separate from the status of comics as art? Are comics like cinema, a medium that accommodates both "films" and "movies," or are comics destined to become like jazz or poetry—an art form that is admired, but only barely viable at the fringes of the commercial economy?

Transcultural Transmedia: The New Global Face of Comics

The world's fastest-growing economies are teaming with young people who are hungry for creative expression. Every popular medium needs a global strategy in the digital era.

The only item on my programming schedule for Sunday was a panel honoring the contributions of Filipino artists who did well-crafted but underappreciated work during the 1970s and 1980s for titles like *Savage Sword of Conan, Creepy, House of Mystery*, and *All-Star Western*. This was one of those "older artists receive long-overdue recognition" panels that tend to be interesting but not terribly crowded. I didn't see any reason to hurry off the floor to line up early.

Big mistake. When I got to the upper level, the line was out the door, around the corner, and all the way down the hall. The panel was in one of the smaller meeting rooms, and I was lucky to get a seat in the back.

The audience appeared to be at least 85 percent of Filipino heritage, including lots of families and kids. They turned out in force to honor the elder statesmen of the business—Alex Niño, Tony DeZuniga, and Ernie Chan, plus their younger colleague Gerry Alangulian. When the older artists took the stage, the applause was sustained and heartfelt, and cheers went up every time they mentioned other well-regarded talent of their generation, such as Rudy Nebres, Nestor Redondo, and the late Alfredo Alcala, who enjoyed legendary reputations in the Philippines even before they brought their skills to the United States.

The artists talked about their craft, the industry in the Philippines, the issues of working with U.S. writers and editors, and the challenges of managing a global supply relationship in the days before the Internet (or even FedEx). The crowd sat in rapt attention, and when Q&A time came, those present declared their affection and respect for all the artists on stage who had served as role models and trailblazers. It was quite moving, and a further reminder, if any were needed, of the worldwide, transcultural appeal of the comics medium.

Seeing these guys get their due provided an unusually gratifying ending to a common story. The comics industry embraced globalization as far back as the late 1960s, for the same reasons as many businesses are embracing it today: to reduce costs with low-wage offshore labor. As DC, Marvel, and other publishers began to expand their lines, they looked to places like the Philippines, Spain, and Latin America, where artists worked quickly in distinctive styles at rates far lower than those paid to Americans. The Filipinos were generally relegated to second-tier nonsuperhero books, although DeZuniga shares creator credit for the enduring DC western character Jonah Hex. Only much later were they recognized for their unique talents and styles in an era in which much of the more mainstream artwork was being hacked out by aging, disengaged industry veterans.

Comics are generally considered to be an American art form, but one reason why the industry has been at the forefront of globalization is because the medium took root around the world during the twentieth century, spawning many vibrant local scenes and styles. Growing up, I kept a copy of Maurice Horn's monumental 800-page *World Encyclopedia of Comics* handy for browsing, and from its pages I learned about the comics of Japan, Europe, Latin America, and Southeast Asia, which seemed weird and exotic to an American kid who had been raised on superheroes. Some of this material started reaching U.S. shores in the late 1970s in *Heavy Metal* magazine, which, for a teenage male in practical terms, meant comics stories featuring naked, big-breasted women. Of course, there was more to it than that. In Europe and Asia, comics gained acceptance as art and literature for adults long before Americans figured out that "Zap! Bam! Pow! Comics Aren't Just for Kids Anymore!"

In the 1980s, more U.S. publishers began importing content, not just labor, for reasons of quality rather than cost. Dark Horse led the pack, bringing acclaimed manga from Japan as well as the work of edgy and sophisticated European creators with titles like *Lone Wolf and Cub* and *Cheval Noir* to the direct market. Most mainstream publishers now tap into the worldwide creative talent pool as a matter of course, and Latin American artists like Fábio Moon, Gabriel Bá, Mike Deodato, and Comic-Con mainstay Sergio Aragonés have large international fan followings. So do Europeans like Jordi Bernet and the late Jean Giraud ("Mobius"), whose reputations in their home countries are enormous.

Many of these artists have not faced the same struggles as their English-speaking brethren in terms of being taken seriously in the wider culture. Comics elsewhere in the world are sold in bookstores and on newsstands, are read in public, and work more closely with other media. Japanese anime cartoons, for example, are produced to help boost sales of the manga (comic books) on which they are based, whereas in the United States, any marketing synergy from media adaptations that spills over into comics seems to be purely coincidental.

This relationship has helped keep the lines between comics as art and comics as pop culture much cleaner in the rest of the world than in the United States. It is understood that some sequential art deals with serious literary themes and some is genre work; the creators are not presumed to share some kind of lowest-common-denominator interests just because they work in the same medium. The annual International Comics Festival in Angoulême, France (which draws more than 200,000 people annually), is about art and

Photo by Jackie Estrada

Mexican-born artist Sergio Aragonés has been doing groundbreaking work in the U.S. comics industry since the mid-1960s.

story, not movies, video games, or transmedia content. People do not attend in costume.

At the same time, association with Hollywood and all the artistic compromises that come with it has its advantages. The revenue opportunities for U.S.-based comics-related properties dwarf those in the rest of the world. Note that 2011's *Adventures of Tintin*, based on the massively popular Belgian character, was produced by Paramount and directed by an American (Steven Spielberg) in lavish 3D animation. Despite its modest success in the United States, it was a worldwide hit, benefiting from Hollywood's unsurpassed production values, brand strength, and marketing hype. It certainly outperformed Europe's other most-recognized comics property,

Asterix the Gaul, last seen in 2008's French-produced *Asterix aux Jeux Olympiques* (which won the French equivalent of a "Razzie" award for worst film of the year, despite doing decent box office in a few European markets).

Because comics are, in the end, a commercial industry as well as an art form, even in Europe, it is likely that the transmedia approach adopted by America, and driven by the American entertainment industry, will become the global model. Other countries in the world with large film industries—India, Hong Kong, and Nigeria—have no problem producing genre action movies, and there is huge potential for cross-licensing and cross-pollination of comics-related content as the global market continues to get more integrated and tastes grow more cosmopolitan.

Then there's Asia. Comics have been part of the landscape in Northeast Asia (Japan, South Korea, Hong Kong, China, and Taiwan) for decades, with a mature publishing industry and well-established transmedia channels involving toys, animation, film, collectible card games, fashion, and everything else you can think of. The manga-and-anime Comiket show in Tokyo draws 500,000 fans twice a year (more than triple the attendance at Comic-Con) and is easily the largest pop culture–themed event in the world. As an art form, a medium, and a business, Asian comics are so distinct that they are almost a separate branch of popular culture in themselves, warranting more attention than I can give them in a book of this scope. They are clearly a significant presence at events like Comic-Con and a major influence in the global market. Most importantly for our purposes, they have served as a primary on-ramp for the next-generation audience, both in their printed version (manga and associated subgenres like Shonen and Shojo) and in transmedia incarnations (everything from Pokémon cards to Transformer toys to anime cartoons).

The growing popularity of manga fueled an expansion of the U.S. market, picking up the slack when sales of mainstream superhero titles started to crumble in the mid- to late 1990s. Titles from Viz, Tokyopop, and others leapfrogged the direct market and went straight to bookstores, where they dominated sales charts and inspired a rich subculture of fans. The comic book adaptation of *Twilight*, for example, is done in manga style and is sold in bookstores, where its female readers can enjoy it away from the withering gaze of purists at the comic book shop. Manga readers tend to be younger and more female than the "mainstream" U.S. audience, and their devotion to the distinct aesthetics of Asian comics sets them apart from the superhero crowd. Anime/manga conventions tend to have a different flavor and vibe from other comics-oriented gatherings, reflecting the profound differences in storytelling style, art, character, and continuity between Asian and Western-style comics.

Many North Asian publishers have already embraced digital distribution as their primary channel, issuing digital editions in advance of paper copies or abandoning paper altogether. Viz announced in November 2011 that a digital-only edition of its top-selling *Naruto* collection would be available ahead of the trade collection—a first for such a high-profile title. Publishers from Japan, Hong Kong, and Korea advertise their digital wares in the Previews catalog of U.S. distributor Diamond and make their presence known to international buyers all over the web. In just about every way, the North Asian approach to integrating comics-based media into pop culture offers an alternative—and potentially competitive—model for the future of the industry that we've been discussing.

The young emerging markets of South Asia, Latin America, the Middle East, and Africa also present some untapped potential for comics as a driver of pop culture. In many of these countries, demographic and economic conditions are similar to those in the United States in the early part of the twentieth century, when comics first became a popular medium. These circumstances—booming cities, incipient modernity, wide disparities between wealth and poverty, governments struggling to rein in corruption and traditional oligarchs, and an ambitious rising young generation with newfound leisure time and disposable income—coexist with the rapid spread of new digital media, particularly mobile devices. The October 2011 launch of a $35 tablet computer in India (part of an inexorable march toward universal digital literacy and access in emerging economies) brings a market of hundreds of millions within the reach of digital comics and comics-related media on the web—and brings the markets of the West within reach of their creative industries as well.

The mix of the modern and the mythological already informs the popular culture of the world's fastest-growing young economy: India. Bollywood films traffic in spectacle, morality tales of good and evil, and genre tropes derived from gangster movies, Westerns, martial arts and action movies, science fiction, fantasy, and musicals. The Indian comics industry is large but relatively undeveloped compared to its potential. It has also been facing many of the same issues as its counterparts in the West, including increasing prices, declining sales, and competition with video games and movies for young mindshare and dollars. However, with the advent of digital and the spread of transmedia properties to the global market, there are huge possibilities for cross-cultural blending that captures both Eastern and Western audiences.

Marvel Comics has tried numerous times to bring its superhero lineup to the subcontinent, with mixed results. The most successful effort, in the mid-2000s, was done in partnership with Gotham Comics and featured a local version of *Spider-Man* whose secret identity was Pavitr Prabhakar, a slumdog Peter Parker from the streets of Mumbai. Marvel also decided to launch the comic books in Hindi and other regional languages, creating localization costs and complexity. For all its potential, India is a tough nut to crack for foreign content, primarily because of distribution issues. That's why digital might hold considerable promise in a country in which mobile phone sales and new connectivity are through the roof.

One company that is betting heavily on this scenario is Liquid Comics (originally Virgin Comics), an all-digital publisher offering a colorful lineup of titles based on classics of Indian literature and Hindu religious themes as well as contemporary genre and super-hero material. Liquid, a U.S.-based venture by three partners with extensive ties to India, has announced the usual slate of transmedia partnerships and licensing agreements that run the gamut from Deepak Chopra to the estate of Elvis Presley (an odd choice until you ask yourself what other American performer made such successful movies in the format that is now identified with Bollywood). In December 2011, Liquid took the logical next step, announcing a digital comics site called Graphic India, with downloadable content, how-to tips, industry news, and hooks to the company's transmedia properties as a way to tap into the vast potential of India's high-tech, pop-crazy young readership. Shortly afterward, it joined the long line of pop culture companies to sign agreements with Stan Lee, who promised in this case to create a new Indian superhero, Chakra—the Invincible.

Who's next to join the bandwagon? Would you believe Archie? According to reports that surfaced in August 2011, the all-American teen is big business in India, selling a reported million units in

2010, and is now developing story lines with specific appeal to that market. It's a strategy that Archie Comics has already employed in Latin America.

Across the emerging economies of the young world, where youthful populations are looking to technology innovation to drive social and economic progress, comics can have a profound impact. The unique words-and-pictures format of sequential art makes it ideal as an educational medium for young readers and for populations with limited literacy. Plain Ink, a start-up nongovernment organization (NGO) founded by educational activist Selene Biffi, helps young people in South Asia find their voice as storytellers through the power of comics. Plain Ink partners with and trains writers, illustrators, and storytellers to "provide enjoyable, inspiring and culturally appropriate content in line with local values and traditions" to sustain the local creative economy, create employment, support the publishing and printing industry, and encourage people of all ages to gain the practical skills they need to create sustainable livelihoods.

Elsewhere in the world, comics have become a vehicle for social engagement, not just entertainment. The Middle East and Africa have produced an impressive roster of acerbic editorial cartoonists whose keen sense of satire flourishes in a target-rich environment of pompous, corrupt, and disingenuous political leaders. During the events of the Arab Spring, the plight of Syrian cartoonist Ali Farzat, who was severely beaten by police following the publication of some cartoons critical of the Assad regime, became a cause célèbre in the international comics blogosphere. Tom Spurgeon, at his influential blog *The Comics Reporter*, is one of the best journalists in any medium at maintaining a truly global perspective, frequently tying news from the comics world to larger events (such as the death threats against Danish cartoonist Kurt Westergaard, whose caricatures of the Prophet Mohammed were deemed blasphemous by Islamic fundamentalists).

The broadening of critical perspectives and connections within the comics community worldwide mirrors a larger trend: the globalization of consumer culture, especially for entertainment and media. Today, the rapid spread of information networks and digital devices in emerging economies with huge young populations has created unprecedented cross-pollination of tastes and styles. In 2010, I was in a dance club in Mumbai where the DJ was spinning not only indigenous Goa-style house music and Bangra, but also the Tex-Mex flavors of the Tijuana-based Nortec Collective and the ethereal electronica of Brazilian chanteuse Bebel Gilberto. Folks in the crowd, some sporting the latest Korean and Japanese fashions, were asking me about *The Daily Show*, which they all watched obsessively through online channels.

In comics and comics-related media, we can see the same evidence of cultural blending in the adoption of the Northeast Asian manga style not only in some North American comics, but also throughout Latin America. The current generation of Indian comics, with a color palette borrowed from Bollywood movie posters and Hindu temple decorations, is influencing design elsewhere in the world. The 2010 film *Scott Pilgrim vs. the World*, despite its commercial disappointment, rivals the UN in its international components: based on a manga-style series of graphic novels from a Canadian creator, directed by a Brit (Edgar Wright), and produced by an American studio, the film blends action, humor, video-game graphic effects, the angst of a 1980s-era John Hughes teen dramedy, and raucous Bollywood-style over-the-top musical set pieces. If the comics industry can move to embrace the broader tastes of the young global audience that is clearly hungry for the kind of entertainment that it offers, the future looks bright in both the commercial and artistic dimensions. It's also a future in which superheroes, the American innovation, may no longer define the medium, becoming diluted by other traditions and other tastes.

One clear sign of the growing global footprint of comics is the spread of comics conventions. The first annual India Comic Con, held in February 2011, was reportedly an enormous success, selling out in advance and hosting huge crowds. The Festival International de la Bande Dessinee in Algiers, Algeria, started in 2008 and focuses on African and Middle Eastern creators, as well as guests representing Europe and North America. These events generate massive amounts of publicity and provide a good time for all, serving as excellent ambassadors of comics culture in all its forms. In a few years, the San Diego Comic-Con may no longer be *the* center, but merely *a* center, of a pop culture industry based in the younger, more vibrant, and restless capitals of a new global economy.

A whole new generation of creators coming of age in these parts of the world may provide the fuel for another "golden age" of comics. Who knows, maybe the next Jack Kirby is today playing cricket with his neighborhood pals in the sandlots of Karachi, or the next Will Eisner is burnishing his storytelling skills in a social media agency in Buenos Aires.

Digital Destiny: Atoms, Bits, and Dollars
Solving the problems of revenue and content security in the digital era creates new business models and new business risks.

As I walked around the exhibit hall Sunday afternoon, trying to catch up with all the people I'd missed during the blinding blur of the previous five days, I kept finding myself in conversations about the digital future of comics: the impending and seemingly inevitable transition from atoms to bits. This topic was the sparking live wire running through a half-million-square-foot exhibition space crammed full of dry old paper. The strategies of the players in the comics industry, ranging from the largest content companies to start-up entrepreneurs to independent creators, provide a rich case study for anyone who is trying to balance the opportunities and risks of migrating a legacy business to online platforms.

In July 2011, the exhibit hall of Comic-Con had the feel of Europe on the eve of World War I: it was palpably the end of one long, fondly remembered, but now exhausted era and the dawn of something new, exciting, and terrifying. The industry was at a tipping point, but no one was sure what it was tipping into. All the players had their own strategies, their own platforms, their own sets of alliances. It seemed as if every second person I talked to was telling me about a plan to create social communities around digital comics, or to build a platform to be the "iTunes of digital comics" (I heard that one a lot) or the "Netflix of digital comics." On the flip side, at least as many folks said they'd die with their paper copies in the last ditch: "Nothing beats the look, the feel, and the smell of old paper."

Just prior to the Con, DC, a major force in the market, moved all in with its announcement that the New 52 would be available for digital download on the same day and date as paper copies appeared in comics shops. The fact that DC was rebooting titles like *Action* and *Detective Comics* that had run continuously since the 1930s as part of the New 52 launch only exacerbated the sense of discontinuity that loomed ahead.

Enthusiasts had been waiting for this particular shoe to drop for nearly a decade. Digital delivery is ideal for comics. It opens up the art form to new possibilities; it creates new avenues for creators to reach fans and fans to engage with one another; it cuts through the fist-sized knot in the distribution channel; it facilitates the rapid spread of international content and access to international markets; and it separates the content side of the business from the distorting effects of the collectibles and nostalgia market, reducing the barriers to entry for younger, less history-obsessed fans.

It is also a huge unknown for an industry and a fan community with a conspicuous cultural preference for the tried-and-true. Digital delivery uproots the traditional ecosystem of printers, partners, and distributors, diverting scarce revenue into a channel populated by unproven   start-ups, rapacious digital content storefronts, buggy applications, and a hardware landscape that changes by the moment. Then there's the piracy risk. In a media world where no content provider or publisher welcomes piracy, the revenue-poor comics industry's posture toward the "online sharing" community resembles that of a starving man guarding his last bread crust from a nest of rats.

While other pillars of media and pop culture have struggled with the disruptions of digital transition and the Internet since the 1990s, comics remained mostly immune, insulated by a small but crucial gap in the technology. Some people swapped scans of comic books online, but reading comics on a computer screen was a poor substitute for the portability and physicality (not to mention collectibility) of the pamphlet or graphic novel. Tablets changed all that, offering an ideal delivery device. Tablets are to comics as MP3 players are to music, and their breakthrough success as consumer devices turned up the heat on publishers to address the distribution issue.

Fans show off digital comics on their tablets—a trend that's turning the industry inside out.

Before we get to that particular elephant in the room, however, it's important to note that some comics have been digital for more than a decade, and are none the worse for wear. The *commercial business* of comics may have dithered and puzzled over the issues raised by online networks for the past decade, but the *art form* of comics was extremely quick to embrace the potential of web-based distribution. Before social networks, before wikis, and before blogs, there were "webcomics," published on homemade sites and communities. They ranged from laughably crude to highly crafted, rediscovering the humor and compact, episodic storytelling that characterized the classic newspaper comic strips of an earlier era.

Webcomics were a perfect match for the 1990s dial-up world of AOL, CompuServe, and Web 1.0. You didn't need broadband speeds to download a couple of panels, and you didn't need Flash or HTML 5 to view static line art. Webcomics, typically only a few panels or pages, can be read comfortably on a PC or on the screen of a tiny smartphone; they did not need to wait for the mass adoption of tablets, the widespread implementation of digital rights management (DRM), or massive online app stores to dish them up to readers. Even pre-Google, you could find digital comics through basic search sites and follow them through syndication technologies like RSS.

At Comic-Con, there is plenty of evidence of the continued vitality of the webcomics community, which has developed a unique identity and audience. The webcomics pavilion, a cluster of colorful booths and tables around aisle 1400, not far from the small press area, is consistently one of the liveliest areas of the show floor, even in the doldrums of Sunday afternoon. These creators interact with their fans all the time online; the social dimension is built into the way they operate. Conventions are just a chance to put faces to the avatars and anonymous trolls.

Webcomics have few barriers to entry: there are no editors to fire off rejection slips and no retailers who refuse to order your books. Consequently, they provide a forum for quirky and creative concepts that no print publisher would touch with a barge pole, leading to unexpected innovations and the discovery of a lot of new talent. The web is also uniquely able to expose hot new ideas at blinding speed, providing a steady source of "overnight success stories" and bottom-up opportunities even as the traditional publishing industry gets harder and harder for aspiring artists and writers to crack.

A case in point is a strip called Axe Cop, one of the most amusing and original comics of the early 2010s. Axe Cop is a collaboration between 28-year-old professional cartoonist Ethan Nicolle and his 6-year-old brother, Malachai. At a family gathering, Malachai had begun spinning awesome, imaginative stories of a kick-ass, monster-slaying cop, which his older brother illustrated in all their surreal glory. Ethan posted the first five episodes of Axe Cop online on January 25, 2010, as a lark. They were an immediate viral hit. According to the FAQ on the strip's website, three days after its debut, AxeCop.com was *Entertainment Weekly*'s "Site of the Day." In four days, the comic had 1,800 fans on Facebook (on a fan-created page), and the number had doubled two weeks later. Dark Horse Comics collected the webcomics in a print edition and signed the duo up for an ongoing monthly series. In 2011, Malachai was the youngest guest ever invited to San Diego Comic-Con. Ethan is the custodian of what must be a very well-funded college kitty for the lad, and the rest is history.

It's not all newbies and wannabes on the web. The popularity and accessibility of webcomics has led established creators like Phil and Kaja Foglio (creators of the steampunk fantasy strip *Girl Genius*) and small presses like Slave Labor Graphics to move their periodical titles online as their prospects in the increasingly superhero-driven direct market dimmed. Even the big publishers like DC, Marvel, and Dark Horse have launched web-only lines to try out artists and concepts that don't have clear market potential for print.

Webcomics have been at the forefront of formal innovations in the medium of comics, incorporating technologies for social media, animation, live performance, and open-ended storytelling as they've developed. One recent example is a project called Trip City, a creator-driven digital community announced in November 2011 that incorporates webcomics, blogs, music, podcasts, and commentary into what the group calls a "Brooklyn-Filtered Literary Arts Salon."

The artistic maturity and diversity of the webcomics scene was well established by the late 1990s, but the economics remained unclear. Comics futurist Scott McCloud made the first serious attempt to address the aesthetic and commercial potential of the new format in his 2000 manifesto *Reinventing Comics,* but he predicated his forecast on the emergence of a technology called micropayments, where viewers would pay very small amounts to read a daily strip. Though the individual amounts (1 cent or less) might be trivial to each reader, the aggregate would be enough to support the creators. Unfortunately, McCloud underestimated the complexity of the underlying system, and the vision he put forward has not yet materialized.

Despite the absence of a direct payment mechanism, some webcomics creators have found ways to earn something from their talents in the new economy. High-traffic webcomics, which are search engine magnets, can be financially viable through advertising, attracting enviable metrics and a young, hip readership that is highly prized by sponsors. Top online strips like Jerry Holkins and Mike Krahulik's *Penny Arcade,* Pete Abrams's *Sluggy Freelance,* and Scott Kurtz's *PvP* are reportedly lucrative enough to provide their creators with a steady living.

Webcomics have also started to spin off into podcasts, online video series, and casual games. The incredibly successful young adult transmedia franchise (books, movies, and merchandise) *Diary of a Wimpy Kid* started out on the web as a more-or-less webcomic on Jeff Kinney's "Funbrain" site. In December 2011, webcomics broke new transmedia ground when Comedy Central tapped *Cyanide and Happiness,* a popular online humor strip featuring the minimalist stylings of Kris Wilson, Rob DenBleyker, Matt Melvin, and Dave McElfatrick, to go into development as a "half-hour animated show featuring the twisted humor of a world populated by glorified stick figures."

Some webcomics have filled the void created by the closure of newspapers and the diminished horizons for editorial and comic strip artists. Webcomics of a technical or political bent are syndicated or published exclusively on some of the most popular sites on the web, including Salon, Slate, BoingBoing, Endgaget, Daily Kos, and the late Andrew Breitbart's family of "Big" (Hollywood, Media, Government, and so on) blogs. While some cartoonists use these outlets for exposure or because their beliefs are in line with the editorial position of the blogs, an increasing number are paid gigs. Expect this to continue as more corporate-owned sites realize the differentiating benefits of comics aesthetics and the communications power of the sequential art medium in a loud and crowded online world.

Creators who haven't found big new media patrons have turned to other means to raise revenues. Some use services like PayPal to put out tip jars on their sites, which often do surprisingly well. Entrepreneurially minded cartoonists parlay their creations into merchandise that they sell on the sites, including branded clothing, accessories, coffee mugs, toys, and so on. They sell their original artwork online and do sketches at conventions, capitalizing on the exposure they receive on the web. A few have used their Internet fame to bolster their careers in teaching, speaking, and fine art. Short-run and print-on-demand services make it cheaper and easier for webcomics cartoonists to collect old story arcs into printed editions for sale on the site or in person, even if they are too small to get into the Diamond catalog for the direct market. Every so often, a highly successful strip like *Axe Cop* gets picked up by a larger publisher, or the creative talent gets access to better-paid freelance assignments.

The web has given birth to more unconventional revenue models for artists and publishers who are willing to take a leap of faith. Jeff Parker and Steve Lieber, Portland-based creators of the critically acclaimed but light-selling suspense comic *Underground*, awoke one morning in October 2010 to discover that their book had been scanned and shared on 4chan.org, a popular spot for discussing and sharing digital content of all kinds. Rather than take up arms against a sea of difficulties, Lieber joined the discussion thread where the scans of his work were posted, introducing himself and responding to a couple of questions from readers. Word spread on social media that the creators had been "totally cool"— and, by the way, the book was worth a look. The "free" availability of the material on a pirate site led to a spike in sales of the printed graphic novel, financial contributions directly to the creators, and other reputational benefits for artists who are trying to distinguish themselves in a crowded and competitive field. Lieber emphasizes that he does not condone piracy and does not advocate that cartoonists routinely distribute their work for free. "The lesson here," he says, "is that your work will be posted online at some point, whether you like it or not, and you need to have a plan for what to do when that happens."

The idea of creators crowdsourcing financial support for their projects takes on a more institutional form at the popular site Kickstarter, where people post proposals for films, comics, art and literary projects, video games, and other such projects. Anyone can go to the site and pledge a financial contribution to the project. Kickstarter has already resulted in several successful comics projects, including a collection called *Womanthology*, edited by Renae De Liz, featuring some of the top contemporary female creators in comics, as a deluxe edition from IDW. Various creators and publishers contributed gift incentives for contributors pledging certain levels of funds, which greatly assisted in making the project commercially viable for the publisher.

With the maturation of print-on-demand technologies, the Kickstarter model of soliciting pledges and funds from fans ahead of publication could be applied to the more routine distribution of printed floppies. Direct market retailers and/or buyers' clubs of comics fans could band together to ensure adequate, cost-effective print runs for titles they enjoy, diminishing the uncertainty and poor visibility of the Diamond preorder system. These custom-printed issues might even feature regional variations, making them more collectible to fans who care about that kind of thing. If the direct market as we know it has a future in the digital world, it probably looks something like that.

10 WAYS WEBCOMICS MAKE MONEY FROM "FREE" CONTENT

1. Traffic and advertising
2. Sponsored by larger sites
3. Springboard for other media deals (books, TV, movies)
4. Generating more freelance opportunities and higher rates
5. Sales of branded merchandise
6. Sales of print-on-demand or e-book collections
7. Sales of original art or commissions
8. Crowdsourced publication/subscriber-based model
9. Tips/donations
10. Leads to paid speaking/teaching/media opportunities

For all the advantages of webcomics as a model for digital comics distribution, the basic problem of *predictable* revenue remains. These newfangled wikinomic theories work fine for creators who are trying to build an audience from scratch or derive a livelihood from one or two creative properties. But these models don't scale in ways that are useful to big media corporations, whose editorial and production processes are more costly and complex. The mainstream publishers are not interested in giving away their content, regardless of what pot of gold might lie at the end of the rainbow. Operationally, they can't afford it. So in the absence of an ironclad e-commerce mechanism, the idea of *downloadable comic books,* as opposed to web-viewable comics content, was a nonstarter.

For most of the 2000s, big publishers treated the web as an R&D lab and a marketing channel, pushing out trial balloons, samples, and occasional "digital editions" weeks or months after the paper copies had been shipped to comics shops. Any tiny revenues that might come through paid digital channels were vastly outweighed by the costs, uncertainties, and political complexities of setting up the system. Anyway, the real money was coming from licensing, transmedia, and bookstore sales of graphic novels.

While publishers were expending their resources elsewhere, several entrepreneurial start-ups—mostly tech-based companies with no formal connection to publishing, comics, or pop culture— emerged to sell digital comics, readable through a browser or on a mobile device like a smartphone. This took some ingenuity, as the tiny screens of phones are not ideal for presenting fully composed comic book pages.

At first, these plucky new ventures skirted the margins of the industry like early mammals hiding in the forest, beneath the notice of the marauding dinosaurs. Then a few started standing erect and building fires, eying the dinosaurs and studying their habits. When a heavenly body known as the Apple iPad struck the media world in 2010, leaving shattered paradigms in its wake, these creatures came

Photo by Ivan Salazar

Digital comics conclave at Comic-Con: left to right, Panelfly CEO Wade Slitkin, ComiXology CEO David Steinberger, BOOM! Studios' Chip Mosher (now with ComiXology), Graphicly CEO Micah Baldwin, and iVerse CEO Michael Murphey.

scurrying out of their caves with fancy new tools, well adapted to a transformed environment.

The breakout success of tablets in the wake of the iPad finally provided digital comics with their ideal platform—and comics provided tablets and color e-book readers with their ideal content. The tech-savvy hipsters who snapped up the first iPads were in the sweet spot to be the long-promised new comics audience (the Trickster crowd): trendy, geek-chic urbanites and well-educated consumers for the new generation of intellectually respectable graphic novels. Tablets also provide the technical platform to make true transmedia content, such as comics embedded in movies, e-books, and video games or comics with real-time or rich media components, a practical reality.

In their first full year as mainstream consumer products (2010), tablets (both iPads and devices running Google's Android operating system) sold 10.3 million units in the United States. The technology analysis firm Forrester forecast that by 2015, total tablet usage will top 82.1 million U.S. adults. Gartner Research estimates that tablets will be a $49 billion global business by 2015, with more than 294 million units sold worldwide. And those estimates came before Amazon shattered the $200 price barrier with the Kindle Fire tablet in 2011. With this kind of engine pulling comics and graphic novels into the consumer marketplace, digital comics have the potential to explode from a niche category with revenues of less than $10 million in 2010 to one of the main drivers of a burgeoning e-book business that is expected to generate more than $2.8 billion by 2015, according to Forrester.

Industry executives understand the potential, but they are determined not to repeat the mistakes of earlier entrants into the commercial digital media arena, particularly those involving piracy. This is a hard problem to address because digital rights management (DRM) technologies are complex, costly, annoying to consumers, and easy to beat. At the end of the day, even with the world's finest DRM for the online files, anyone with a camera or a scanner and access to a printed issue can upload a scan in a matter of minutes. Apple tried a rights-managed approach to selling music through the iTunes Store in the mid-2000s, using a protected file format that was playable only using its technology. The effort failed largely because the MP3 format was already widely established, and consumers—especially the Net Generation young people who are the pop culture target market—will always prefer an open system to a restrictive one, all other things being equal.

In comics, though, few mainstream consumers had had much exposure to the open formats like CBR and CBZ (compressed JPEG containers) used by the illicit scanners and BitTorrent traders. Publishers and distributors figured that if they could establish a rights management regime as the default for digital comics when they first hit the market in earnest, they could marginalize the pirates and anchor their e-commerce strategy on a secure foundation.

Several digital comic start-ups, including ComiXology, iVerse, and Graphicly, had already built platforms to sell comics from multiple publishers on mobile phones and browsers. They had solved the rights management issue by using secure files that ran only in their own application environments rather than "open" formats that could be shared and traded freely. While most publishers rolled out digital storefronts that licensed existing technology (principally ComiXology's display engine), a few, notably Dark Horse, developed their own apps and formats as well.

Most of these distribution schemes make comics available through the cloud, meaning that the files themselves reside primarily online rather than on the user's own device. This gives readers access to their comics libraries across any device running the app without having to transfer or reacquire the files, and without the risks of a hard-drive crash or loss of the device. The apps used to read the files are free and are available for most systems and devices, so users don't have to pick a winner in the Apple-Google-Microsoft-Amazon wars. That convenience, plus the social legitimacy of buying rather than stealing content, presumably helps justify the price and restrictive terms of use governing digital comics.

Though most publishers have their own branded online portals and apps, the emergence of independent digital distributors brings order to the market by providing a few simple points of access where fans can build diverse libraries of digital comics without needing an app (and an account) from each publisher. Publishers can outsource some of the risk and responsibility of managing the content and technology to the distributors, while keeping control of the pricing and license terms. The distributors also insulate publishers from direct competition with their brick-and-mortar retail channel and provide a dedicated, comics-friendly front end to vast app stores where it might be hard to find and differentiate comics from a sea of other options.

Problem solved? Not quite. While the distributors' proprietary file formats and cloud-based strategies assuage the publishers' concerns about content security, they create some new problems that are likely to haunt the industry in the future.

The lack of a cross-industry standard file format means that if you buy a digital comic through one distributor's platform, you can read it only using a compatible application. You can't open it in a "generic" reader, and you can't transfer or consolidate titles that you bought from multiple sources into one library. There's no inherent reason why people can't use multiple applications to read different titles, but mainstream comics fans are an orderly and habit-driven lot. Once fans begin building a collection on a single platform, they are likely to stick with it to keep everything organized, accessible, and convenient. Every subsequent purchase will lock them in further and reduce the incentive to buy through other, incompatible apps.

The uncertainties of the cloud model also feed into the cycle. Consider this: if Apple went out of business tomorrow, all the people who bought music from the Apple store would still be able to play their MP3s from their hard drives. If Marvel stopped publishing tomorrow, Joe Quesada would not sneak into your basement and remove all the old issues of *X-Men* from your collection. But what happens to proprietary, cloud-hosted content if the service provider vanishes into the mist? What if you try to access a digital comic that you purchased, and the platform that hosts and enables you to read that particular type of file is no longer in business? This element of uncertainty means that small shifts in momentum could easily trigger a mass flight to the safer harbors of the market leader, accelerating trends toward consolidation.

Once one provider shows signs of achieving critical mass, market momentum will take care of the rest: publishers will disdain less popular channels and formats and will work with the leader; new fans will go where the best and most content can be found. Competitors will wither on the vine, leaving the leader with the lion's share of the market.

This set of user behaviors and dynamics, arising from the peculiarities of the superhero-driven comics market and its hard-core collector audience, favors the emergence of a single digital comics clearinghouse rather than a diversity of distributors, all offering differently formatted, mutually incompatible versions of the same comics at the same price.

If that happens, publishers will find themselves dealing with a monopoly digital distributor, just as they are currently dealing with a monopoly print distributor. The only way to break the emerging monopoly without drowning the market in a flood of standalone, proprietary technologies is to open up the protected file formats, allowing people to move and organize their digital collections between applications and providers. But that would strip away the technical protections that prevent wholesale copying, sharing, and redistribution of the digital comics.

Given the choice between monopoly and piracy, it seems pretty clear which the industry will prefer to tolerate.

These conditions set the stage for a winner-take-all battle to become the preeminent digital comics distributor, and as 2011 dawned, the race was on. The three leading contenders, ComiXology, iVerse, and Graphicly, all angled for advantage, with each company pursuing different strategies to create critical mass around its platform.

Graphicly, a feisty and well-funded start-up that was cofounded by tech entrepreneur Micah Baldwin, is especially aggressive in embracing social media and looking past the dysfunctional direct market to a new model for getting graphic literature out to that giant potential audience glimpsed at the Trickster party. In April 2012, Graphicly closed its Android and iOS marketplaces and announced a new focus on facilitating distribution of graphic-heavy ebooks, such as cookbooks and textbooks, as well as comics, across multiple platforms.

iVerse, which announced a $4 million infusion of capital from private equity in November 2011, is also banking on an enhanced content strategy with its Digital Comics Reader in addition to its Comics+ application. It is partnering with Diamond, the print distributor, on a new digital service, and it is trying to broaden the market to kids, video-game fans, and those outside the super-hero crowd. In February 2012, CEO Michael Murphey announced an ambitious system, offering a new way for brick-and-mortar comics shops to participate in digital revenues through their Diamond accounts, claiming lower costs and less competitive risk than other affiliate programs. iVerse has also presented an offline alternative to the proprietary/cloud-based file model, although the program's details and its potential for widespread industry adoption remain unclear.

Then there's ComiXology, which began 2011 in a great position to claim the leader's mantle and ended the year as the prohibitive favorite to lock things up: quite a journey for a company that is still barely out of the start-up phase. ComiXology began in 2006 as a project of David Steinberger, a business student at NYU, and partners John Roberts and Peter Jaffe, to create an online community to help comics fans identify and rate upcoming titles from the direct market Previews catalog. After the team won a business plan competition in 2007 and got some seed money, ComiXology added tools for fans to preorder comics that they wanted from local retailers, a set of store and inventory-management tools for comics stores, and finally a comics reader app to enable users to read comics on their mobile devices and the web.

ComiXology's special sauce for the reader application is a patent-pending technology called Guided View, a concise and intuitive way to represent the multipanel comic book page as a sequence of frames on a mobile device while maintaining the integrity of the design composition and the experience of reading a printed comic book. Steinberger, a trained opera singer, was reportedly inspired by the musical principles of harmony and dynamics when designing an application for making comic pages "sing" within the confines of a digital display. ComiXology was also among the first to integrate Apple's in-app content purchasing technology, making it possible to order and purchase comics directly from the application with one touch.

In contrast to Graphicly, iVerse, and some of the others, ComiXology does not seem terribly interested in delivering comics through social channels or in building in a lot of extra features to augment the art and story. Steinberger espouses a belief in the integrity of the comic book format as its own medium, and the company has gone out of its way to recruit rather than antagonize the direct market with an early and widely adopted affiliate program.

ComiXology recognized that in the short term, its most important customers were not the end users and not the creators, but rather the publishers, who were in need of a trusted partner. Steinberger and his team worked behind the scenes to get their technology adopted as the "white label" engine powering the largest publishers' branded applications, while also increasing the visibility of their own Comics by ComiXology app on readers' devices. They lined up an impressive array of content providers, including almost all of the top names in the industry, and while most publishers hedged their bets by dealing with multiple distributors, ComiXology won exclusive rights to distribute DC Comics on Apple's iOS devices. That turned out to be a very big deal.

When DC relaunched its comics line in September 2011, the market response was tremendous. All 52 first issues sold out, driving comics sales to heights not seen in nearly a decade while revving the digital engine to levels that surprised even seasoned industry observers. If you wanted to buy copies of *Batman, Superman, Justice League,* and the others to read on your iPad or iPhone, you could use DC's own application, you could go to your comics store's "digital storefront" (if it had one), or you could get them through your ComiXology-branded app, but in all cases they were coming via ComiXology technology and were not available to users of other systems.

ComiXology's DC exclusive helped make it the top downloaded iOS and Android app throughout the fall of 2011, unseating even the mighty Angry Birds on Wednesdays, the day the new comics were released to the market. In November 2011, the company announced its biggest and potentially most important deal yet: featured presence on Amazon's Kindle Fire tablet to buy comics through the Amazon store and view them on the ComiXology app. This has boxed in the other digital comics players, forcing them to adopt strategies that sell around the DC exclusive and focus on other aspects of the audience. Both Graphicly and iVerse have courted independent creators, small presses, and self-published authors more assiduously than ComiXology and offer greater social media integration, in an apparent attempt to fuse the economics of paid digital downloads with the vitality and diversity of webcomics. Both appear to be betting on technological enhancements to comics, from hyperlinked exclusives to rich content (video, animation, and games), based on the trajectory of their development and acquisitions. iVerse brings Diamond's power to the table (albeit nearly a year after the digital market began taking shape in earnest).

As long-term strategies, these plans might work. Certainly the investors who wrote those companies nine-figure checks think so. But in the superhero world that defines the traditional comics market mainstream, ComiXology, harnessed to the DC juggernaut and glowing white hot from the Kindle Fire, is running away from the field. In March 2012, ComiXology announced that customers had downloaded more than 50 million titles since the company started doing business, with 5 million of those downloads coming in December 2011 alone (compared to 6.4 million print comics and graphic novels sold through the direct market in the same period). Those are staggering numbers and represent a growth curve undreamed of by the most optimistic industry observers. Though industrywide figures are difficult to ascertain for comparison, anecdotal evidence suggests that ComiXology is outselling its competitors tenfold or more.

If this trend continues, the digital distribution wars will be over before most consumers realize that they had a choice. But we are still in the early days. There are plenty of companies in the media-publishing-technology-distribution space with enough cash to buy and sell the entire digital comics market many times over anytime they choose. If an Amazon, Apple, or Netflix wanted to get directly into the digital comics business, it could make a strategic acquisition (potentially changing the terms of service in unexpected ways) or set itself up as a more-than-credible competitor overnight. If an Adobe or a Microsoft came forward with a secure standard file format or DRM scheme for digital comics that was not tethered to a distributor or an application, its entry into the market would change the game instantly—and make a lot of early adopters of proprietary platforms look like suckers.

Even if one player establishes an insurmountable lead in the digital distribution market, size and scale do not offer protection from user dissatisfaction in today's social media marketplace. As Facebook and Netflix discovered, the more people rely on a service, the harder it is to change the privacy or pricing policy, or even tweak the user interface, without incurring some backlash. If enough users get fed up with a digital comics provider, they can tarnish the distributor's reputation in the tight-knit fan community, potentially even casting a shadow over the distributor's future business prospects. That could trigger a stampede of users who are desperate to "back up" their purchases from illicit sources so that they don't lose their investment in cloud-hosted content, tearing the scab off the whole piracy issue once again.

There's also another irksome issue for detail-minded comics collectors: when digital content is hosted in the cloud, it can be updated, corrected, redacted, or withdrawn from circulation at the source without the buyer's consent or control. A comic that you thought you bought may no longer be available to you, or may have been altered by the publisher after you purchased it. In a hobby in which misprints, early shipments, and controversy become overnight collectors' items, this "feature" of remotely managed digital comics not only smacks of paternalism, but also seems like a step backward from the certainties of print.

The point here is not to dwell on every far-fetched negative possibility, but it's worth keeping in mind that the cloud-based model comes with troublesome issues that haven't been fully worked out anywhere in the IT industry or the content business, as much as some parties would like to present the system as a fait accompli. Publishers and distributors may have collectively decided that deploying rights-managed, cloud-hosted media is better than giving consumers unfettered access to the data, but consumers may not be convinced. If something happens to break the customers' trust, comics' digital destiny could end up in the ditch.

The biggest uncertainty around *all* media distributed online, not just comics, is whether the problematic digital channel increases the total market or cannibalizes sales from more reliable traditional retail outlets. Are the folks who are paying for downloaded content (or stealing it, for that matter) just old fans looking for their favorites in a new format, or is there a whole new market of digital-only customers waiting to be tapped? Is the current estimate of 300,000 regular comic book readers a floor or a ceiling? Can comics (or any niche content segment) grow their market just by providing more and bigger doorways to the same giant funhouse?

A lot of the conflicts between the direct market and the publishers concerning digital comics are predicated on the assumption that when it comes to the superhero-fantasy-horror comics mainstream, it's a zero-sum game, that every dollar spent on downloads comes out of the hide of the retailers. ComiXology's David Steinberger does not share this view, and has stated publicly that he believes that the direct market audience wants the brick-and-mortar retail experience, whereas digital-only customers represent a blue-sky opportunity to bring in entirely new readers. Retailers usually respond, "Yeah, that's what you *would* say!"

For years, the vocal opposition of direct market retailers has won that argument and "wagged the dog" in terms of creating artificial roadblocks (delayed availability, higher prices for digital copies) in the publishers' digital marketing plans. Only a company like Archie Comics, which still distributes primarily to newsstands rather than through comic book stores, has had the freedom to pursue its own digital strategy early on (which it did, rather successfully, when it recognized that its younger audience was composed primarily of Net Generation digital natives).

Because of this touchy political situation, the publishers cannot appear to be making too strong a push to appeal to customers directly, as that would put them in competition with their own retailers. They can't adopt more flexible pricing models or marketing strategies that bring more customers into the digital channel if doing so is perceived as threatening the lifeblood sales of printed products.

But competition may be forcing the issue. As of 2012, same day as print digital (simultaneous with print) release is standard in the industry. Some publishers are doing low-cost "digital-first" releases for titles that might not have enough viability in the direct market. All the online distributors and the publishers who sell direct to consumers offer digital backstock titles at significant discounts, sometimes as low as 99 cents or even free. Marvel is doing discounted pricing for complete story arcs; Archie is first to market with a monthly subscription model through the iVerse service;

various publishers are starting to discount digital graphic novels on Amazon.

Will this kill the direct market? It is still early, but sales data from the triumphant fall of 2011, following DC's successful New 52 relaunch, showed that the market had in fact expanded in all dimensions. Digital was bringing in new readers, while the shops held their own and even made some headway with lapsed readers and traditional customers. *Justice League #1*, for example, sold more than 500,000 copies (with digital running at about 10 percent of that)—stunning numbers in the context of recent comics sales. Print sales soon entered their usual cycle of decline, but they are declining more slowly and from significantly higher levels than was the case as recently as the summer of 2011. Meanwhile, the digital channel continues to expand. Fifty million is a mighty big number for such early days of the market, and the math gets better as tablets and e-book readers continue to increase in features and popularity while falling in price.

If that trend can be sustained, the future of the "mainstream" industry looks brighter than it has in decades, despite the inherent fragility of a business model that depends on the continued health and growth of a single distributor. The clannish, dysfunctional comics industry could end up lighting the way forward in digital distribution for other content-driven businesses, succeeding where much higher-stakes media like music and video have failed. By backing into the future, the big publishers may have stumbled onto a payday—at least for the time being.

There's something else to consider: all of these concerns about monopoly, rights management, and zero-sum games matter only when you are talking about the mainstream comics business, with its ties to the larger world of licensing, entertainment, and transmedia. Superman, Spider-Man, Walking Dead, and Wolverine are brands as much as they are story sources, even though they are based fundamentally in the comics medium. If they are to continue as revenue-generating comics properties, they need distribution capabilities and revenue models that are scaled to a mass market. They need a digital channel that at least resembles the current print channel, with all of its built-in complexities and protections.

But what if the future of pop culture looks more like the world of webcomics and indie publishers than like the world of superheroes? In this scenario, technology providers don't need to be concerned about lock-in, standardization, and rights management, and don't need to tiptoe around the delicate sensitivities of retailers. The artificial constraints on pricing and availability of digital content do not apply. There is room for greater innovation and less mediation between the content creators and the audience. As with webcomics, anyone can play, and good ideas will find their way to the market; as with the burgeoning world of direct-to-web videos, do-it-yourself projects from talented creators can end up influencing and outperforming big-budget, A-list blockbusters.

This is the model that's taking hold in the graphic novel space, where a diverse group of developers is working with publishers and creators to create custom apps to enhance the content of graphic e-books. The graphic novel and indie market has never been dominated by collectors and obsessive completists, so there is no compelling need for ordinary readers to "standardize" on one application for reading graphic novels. Amazon offers its own graphic novel reader application for the Kindle Fire, but consumers have many alternatives to choose from.

One example is the digital edition of Eric Shanower's epic Trojan War–themed graphic novel *Age of Bronze*, released in monthly segments starting in October 2011. The custom app uses the "Seen" engine, created by publisher Throwaway Horse LLC (which also published illustrated annotated versions of *Ulysses* and *The Waste Land* in digital format), to offer a page-by-page interactive reader's guide, plus additional content such as character profiles, maps, and a built-in discussion board where users can interact with the creators and one another. The annotated twenty-fifth-anniversary edition of Art Spiegelman's *Maus*, called *MetaMaus*, offers the same kind of rich bonus features and integration, albeit in the slightly antiquated format of a DVD that comes with the physical book. Many other media enhancements, from semianimated motion comics to full immersive, interactive experiences, are certain to appear soon, taking advantage of the converged platform of the tablet.

In contrast to the walled gardens of the big publishers—constrained by costs, scale, and legacy business concerns—this grand bazaar of grassroots, entrepreneurial innovation from independent developers and creators has more pricing flexibility as well as a greater latitude to innovate. In a consolidated market with a single supplier, it may be possible to sustain artificially high prices and margins, but not in a situation in which many small app developers and distributors are competing for share. In an interview with *Publishers Weekly*, Robert Berry, cofounder of Throwaway Horse, explained, "People are used to getting more from digital content for less. We don't want to undervalue Eric [Shanower]'s work, but 99 *cents* seems to make new audiences try new material. We want new readers to see his work and that means keeping it at an affordable price."

Pricing flexibility is a competitive requirement, especially as distributors make better content formatting and marketing tools available to self-publishers. Over the 2011 holiday season, four of

Amazon's top 10 digital graphic novel bestsellers, including the number one title, *How to Be a Super-Villain (a Children's Colorful and Fun Picture Book and Entertaining Bedtime Story)* by 14-year-old Rachel Yu, were self-published. These do-it-yourself offerings outsold *Superman, Batman, Watchmen*, and titles by some of the top professional talent in the comics industry. In this upside-down model of the industry, distributors replace publishers in the value chain; big brands and popular characters lose their pricing power in an environment where anyone can come to market at a low price point and win customers on an equal basis. If that's the future of digital comics, then everybody in the business needs to rethink their assumptions.

The big publishers appear to have put aside their reluctance to issue digital comics in the 2010s, but they still need to build fences and charge tolls to maintain the value of their IP assets. Two decades' experience has shown us that the Internet is where fences go to die, and where money comes through the tip jar, not the tollbooth. If the online world continues to collapse barriers to entry and empower creativity from the bottom up, the big publishers' efforts to safeguard their content through sophisticated app-based distribution schemes will amount to little more than very expensive sand castles in the face of a rising tide. At best, a successful paid digital strategy will protect the core business but inhibit future creativity at the margins. At worst, publishers may alienate a generation of potential new readers, rendering any gains with the aging mainstream market short lived.

Comics indeed have a digital destiny, one that represents a break from the old habits and mores of the print era. But whether that destiny leads toward a cloudy future of consolidation, centralized content management, and monopoly or toward grassroots innovation, experimentation, and spontaneity is the biggest uncertainty facing comics (and all content, media, and publishing) as we head deeper into the second decade of the century.

After Hours: Dead Dogs and Englishmen
All creative content businesses rest on the talent of the creators.
The culture of creativity will outlive any changes in business models, technology, or industries.

At 5 p.m., the doors of Comic-Con closed for 2011. The collective sigh of relief from retailers and exhibitors could be heard echoing off the cliffs of Del Mar. A stream of exhausted, blissed-out, costumed refugees staggered out into the streets of San Diego, toting cartons of swag and prized collectibles. Organizers reached for the champagne to celebrate another year of record-setting attendance, media coverage, and execution free of any major glitches.

After a too-short rest break at the hotel, Eunice and I ventured out in the early evening to the super-secret location of the final event on our Comic-Con agenda, the Dead Dog Party. Bob Chapman, the owner of Graphitti Designs, one of the main providers of T-shirts and other comics-themed fashion accessories, has hosted the party annually since the early 1980s. He and his wife, Gina, invite friends, professional associates, and comics industry types— no guests. If you don't have your own invitation, you don't get in.

This party is the last, and sometimes the only, chance for the old inner circle of professionals to get together in a completely informal environment, with all the craziness and obligations of Comic-Con behind them. Despite the size and scope of the business, there is a remarkably small group that's been at the center of the industry for decades, and when they get together, it is like a family reunion (albeit with the usual assortment of rivalries and personality conflicts).

The hundred or so people attending the party represent a cross section of the American comics scene going back nearly 50 years. Jim Steranko, the first real superstar (in the Andy Warhol sense) comic book artist, who lit up the pages of mid-1960s Marvel comics with his chrome-plated pop art designs and beguiled fans with his celebrity persona, was laughing with a few cronies in the corner. His trademark pompadour had gone a striking white, and he sported dark glasses to go with his immaculately tailored suit.

At the bar, Bill Sienkiewicz, another radically innovative artist who had brought fine art, painterly, and mixed-media techniques to the pages of mid-1980s classics like *Elektra: Assassin* and *Big Numbers*, chatted with the erstwhile enfant terrible of the late 1990s independent scene, Paul Pope. A few seats away, longtime industry reporter Heidi MacDonald shared a few laughs with Paul Guinan and his wife, Anina Bennett, two Portland-based creators hoping that their steampunk creation, *Boilerplate*, was bound for transmedia success as a graphic novel and an upcoming film. The young Brazilian twins, Gabriel Bá and Fábio Moon, whose heartfelt acceptance speech at the Eisner Awards on Friday night had charmed the audience and announced their arrival as the next major talents on the global stage, breezed in as the party was moving into high gear, fashionably dressed as if for a night of high-end clubbing in São Paolo.

Eunice and I hung out with Jackie Estrada, who had arrived on her own while Batton waited (and waited and waited) for the events services staff to collect the last of the Exhibit A load-out items from the convention center loading dock. Batton finally turned up close to 11, exhausted but still ready to party.

Shortly before midnight, Frank Miller made his big entrance, smiling ear-to-ear under his broad-brimmed fedora. Despite Miller's

Photo by Jackie Estrada

Still some life in these dogs: artists Bill Sienkiewicz, Walt Simonson, Frank Miller, and Dave Gibbons at the Dead Dog Party.

forays into film, he remains firmly committed to comics and was at the Con to announce the imminent release of his new graphic novel, *Holy Terror*, the flagship title of a new venture called Legendary Comics. Miller's art and political sensibility draw polarized reactions, but at an industry party, he's undeniably the center of attention. When I spotted him at the door, he was accompanied by artist Dave Gibbons of *Watchmen* fame, Bill Sienkiewicz, and Walt Simonson, another trendsetter of the 1970s and 1980s.

For someone outside the industry looking in, but possessed of a deep appreciation for what these people have contributed, it was a privilege to be in the room with so much talent and to see the inner workings of the culture at such close range after the mediated sensory overload of the Con.

The gang partied on until the wee hours, and after closing down the bar, a few of the heartiest souls took the revelries back to the hotel lounges and rooms, unwilling to let go of the camaraderie of the Comic-Con scene until it was pried from their fingers by the first rays of dawn. We'd called it quits well before that and retreated to the Marriott to prepare for our flight back on Monday afternoon.

The San Diego Comic-Con in the 2010s is an exhausting odyssey through the kaleidoscopic madhouse of contemporary popular culture. It is uplifting to consider that at the end of it all, the comics business comes down to the individual visions and talents of creators: people with imaginations and stories to tell in the most profound and ancient human tradition. Changes in the business might disrupt their income, changes in technology might affect their craft, but nothing will silence their voices.

CHAPTER ⟨7⟩

JUST WAIT TILL NEXT YEAR

t's July 15, 2017, and Eunice and I are packing to attend Comic-Con. Though we miss the hotels, restaurants, and familiar scene of San Diego, we are happy that Long Beach is able to accommodate the more than 500,000 attendees without all the hassles that had finally forced the move a couple years back. We're also stoked that the $250 five-day pass also includes a day at the new Disneyland Comics Kingdom.

Before we fly out, I need to stop at the local Starbucks and top off my Amazon ComiXology playlist on my FireFive. I could do it online, but I'd rather go hang out with Chris and my buddies. Starbucks was smart to hire him and a bunch of the other old retailers to run its Graphics Lounges. I'm glad the digital providers realized that you can't completely replace the social atmosphere of retail online. Eunice, ever the contrarian, goes to the Apple iCandy Bar instead. All her girl-geek pals are such iToons zombies!

Scanning through the online events guide for the Con, I see that Jim Lee, SVP of visual transmedia, and Geoff Johns, SVP of narrative transmedia, for Facebook Time Warner are scheduled to join chairman Mark Zuckerberg to announce the new line of exclusive social gaming apps. Naturally, that's scheduled directly against Disney's sneak preview of *Power Man/Iron Fist—The Musical*, set to open on Broadway and in London this fall, with day-and-date 3D motion comics and video-game tie-ins.

At least we know what we'll be doing Friday night: catching the recently reunited Radiohead when the band opens for Kirby Krackle at the EA-sponsored Eisner Awards afterparty. I remember a few years ago when it seemed that Comic-Con couldn't get much bigger. I wonder what it will look like in 2025!

It's July 15, 2017, and Eunice and I are staring at the hole in the calendar where Comic-Con used to be. Sure, if we're feeling adventurous, we could try to figure out a way to get to the Graphic Literature Makers Faire in Sydney. There is also some kind of webcomics thing in San Francisco that's supposed to be getting really good, and of course there's the big Masters of Twenty-First-Century Comics exhibit at MoMA in New York.

Still, nothing quite fills the gap that was left when SDCC called it a day. It had grown so fast, fueled by all that Hollywood money that, it turned out, could dry up even faster than it appeared in the first place. Some say that comics will make a comeback on the big screen. Maybe, but why make movies about characters that no one cares about? The big entertainment companies have shuttered their comics divisions, and the direct market is dead. You can still buy Superman underwear, but you can't buy *Superman* comics anymore.

At least people are still reading the good stuff. Graphic novels on the *New York Times* bestseller list are outselling prose books in both print and electronic format. Indie titles are going strong as webcomics and selling pretty well on their own apps or through Graphicly. I guess if Robert Crumb can get a National Medal of Arts and the collected works of Daniel Clowes are Penguin Classics, then comics have truly arrived as world literature.

It's July 15, 2017 and, as usual, Eunice was right about the hotels. The longer you wait, the deeper the discount. After last year's Comic-Con failed to break 50,000 attendance and had to scale back the exhibit hall again, all the big hotels started to panic and dump rooms on the market at ridiculous rates. We got the Marriott for $129 and practically had the place to ourselves.

Still, 50,000 is a pretty good-sized show just for comics. It's fun to hang out with the familiar faces in the dealers' room, swapping back issues and comparing original artwork. It's amazing how much you don't miss all the movie stuff and video-game noise, and how much nicer it is to be able to just attend panels when you feel like it instead of lining up all day.

A few years ago, when the digital thing went bust and Hollywood moved on, you wouldn't have guessed that comics would survive. Fortunately, they came up with that whole print-on-demand, service-bureau model that brought costs down so much and saved the direct market. Now even the smallest publishers and creators can make money, stores get the books they need, fans are happy, and the collectibles market is off the charts. Sure, everything is on a smaller scale these days, but at least the hobby has returned to the people who love it.

It's July 15, 2017, and we're packing our bags to head to San Diego—now just one stop on the global convention circuit that includes Rio in October, Angoulême and Tokyo in January, and Mumbai in April. There's so much going on this year, between all the new seasons of our favorite titles launching in September in interactive motion format, the amazing wave of young talent coming out of Latin America, crazy Bollywood versions of superhero and comic films, and the hard-edged action material from North Africa.

Right now, the hardest part is going through the event guide and figuring out what's happening in the exhibit hall. There are a lot fewer of the big booths than there were 8 to 10 years ago, but it seems like there are dozens of new studios, creative shops, digital publishers, game makers, and projects popping up every year. Since Disney and Warner decided to license out the Marvel and DC characters to autonomous creative shops rather than manage big, centralized comics divisions, even the tired old super-hero stories seem fresher. Kids can pick up an issue of *X-Men* without needing a Ph.D. in Marvel Universe history, and that's brought a bunch of new readers into the hobby.

Meanwhile, the range of subjects and genres keeps getting more interesting. Most of the top TV and web series are either based on comics properties or part of cross-media story lines, and most of them are coming from independent producers.

Things are a lot more complicated with all the technology and globalization pervading the industry these days, but at least comics, with all their amazing, innovative, and diverse potential, have been embraced around the world.

Four Paths to the Future

In the introduction, I wrote that various forces are pulling popular culture in multiple directions at once. Walking around the 2011 Comic-Con, from the exhibit hall to the conference rooms to the parties and private meetings, you could see those forces at work: the lure of digital technology, dragging publishers into an uncertain new marketplace; the centrifugal force of consolidation, as corporate pop culture conglomerates attempt to weave their diverse holdings into a coherent portfolio across all media; the amplification of individual creative voices connecting directly with their audience; and the aspirations of fans who want to participate in a culture that is rich, spectacular, exciting, familiar, and uniquely theirs.

When we look to the future of the pop culture business, the overall trajectory of these forces matters much more than do individual events and specific developments. Comics are certain to evolve as a medium, a business, a hobby, and an art form. We've already seen profound changes in the past 18 to 24 months, and we are likely to see changes move even faster as new delivery platforms like tablets reach critical mass in the consumer market. We can extrapolate from current trends to speculate about how comics will blend with other communications media in the near future and what those blends might look like. Every day, in offices, in conferences, and around the blogosphere, people are prognosticating about new developments in the business and the technology affecting popular culture, while others are putting these developments into action. Trying to capture those specifics in a book, especially one written at a moment of maximum change and uncertainty, is like throwing darts at a moving target.

The larger issue is how these changes will affect the role of comics culture within the entertainment industry and what that means to the whole spectrum of creative, technology-based, marketing communications enterprises that take their cues from popular culture. Will the broader reach and richer functionality of digital distribution open up new markets and new audiences, or will it end up killing the existing channel without replacing the revenues quickly enough? Will popular culture continue to benefit from the critical and institutional acceptance of literary, art-oriented comics and graphic novels? Will a more consolidated, centrally managed media industry allow fans to co-own and co-create the content that engages them, or will it try to keep them at arm's length through litigation, rights management, and legislative attempts to clamp down on online activity?

To address those questions, we need to change tools from the microscope (or perhaps kaleidoscope) that we used to observe the goings-on at Comic-Con to some wide-angle binoculars that can scan the far horizon.

My preferred technique for taking the long view is known as scenario planning. Scenario planning is a strategic method for creating stories about the future. It extends beyond making simple predictions and spotting trends; it lets you see how those trends interact with one another and with larger externalities to form coherent worlds with flavor, logic, and character. This is a useful exercise if you are writing science fiction (or comics!); in business, it can help companies avoid billion-dollar mistakes.

Once you've built scenario models, you can use them to test strategies and ideas that are specific to your industry or your firm and tease out issues that would not otherwise be apparent. As an analyst and consultant, I have used scenario planning to help my clients see how larger trends and uncertainties affect their business, their markets, and their world. The method underlies all my published work, including this book. Here's how it works, by way of a relevant analogy.

One of my favorite comics from the late 1970s was a Marvel title called *What If?* that explored the flip side of established story lines: *What if . . . Spider-Man Joined the Fantastic Four? What if . . . Captain America Survived World War II?* Each issue not only told a story, but constructed a whole parallel world of different outcomes starting from a single changed premise, with consequences that rippled through the whole Marvel universe. Scenario planning is a little like that. Instead of looking at the future as the inevitable end point of trends that are at work in the market today, scenario planning requires us to consider the disruptive possibilities that we don't expect, the "black swans." It helps us separate stable trends from assumptions: the "known unknowns" from the "unknown unknowns," in the words of former defense secretary Donald Rumsfeld, who knows a few things about basing big strategies on flawed premises.

This is important because the big picture determines how a lot of the little issues will work out. It's not enough to ask where the next big transmedia property will come from, or how creators might make money from webcomics in five years. To really think strategically about the future of the business, you have to ponder potential changes at a macro level. *What if . . . Hollywood gets bored with comics? What if . . . print-on-demand technology saves the direct market? What if . . . the comics and entertainment industries of India and Latin America start to surpass those of North America, North Asia, and Europe? What if . . . a security issue or business disruption shakes consumers' faith in digital e-commerce?*

All of these uncertainties are worth considering, but the scenario-planning process requires us to identify *two* overarching questions that capture as many secondary risks and opportunities as possible. So what are the biggest uncertainties in the relationship between comics and popular culture in the early 2010s?

The last decade has seen a rapid, frenzied ascent toward "peak geek." Comics culture sits at the center of the entertainment industry zeitgeist, driving some of the most important commercial, creative, and distribution decisions. From the vantage point of 2012, it looks like it will be there forever. But what if the hour of the nerd passes, for reasons that have as much to do with the ordinary cycles of popular taste and generational procession as with any developments within the related industries? Over the last decade, comics culture has expanded by bringing in a lot of loosely affiliated fans. An audience that is cheaply won can be quickly lost, and a world in which comics culture retreats back to the edges of social acceptability looks very different from one in which it becomes permanently embedded in the media landscape.

We're also at a moment when two different business dynamics are fighting for supremacy. The tension between centralization at the top of the pop culture industry and the radical democratization of the tools for individual expression and creativity from the bottom up is the matter/anti-matter reactor powering the twenty-first-century creative economy. We can remain at warp speed only if the forces remain in balance, yet they are always struggling to annihilate each other.

On one hand, we can see how the priorities of big companies like Disney, Time Warner, NBCUniversal (plus or minus Comcast), Amazon, and Apple are dominating and shaping the development of technology, the regulation of intellectual property, the licensing of content to fill up the channels owned by these entities, and the market positioning of comics culture in the mass media. Their strategies are all aimed at shaping a landscape that makes it easier for them to monetize their IP assets with minimal concessions to creators, consumers, partners, and fans.

At the same time, the global spread of digital devices and networks has obliterated barriers to entry for an audience of billions. New disruptive entrepreneurial ventures are springing up everywhere; ordinary people and fans are becoming creators, worldwide sensations, and brands overnight. Subcultures form around new styles and blends of styles faster than anyone can follow. These innovations don't require anyone's support or anyone's permission to break through, rise up, and challenge incumbents. In the world of popular culture, we see this in everything from self-published digital comics that rise to the top of the bestseller charts to self-produced videos that draw more eyeballs than network fare costing millions per episode. We see the struggle between self-created and self-managed fan communities and efforts to galvanize nerd culture into a more predictable form of consumerism. A world in which a thousand flowers bloom looks very different from one in which pop culture content is managed and regulated by a few big players.

If we want to think honestly and objectively about the future, we need to consider that either outcome of either uncertainty is possible. Comics culture could continue to increase in relevance to the overall pop culture/entertainment world, or it could decline. Innovation in the business of pop culture could come from the corporate centers of the global economy or from the entrepreneurial edges.

If we envision each possibility as the pole of an "axis of uncertainty," and then plot the two axes to form a matrix, we end up with the diagram seen in the figure given here.

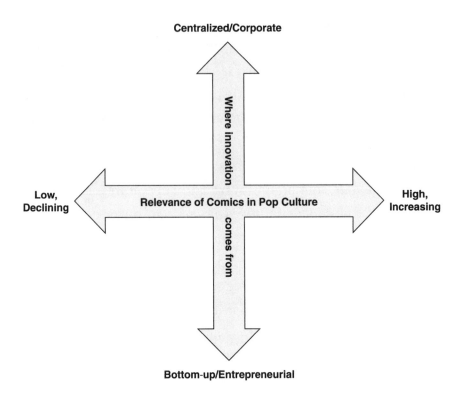

Critical uncertainties in the future of popular culture

Each quadrant of the matrix represents a different permutation of uncertainties. For example, the northeast quadrant represents a world in which innovation is driven by centralized, corporate forces, and comics remain culturally and commercially viable. The southwest quadrant represents a future in which fans and entrepreneurs are driving the pop culture discussion, and comics culture is less important in the mix. Mix, match, rinse, repeat, and . . . presto! Four different futures, each occupying a different quadrant.

The next step is to give the scenarios names that fit their characters. In this example, I've chosen "Endless Summer" for the triumphant fusion of comics, Hollywood, and the digital entertainment commercial complex; "The Expanding Multiverse" to suggest the explosion of creative possibilities in a world in which popular culture embraces a diversity of comics forms, content, and distribution models driven from the bottom up; "Ghost World" to represent a world in which independently produced, artistically oriented comics are divorced from the mainstream popular culture; and "Infinite Crisis" as an allusion to the world in which comics are trapped in a death spiral with a shrinking community of aging, continuity-obsessed fanboys, once again outside the mainstream.

That gives us a grid that looks like the following figure.

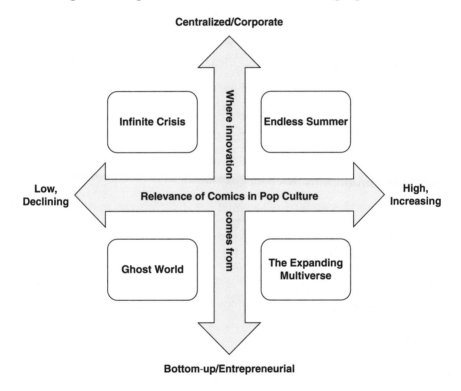

Future of comics scenarios

The scenarios represent unrealistically stark choices, but that's part of the point. Like those clownish political debate shows on cable news, we want to entertain the most extreme and polarized perspectives in the hopes that insight might arise from contrast. The real future will probably fall somewhere in the middle, blending features from three or more scenarios. By understanding the choices in their purest form, we can be prepared for the widest range of possibilities.

Once we've identified and named our scenarios, we can start to tell stories about what these worlds look like. Telling stories about possible futures is one part of my job where being a comics fan helps, because you need to apply the same kind of rigorous, continuity-based thinking that governs comic book universes. This process allows us to draw out additional details and inferences about external conditions, such as political, economic, and social factors, that flow logically from the two assumptions regarding the primary uncertainties. If you believe, as I do, that there are certain social cycles and relationships that recur in recognizable patterns, you can apply a knowledge of history and other analytical techniques, not just intuition, to the development of the scenario stories. You can also use the scenarios to chart a path from the present to each future so that you can get your bearings as events unfold.

Here are quick thumbnails of the four scenarios. You may recognize them as the basis for the stories from the start of this chapter, and from their cameo appearances earlier in the book.

Endless Summer

In this world, the big bets have paid off. Large corporations have successfully fused the aesthetics and content of mainstream comics with various other media, creating seamless synergies across brands. The audience for movies, video games, books, comics, toys, and fashion is expanding. Consumers with no prior affinity for comics culture are brought in through new media channels and digital distribution.

The top creators are highly paid superstars, and big publishers dominate the industry. Opportunities are abundant for both full-time staff positions and agencies that serve the big players. However, the corporate content owners are moving to restrict creator ownership, using their leverage and their access to the market to drive harder bargains. Most artists, with fewer options for reaching their audience outside of centrally controlled channels, are falling into line.

Content owners have won their fight for restrictive legislation covering online media. Digital media are subject to heavy rights management, and they are distributed through one or two "standard" providers. Pirates and illicit traffickers are aggressively prosecuted; other bottom-up channels that might pose a threat to the consolidated media companies are just collateral damage. The direct market is gone. Some of its staff members and inventories have been subsumed into larger national retailers, but most distribution of paper comics is handled through online storefronts.

Geek culture remains ascendant in the mass media, both in entertainment and in commentary. "Nerdlebrities" are authoritative tastemakers, though their voices seem less credible when they are amplified through big-media channels. Product placement and sophisticated marketing throughout these channels is pervasive, blending the boundaries between content, personal opinion, and advertising. Comic-Con, the undisputed center of the North American media/pop culture universe (and thus the world), has expanded even further to accommodate the nearly half-million fans who attend each year. All traces of the old culture of fandom have vanished, driven to the edges at smaller regional shows with a distinctly nostalgic flavor.

Endless Summer is the world we can see most clearly in the summit of "Peak Geek" in 2012, and a lot of industry investment and momentum is going into making sure that this is the future that materializes. It is also a brittle future that's ready to crack, as consumer dissatisfaction and disengagement fester under the placid surface.

Ghost World

In Ghost World, pop culture gets bored with comic-themed entertainment, but the art form thrives, driven by individual creativity and business ingenuity.

Continued economic stagnation and political unrest lead to an era in which music and political engagement are the defining elements of youth culture; superheroes are seen as reactionary power fantasies for juvenile mentalities, unserious and vaguely embarrassing. In Hollywood, the big comics-based franchises are exhausted for a generation, and the second-string material does not perform. DC and Marvel, no longer strategic to their corporate owners, close down their publishing operations, although reprints and collected editions of top titles continue to be available in print and digital form. The direct market collapses, pulling most of the smaller mainstream publishers down with it. Lots of creators lose their jobs.

None of this affects the independent/alt.comics world, which continues to cater to a more sophisticated audience and digs deeper into cultural and academic institutions. Small presses publish handsome print editions for collectors. Webcomics prosper, and independent or self-published digital comics often top the sales charts. Artists and publishers work with a variety of developers and distributors to create customized comics apps for different platforms. A few sites aggregate and distribute these apps, as opposed to selling the digital comics themselves.

Creators are celebrated for their artistic genius and innovation, but are not well known to the general public. Festivals and indie-oriented conventions are popular, but unit sales are low. Commercial work is held in low regard by the connoisseurs who serve as gatekeepers for the seriousness and ambition of the medium. Some comics publications serve as exhibition catalogs for creators, who make more by selling their originals as fine art. In the wider culture, comics have acquired the patina of a luxury brand, associated with the tastes of an affluent, well-educated elite.

This same bifurcation between independent, art-oriented work and commercial entertainment is pervasive across the rest of the pop culture spectrum. While Hollywood does its usual blockbuster thing, there is a renaissance of indie films that reach their audience through online channels; casual games have an audience that the big platform players can't reach; fashion and music are dominated by niche markets and microbrands.

Ghost World is a "low-gear" future, one in which the scaling mechanisms of brands, big media, and centralized distribution do not function as they do now. There are few shortcuts to mass popularity beyond individual talent and effort.

Infinite Crisis

Infinite Crisis is a top-down retreat from "peak geek." Popular culture moves on to embrace less nerdy enthusiasms, while the mainstream business of comics putters along in its timeworn niche.

A slow-growing economy and a conservative political culture make everyone risk-averse. After a string of big-budget flops, Hollywood reassesses its relationship with comic book properties as fodder for blockbusters, preferring the safer harbors of comedies, remakes, thrillers, chick flicks, and a despicable but profitable new genre of "reality cinema." A few comics-themed titles are released direct to video or as web series, but these don't catch on beyond the niche fan base.

The traditional comics audience continues to support the mainstream publishers, but it demands tried-and-true material and creators. A series of business and technical failures in the rights-managed digital comics space sours a lot of people on the whole concept. Amazon tries to "re-Kindle" the market and gains some traction in graphic novels, reprints, and self-published work, but the price structure does not support producing comics on a periodical basis for such a small audience.

Fortunately, advances in print-on-demand technology keep the direct market viable. Retailers and customers form "buyers' clubs" to support titles that they like, using Kickstarter-like crowdsourcing to aggregate financial resources for worthy titles and projects. This model takes off in other creative industries as well.

The narrow tastes of a shrinking readership means that there is not much diversity of subject matter. Audiences and publishers have retreated to their comfort zones. Older fans and older values predominate. Alternatives move online, where they have less and less to do with the comics industry or pop culture. The conservative cultural climate makes institutions like libraries and museums less eager to embrace comics than they have been in the past.

Eventually, comics lose their grip on the popular imagination. The comics-crazy pop culture of the early 2010s is viewed with the same mixture of unaffectionate nostalgia and "what were we thinking?" bewilderment as the disco era. Comics fandom retrenches to where it stood in the pre-*Dark Knight* days of the early 1980s: far removed from the mainstream, waiting to be rediscovered by a new generation.

Expanding Multiverse

This is a world of vibrant economic growth and rapid development, driven at the edges by innovative young populations around the world connected by networks and mobile devices. A diverse, global, and more female audience embraces comics and comics culture as the vehicle for creative expression in all kinds of ways.

A steady stream of successful innovations has opened up the medium of comics, allowing it to expand in multiple dimensions at once. Business is strong, attracting new talent and investment. Sales of digital comics and books complement each other. An improved economy allows retailers to invest in better stores and strategies to translate the wider audience for comics into a strong community of consumers for print and comics-related merchandise. Fans are participants in and co-creators of their entertainment through various social channels. Comics are a common language for literature, entertainment, education, and business communication.

Formats and distribution options abound, from traditional periodicals to graphic novels to digital and interactive media. Digital comics create more interest in print, and a new generation of direct market retailers fills the gap left by the demise of megabookstores. Large media companies prosper, but there is a lot of innovation at the edges and a lot of room for small publishers and independent creators to reach the market.

The online climate remains open and lightly regulated, enabling greater freedom to mix and mash content. Entrepreneurs and start-ups drive rapid, unexpected improvements in technology, business, and society. Culture is inclusive, focusing on creativity.

Transmedia channels and "on-ramps" like young adult fiction bring a new, more diverse generation into comics culture, which they proceed to reshape in their image. Emerging economies (India, Brazil, and others) replicate the social conditions for a "Golden Age" of comics, and the burst of new talent coming from these huge creative centers inspires others.

The dynamic expansion of the market in this future has temporarily kept the forces of backlash and consolidation off balance, but sooner or later, things will cool down. A shakeout, and possibly a crackdown from discomfited traditional authorities, waits in the wings.

Each of the four scenarios provides a plausible and coherent future based on current social, market, and technology trends, but each has a very different flavor and implies a very different set of strategies for those in the pop culture space. Business choices that play well in one or two of these futures may fail disastrously if alternative scenarios materialize.

By drilling down into the scenarios and following the logic, individual stakeholders can better define the scenario conditions that affect their own futures, ranging from strategic business investments to the prospects of professionals working in the industry. The figure given here shows how different aspects of the comics/pop culture landscape look through the lens of each scenario.

Implications of future scenarios for comics

	Expanding Multiverse	Endless Summer	Infinite Crisis	Ghost World
Who is the comics audience?	Smart, global cultural vanguard and curious people everywhere	Mass market consumers of popular entertainment	Aging fans	Connoisseurs
Who are the creators?	Anyone with fun, cool story ideas	Creative superstars	Fanboys turned pro	Serious artists
Who are the publishers?	Big variety, from established to newcomers, multinational, media companies, game companies, individuals	Mostly big media companies	The usual suspects	Specialty publishers, art galleries, independent creators
How are comics distributed?	Multiple digital services and pricing options, rejuvenated direct market, lots of experimentation in formats, blurred boundaries between formats and genres	One predominant digital distributor, one print distributor, online book sales, lots of tie-ins with movies, online, games, fast food, merchandise, etc.	On paper, on Wednesday, at the comic store (via print-on-demand); digital only as an add-on	Deluxe limited editions, print-on-demand; pirated scans of back issues
What's the role of digital comics and digital technology?	Digital is the default option for most readers. There are good platforms for mobile comics and lots of social channels for finding and discussing comics.	Digital comics are a keystone of the integrated media plan. They are often linked to other media (film previews, product placement, videogames, web videos, etc.)	Digital comics are promotions and samples, and for collections of back-issue story arcs. Independent creators publish online.	Creators use self-published digital comics as ways to get attention. Digital editions of new and archival material are available but not as popular as the paper copies.
What does a "comic" look like?	Combination of digital (web and app based), paper, live performance, social content	Mixed media, 3D, interactive, apps with games and stories	Print-on-demand pamphlet with regional variations, often collected in trades or digital collection of back issues	Experimental formats (*RAW*), well-designed hardcovers (*Cages, Asterios Polyp*) or library editions, self-published digital and web-comics.

(continued)

(continued)

	Expanding Multiverse	Endless Summer	Infinite Crisis	Ghost World
What motivates creators?	Rewarding creative career	Money and fame	Nostalgia, sense of belonging	Artistic ambition, serious purpose
What genres are popular?	Fantasy and adventure, humor, quirky personal stories, historical drama, romance, tween-teen content	Action, super-heroes, mystery, serialized drama, "reality" comics, porn	Superheroes, retro genres (hard-boiled, horror, jungle adventure, etc.)	Personal nar-ratives, serious fiction, journalism, biography, satire, avant-garde
How are sales doing?	Great!	Great for top sellers, OK for everyone else	Bad and getting worse	Small but stable
What keeps publishers awake at night?	Competing with self-published works, global alliances, staying ahead of trends	Protecting IP, locking up talent, making the best licensing deals	Maintaining mar-ket share, paying the bills	Getting titles reviewed, reputa-tion of brand and creators
Status of IP protection	More open climate encourages co-creation, fan fiction	All content is rights-managed and aggressively protected	Publishers con-stantly litigating against creators and pirates	Most IP is creator-owned
Perception of comics in the pop-culture universe	A mass medium for communica-tion, storytelling, education	Part of the trans-media mix, source of high-value IP	Do they still make comics? Only nerds read those things!	"Graphic stories/ novels" are for hipsters, academics, and intellectuals
What's next?	Continued market expansion; hybrid-ization of forms; potential overex-posure; shakeout; crackdown	Overexposure; next new thing comes along; new gen-eration rediscovers "classic" print and art comics	Collapse, rejuve-nation, purification	Halting attempts to restart com-mercial industry; popular characters lapse into public domain; comics become specialty taste, like poetry

So which of these actually *is* the future of pop culture? That's what's being hashed out now within the industry, online, and at places like San Diego Comic-Con. Every one of those future scenarios has a motivated constituency that is actively trying to realize its preferred vision.

For the entertainment industry, banking on continued media convergence and the rising value of comics-centric IP, "Endless Summer" solves many problems, especially the biggest one: where is the money coming from? The fact that this future suggests a regimentation of both the creative industry and the fan base, and the reduction of comics culture to a more motivated form of consumerism, is at best an unintended consequence and at worst a deliberate strategy to reduce market friction, cut costs, and promote consolidation. It's a future in which the freedom of large IP holders to derive high rents from their properties (locked in place by restrictive Internet legislation jammed through Congress) trumps other kinds of freedom online, and in which competitive risks can be managed and disposed of easily by incumbent market leaders.

The name for this scenario, "Endless Summer", intentionally represents a paradox: an unsustainable status quo that flows from the ambitions of its most fervent advocates. Subcultures such as comics, which drive the larger entertainment dynamo, work best precisely because they are so unruly and difficult. Large businesses that expend huge amounts of resources to corral rabid fans and domesticate crazy artists in the pursuit of more predictable, manageable revenue streams may find that they have only succeeded in draining their IP assets of value and sowing once-fertile fields with salt. It's an ancient problem—killing the golden goose—but it's as relevant to the twenty-first-century creative industries as it was in the time of Aesop.

"Ghost World" may seem unattractive to those with a stake in the more commercial, entertainment-oriented aspects of comics, but it's paradise for the people who take the art form seriously and want to see the future of comics in the hands of the medium's most thoughtful and ambitious practitioners. Alt.comics fans may not wish for the demise of the mainstream (although some do); however, the divergence of the creative communities and the audience make it possible to envision a situation in which art thrives by catering to sophisticated elites, while commerce withers when the fickle mass audience moves on.

"Expanding Multiverse" sounds great to fans and creators because of its vibrant, optimistic character. It's the kind of future that everyone favors in theory, but that can emerge only if big vested interests get out of the way (or are moved aside). It is, for example, much less predictable in terms of revenue for the big content owners, and much more competitive. It's a world in which self-published graphic novels routinely outsell and put pricing pressure on incumbents, and in which fans have a greater say in the co-creation of brands, stories, and conversations about them. The cosmopolitan, "creative-class" flavor of this future is very threatening to enemies of modernity and artistic experimentation, both in the United States and abroad. But it's a vision that a lot of people at the grass roots can work toward if they know that it's a possible end point.

You might think that "Infinite Crisis" holds limited appeal, being both a commercial and an artistic dead end. But don't underestimate the pull of nostalgia, which lies at the very heart of comics fandom. Comics culture teems with ill-concealed disdain for the poseurs and voyeurs who have blown up fandom, transformed Comic-Con into an unimaginable expense and hassle, and dragged comics into an incestuous union with Hollywood, video games, *Twilight*, and the makers of trinkets and baubles. There is also a large, vocal audience for whom "comics" means "superhero comics," and all that artsy stuff is just irrelevant. To this day, underground comics from the 1960s are not listed in the hobbyists' bible, *The Overstreet Comic Book Price Guide*, reflecting an antediluvian prejudice against experimental material that remains pervasive in the direct market mainstream. These folks yearn for simpler times when fans gathered to share their love for a misunderstood and despised art form, flaunt their hard-won knowledge, and fly their geek flags outside the glare of the media spotlight.

I sympathize. That's the comics culture I grew up in, where I gained my lifelong appreciation for the art form and the creators who made it great. It's a culture that lives on in smaller shows around the country and in private communities on the Internet. If its advocates were content to age gracefully, it could persist for decades as a vibrant subculture. But in this time of change, the power of reaction is strong. The digital train may have left the station, but there is still time for an army of discontented old-time fans and retailers to throw themselves on the tracks and bring the whole thing to a halt. If that happens, "Infinite Crisis" becomes a road map for retreat and collapse.

Strategies for Success

Scenario planning is useful as a thought exercise, but it is very rare that the actual future unfolds neatly as one quadrant or another. Instead, we'll see events and developments pushing sometimes one way, sometimes another, and usually toward some blended outcome that includes aspects from several scenarios. Walking the floor of Comic-Con, I used my scenario map as a compass, with the needle pointing toward different quadrants as I observed the various activities and subcultures.

This is where the strategic value of scenario planning lies. If you have a sense of the range of possibilities and their implications, you can recognize new developments, put them in context as they occur, and make adjustments accordingly. In other words, if you start to recognize that events are tipping toward the Ghost World/ Infinite Crisis end of the spectrum, it might be time to unwind investments that depend on continued licensing revenues and air cover from the entertainment industry. If the large corporate media players are stymied in their efforts to consolidate the pop culture market, it might be a good time to look at revenue models that are based on audience engagement and co-creation rather than on extracting rents from owned IP.

At the same time, there are some strategies that play well across all the scenarios, and some decisions that players can take now or in the near future to avoid some of the less-desirable outcomes. Here are a few that suggest themselves based on the scenario logic.

- **Find ways to strengthen and preserve the traditional retail channel.** Some industries can survive without a physical retail footprint. Comics can't. The social capital, knowledge, and customer relationships owned by specialty pop culture retailers are irreplaceable. Impulse purchases, credible recommendations and upselling and cross-selling are the lifeblood of the industry. The physicality of the product is intrinsic to its appeal for a large segment of the current market, and may serve as a differentiating advantage for some portion of the younger audience. Some ways to support the retail channel are to enhance digital affiliate programs to allow for more customization and pricing flexibility; investigate print-on-demand and buyers' club models to reduce the costs of logistics and distribution and reduce the inventory risk carried by retailers; and provide co-op funds for retailers to refurbish store environments.

- **Develop a standard secure digital format.** Making digital media portable across various commercial platforms rather than forcing every distributor to use its own proprietary system will remove a lot of the instability from the current environment, reassure consumers that their investments are not at risk, avoid useless duplication of costs, and diffuse the market-consolidating pressures to create a monopoly digital distributor. Considering the central importance of digital distribution to the future of transmedia, consumer electronics, and publishing, this is more than a tactical suggestion for publishers and distributors; it's a market imperative.

- **Develop properties and entire genres that are transmedia-ready, without built-in allegiance to one preferred medium.** Think in terms of stories where different media can carry different threads of the story line, each best suited to its own format and mode of expression. Devices that bring video, gaming, prose, and graphic media together through a common platform offer a unique opportunity to create content that plays well across the spectrum, captures multiple audiences simultaneously, and avoids the "Hall H problem" of slavish fidelity to niche-market source material.

- **Look for ways to formalize, institutionalize, and scale the successful business practices of bottom-up publishing models such as webcomics** as a way to keep the creative, independent side of the business sustainable. Distributing new, personally produced content on the web is a viable strategy across all the scenarios and a critical way to keep new voices and new ideas flowing into the creative industries. But the revenue opportunities need to become more stable and more predictable so that more creators can feasibly pursue their profession and make a living. Sponsorships, crowdsourced funding, cottage-industry merchandising, and personal brand building are all possible areas for continued innovation.

- **Do not neglect "casual fans"** and members of the 20- to 35-year-old generation whose pop culture tastes are not as detailed and specialized as those of traditional comic fans. Be mindful that young consumers of digital content despise restrictive rights-management systems and rebel against efforts to control, channel, or silence their ability to share and collaborate around their media passions. Most of all, don't gratuitously alienate women and kids in the process of pursuing adolescent males; they are the future of fandom. Comics culture has fought long and hard to liberate itself from the stigmas of illiteracy, deviance, juvenilia, and geekdom. It can consolidate those gains by continuing to produce and publicize work in a range of subjects, styles, and formats, and by integrating sequential art into other media channels.

- **Recognize the global potential of transmedia entertainment and literature,** especially with the rapid spread of delivery devices such as tablets and high-speed wireless networks. Emerging economies not only are increasing in buying power with the establishment of indigenous consumer middle classes, but are also becoming centers of the creative/knowledge economy. The talent coming from these regions will transform the media landscape. Strategies that embrace rising young markets—particularly the vast English-speaking markets of South Asia and Africa—are well positioned for success in nearly any future scenario.

- **Find a balance between the protection of intellectual property and satisfying the desires of fans to participate in their media passions.** Co-creation, mashups, and sampling of media are inevitable features of a digital environment; sharing and free distribution of content are by-products of open networks. Trying to close off these aspects of the media landscape through legislation, restrictive technologies, and litigation antagonizes the most vocal and active segments of the fan base, and will ultimately fail. It also constrains innovation in ways that will eventually damage audience engagement and leave industry leaders brittle and vulnerable to new competition.

This guidance is intended primarily for stakeholders in the pop culture/entertainment/communications industries, but the scenarios outlined here have interesting implications that ripple through the worlds of business and education. A world in which comics are a coequal feature of the transmedia landscape and a popular format for training, education, and advertising has important differences from one in which they are a marginal or forgotten medium, a discredited subculture, or an affectation of elite sophisticates.

Scenarios are not a crystal ball, but they can serve as a kind of GPS system to give us clues to where we are heading and what individual developments and innovations mean in the greater context of the business, the economy, and the culture. Armed with that kind of knowledge, comics and the pop culture industry (or any industry) can stop backing into the future and start to face front.

In one of the great *X-Men* stories of the early 1980s, a future version of Kitty Pryde travels back in time and inhabits her younger self to warn her teammates of terrible events that may unfold if their next battle goes the wrong way. Even armed with this knowledge, and with the ability to affect the unspooling of the timeline, it is unclear that her presence made any difference. In the final panel, the characters muse on the nature of uncertainty. "Does that mean we changed the future?" asks the Angel. "I do not know," responds Storm. "Cliché though it sounds, only time will tell."

The world of comics is changing faster and more dramatically than ever before in its history. These may well be the days of future past: the industry, the market, the profession, and the hobby could be as unrecognizable in five years as a world taken over by giant robots. That's incredibly disorienting for any culture, but especially one as grounded in nostalgia and continuity as comics. It may not be possible to stop or even slow changes driven by external forces, but if you are careening ahead at high speed, it is a good idea to know where you are going.

For five days in July, the 2011 San Diego Comic-Con gave us a glimpse into a whole spectrum of futures for comics and pop culture. It pointed the way toward amazing technological innovation and new ways of engaging a growing global audience; it also pointed the way toward catastrophic disruptions in the business that could dissipate decades of accumulated social capital and sunder the bonds that hold comics culture together.

Even those of us who lack mutant abilities can apply visioning techniques to better understand the choices facing us, whether we are industry decision makers, creative professionals, outside stakeholders, or fans. This is a moment not of foregone fate, but of deliberate decision. The panel lines are ruled on the pages; it is still up to us to fill in the pictures and finish the story.

ENDNOTES ⊂⊃

Introduction

p. 3 hereafter "known as Comic-Con": Note that the term "Comic-Con" (with a hyphen) is a registered trademark of the Comic-Con International: San Diego. Other shows are "comic cons" (no hyphen).

p. 3 "contributes an estimated $163 million to the local economy": http://www.visitsandiego.com/pressroom/details.cfm/newsid/201.

p. 3 "upwards of 130,000 people": Comic-Con might be one of the few events that systematically underreports its attendance. Rumor has it that the official estimate of 130,000 is for the benefit of the fire marshal, and that the real number is closer to 150,000.

p. 3 "sells out almost instantly": The speed with which Comic-Con sells out is now pushing up against the laws of physics. For the 2012 show, anyone interested in attending had to apply for a member number well in advance just to be given a chance to purchase an admission pass. When the passes went on sale the morning of March 3 to this select group, the online queue reached into the 10,000s in the first few seconds, and Comic-Con reported a complete sellout in less than an hour. Small follow-on lots of badges would go on sale throughout the spring and sell out in seconds.

p. 7 "Comic-Con history book that came out in 2009": *Comic-Con: 40 Years of Artists, Writers, Fans and Friends* (Chronicle Books, San Francisco, 2009).

p. 8 "links at his Comics Reporter site": http://www.comicsreporter.com /index.php/resources/out_and_about/33639/.

p. 8   "the monograph by Douglas Wolk": Douglas Wolk, *Comic-Con Strikes Again*," Kindle Edition, August 2011. Douglas and I were working on our projects at the same time – we ran into each other at the ICv2 event – and I salute his alacrity at getting his work out so quickly, in part by walking the talk when it came to digital publishing. I strongly recommend all of his writing on comics, particularly *Reading Comics: How Graphic Novels Work and What They Mean* (De Capo Press, 2007), to anyone interested in issues related to the aesthetics of the medium.

p. 10   "what new problems are they encountering?": For a more detailed discussion of the disruptive role of entrepreneurship worldwide, see R. Salkowitz, *Young World Rising: How Youth, Technology and Entrepreneurship Are Changing the World from the Bottom Up* (Hoboken, NJ: John Wiley & Sons, 2010).

p. 11   "different orientation toward digital technology": For a detailed treatment of this subject, please see R. Salkowitz, *Generation Blend: Managing Across the Technology Age Gap* (Hoboken, NJ: John Wiley & Sons, 2008).

Chapter 1

p. 16   "unique use of words and pictures to tell stories": For an authoritative analysis of comics and sequential art as a medium, you can't beat Scott McCloud, *Understanding Comics* (New York: Harper, 1994).

p. 21   "The most desirable tickets for the 2011 convention": http://www.nctimes.com/business /article_0dd24a8a-a75d-53ae-a16e-3c0c244d5e0c.html.

p. 22   "a rising tide of hassles, costs, and inconveniences": For those of you not lucky enough to be married to an über-organized geek goddess or god, Doug Kline's *Unauthorized San Diego Comic-Con Survival Guide* is an essential resource to help navigate the hassles of Con attendance; http://sdccsurvivalguide.com/.

Chapter 2

p. 27   "'bestsellers' in a given month rarely broke 75,000": DC's "New 52" launch in September helped lift sales into the 170,000–200,000 level for many titles (and over 360,000, and possibly considerably more in later printings, for the bestselling *Justice League #1*), according to industry data, but that burst of activity was still several months in the future at the time of Comic-Con 2011, and the overall trend remains ominous; http://www.hollywoodreporter.com/heat-vision /dc-comics-marvel-sales-figures-277720.

p. 27   "the top-selling Batman title that month":
http://www.comichron.com/monthlycomicssales/2011/2011-07.html.

p. 28   "a future . . . that does not include comic books: "Is the Comic Book
Doomed?" was the subject of a panel during the 2011 Con, which I did
not attend. Summary here:
http://www.comicbookresources.com/?page = article&id = 33573.

p. 31   "the industry group ICv2": The group's name stands for "Internal Cor-
respondence," the name of the association's original printed newsletter.
"v2" (version 2) indicates we are now in the digital era.

p. 33   "graphic novels were down more than 5 percent in 2010": Sales would
continue their plunge, down another 11.6 percent for 2011;
http://www.newsarama.com/comics/december-2011-comic-book-sales-
charts-120106.html.

p. 34   "leaving the manga business and restructuring":
http://www.animenewsnetwork.com/feature
/bandai_downsizing_ken_iyadomi_interview.

p. 34   "most manga sales come through bookstores":
http://www.comicsbeat.com/2011/08/19/with-borders-gone-manga.

p. 37   "comics may be the "killer app": Amazon seems to think so. Comics,
graphic novels, and the ComiXology app featured prominently in the
marketing of the Kindle Fire during its launch in the fall of 2011.

p. 38   "taking the entire direct market down with them": Some retailers and
analysts dispute this point; http://www.newsarama.com/comics/digi-
tal-and-future-of-comic-book-shops-110810.html.

p. 38   "can't take more than a few steps without setting it on fire": For a good
example of the retailer's view on the move to digital, see
http://www.comicbookresources.com/?page = article&id = 34091.

p. 39   "consumers who expect digital comics to be free": I wrote about this
problem back in 2006; http://www.worldfamouscomics.com/tony
/back20060808.shtml.

p. 39   "about 1 to 3 percent": http://www.icv2.com/articles/news/20448.html.
By 2012, digital sales were running 10 to 15 percent of print and higher
on some titles.

p. 39   "ComiXology, had made a series of announcements":
http://www.newsarama.com/comics/ComiXology.

p. 40   "a few smaller publishers were experimenting with day-and-date":
BOOM! Studios was the first publisher to market with day-and-date digital. Though the results were encouraging, digital sales remained a tiny
percentage of revenues generated by print products.

p. 40   "its entire line will be available same-day digital by April 2012": At the SxSW Conference in March 2012, Marvel moved the digital conversation forward with an ambitious strategy involving augmented reality and new storytelling modes.
http://www.fastcompany.com/1824133 /marvel-announces-big-new-digital-comics-push-but-will-it-fly.

p. 40   "too high a barrier for a lot of readers": One informed industry source claims the opposite is true: digital sales did not take off until the undiscounted price for a download rose to $1.99, giving publishers room to create gradations of pricing to influence value perception.

p. 41   "retailers will retaliate by canceling orders": This fear is well founded. When publisher Dark Horse Comics intimated that it was reducing day-and-date digital pricing to $1.99 (compared to $2.99 for print) in December 2011, retailer backlash was so forceful that the company was forced to "clarify" its position, saying that the $1.99 pricing applied only after the title had been in-market for a few weeks.

p. 42   "one of the most perceptive observers of the comics industry": See www.comicsbeat.com for one of the web's best daily discussions of issues affecting every aspect of the art, business, and hobby of comics.

p. 49   "*Supernatural Law* moved online": It can be found at www.supernaturallaw.com.

p. 52   "retailers grew skittish": Exhibit A found a creative solution to the self-publishing dilemma, mounting a successful campaign on the crowd-sourced creative financing site Kickstarter to fund its new trade edition in 2012.

p. 56   "Lucasfilm showed up with a slideshow": There are great pictures of that historical moment at EW.com: http://www.ew.com/ew /gallery/0,,20399642_20511617_20990681,00.html#20990681.

Chapter 3

p. 62   "posted on the Comic-Con website": http://www.comic-con.org.

p. 68   "He expounded on these ideas": Grant Morrison, *Supergods: What Masked Vigilantes, Miraculous Mutants and a Sun God from Smallville Can Teach Us About Being Human* (New York: Spiegel and Grau, 2011).

p. 72   "to changes in solar activity in 11-year cycles": Ibid., pp. 301–302.

p. 72   "first put forward this idea in their 1991 book": William Strauss and Neil Howe, *Generations: The History of America's Future 1584–2069* (New York: Perennial, 1991).

p. 73 "restore a clichéd trope to mass-cultural relevance": One retailer described the effect of early sales as "DC's stimulus package" to the direct market: http://flyingcolorscomics.com/ via http://www.comics-beat.com/2011/09/23/new-52-stimulus-flowing-freely-into-comics-shops.

p. 74 "behind the convention center": There's a nice recap here: http://popwatch.ew.com/2011/07/20 /twilight-comic-con-fans-breaking-dawn/.

p. 76 "high numbers of females of any age": That's not to say that women were entirely absent. The "matriarchs" of comics fandom include people like Maggie Thompson and Pat Lupoff, who were present from the earliest days, and our friend Jackie Estrada, who was at the first San Diego Con in 1970 and every one since.

p. 77 "the hardest-core male superhero reader": And please, *please* note for the record that I am not suggesting that all female comics fans are into *Twilight*. Many hard-core girl geeks have just as big a problem with the soft-edged premise as guys do.

p. 77 "young adult fiction": I am apparently too old and too male to have noticed the obvious recent addition to this list, *The Hunger Games*, until it was nearly too late to mention it in the text!

p. 79 "gratuitously offensive characterizations of women in their books": A disturbing trend in the depiction of women as crime victims in certain superhero comic books is known in fandom as the "women in refrigerators syndrome." http://en.wikipedia. org/wiki /Women_in_Refrigerators#Women_in_Refrigerators_Syndrome.

p. 79 "employing more female creators": Questions about the poor representation of female creators in DC's New 52 launch dogged DC President Dan DiDio throughout the 2011 Comic-Con—only the most recent example of an oft-expressed concern.

p. 80 "created by comic industry veterans": Specifically, Joe Casey, Steven T. Seagle, Duncan Rouleau, and Joe Kelly of Man of Action Studios. www. manofaction.tv.

p. 82 "The room frequently shook with laughter": For the moderator's perspective, see http://www.hitfix.com/blogs/whats-alan-watching/posts /comic-con-2011-fxs-wilfred-charms-horrifies-and-amuses.

p. 85 "properties like *Breaking Bad*": http://www.amctv.com/shows /breaking-bad/the-interrogation.

p. 89 "*the* coolest place in the comics universe at that particular moment": Chip is now performing that function for ComiXology, the digital comics distributor, as vice president of marketing, public relations, and business development.

p. 91   "a host of smaller publishers track in the single digits": Current market data is tracked by ICv2 and can be found at sites like Newsarama and The Beat, which also provide analysis.

p. 93   "DC provided evidence": See http://dcu.blog.dccomics.com/2012/02/01 /dc-entertainment-officially-announces-%E2%80%9Cbefore-watchmen %E2%80%9D/ for the announcement, http://www.fastcompany .com/1813669/whos-watching-the-watchmen-even-prestigious-comics-are-just-grist-for-the-entertainment-mill for my discussion of it, and http://www.fastcocreate.com/1679856/alan-moore-on-watchmen-s-toxic-cloud-and-creativity-v-big-business for Moore's take on the proceedings.

p. 93   "Marvel successfully sued": ComicBook Resources was just one of many sites that discussed the details of this complex situation in which writer Gary Friedrich sued Marvel over the Ghost Rider character, lost, and was ordered to pay $17,000 in damages for money he made selling prints and other merchandise at trade shows. Many were concerned the case would cast a pall over the ability of artists to sell drawings of corporate-owned characters to fans at conventions or through the Internet, a significant source of income for some creators in the industry. http://www .comicbookresources.com/?page=article&id=36893.

p. 94   "reportedly in development at Showtime": According to this March 2011 report from the insider blog *Deadline Hollywood*: http://www.deadline.com/2011/03 /showtime-developing-comedy-series-adaptation-of-comic-chew/.

Chapter 4

p. 107   "this offbeat, genre-crossing movie": Fortunately, it appears destined to have a long afterlife in video as a cult classic.

p. 110   "the vibe just isn't right": Note that animation often solves this problem effectively. Some of the best-loved and most successful adaptations of superhero comics in recent years have been cartoon series (*Batman: The Animated Series*, various incarnations of *X-Men*, and so on), but these seem to reach their maximum audience via TV or direct-to-video features, and rarely, if ever, get theatrical release. One notable exception is the animated 2004 film *The Incredibles* (Disney/Pixar), which is considered by many to be the best superhero movie not based on a pre-existing property.

p. 110   "a masterpiece of graphic storytelling": Including *Time* magazine, which put *Watchmen* on the list of the 100 most important novels of the twentieth century.

p. 111   "a movie that pleased no one": That is, it dramatically underperformed commercial and critical expectations. It was not a flop—according to the industry site Box Office Mojo, it (barely) made back its $150 million production cost with domestic and foreign box office, and it scored a 65 percent on the film critic aggregator Rotten Tomatoes. Many comic films have done worse, but few have had higher hopes for massive success.

p. 111   "ill served in film adaptations over the years": His other credits include *The League of Extraordinary Gentlemen, V for Vendetta,* and *From Hell,* all of which are considered classics in the comics medium; in addition, he created the character John Constantine, a complex and cynical British supernaturalist, portrayed by Keanu Reeves in the 2005 film *Constantine.*

p. 120   "the medium of comics and its history": At his highly entertaining blog, "The Fate of the Artist": http://eddiecampbell.blogspot.com/.

p. 121   "did not believe his current work benefited": Eddie's position on this was not as definitive as I represented it in the text. He decided to attend the 2012 Con and I was never happier to be wrong: His presence adds much to the proceedings.

p. 123   "others are likely to follow suit": The acclaimed graphic novelist Chris Ware took a big step down this path in September 2011, announcing the release of his latest work, "Touch Sensitive," as an iPad digital exclusive through his publisher, McSweeney's: http://www.tuaw.com/2011/09/20/chris-ware-releases-ipad-only-comic-via-mcsweeneys-app/.

p. 129   "had him killed in an explosion": Naturally, no one stays dead permanently in comics. DC revived the character later, and he now headlines his own book, *Red Hood and the Outsiders.*

p. 135   "properties that have no relevance to the current day": Or ignore better-known simplified versions of their characters that may have appeared in other media in favor of versions that "respect" every obscure continuity point that longtime fans might seize on.

p. 140   "hilarious innuendo capped with a full-on kiss on the lips": See for yourself at http://www.youtube.com/watch?v=a8NxWnMhlso or search for "Jonathan Ross Snogs Neil Gaiman."

Chapter 5

p. 146   "my local comics store, The Comics Dungeon": Located in Seattle's Wallingford neighborhood, owned by G. Scott Tomlin, and managed by mighty Chris Casos.

p. 146 "Diamond has the market to itself": Diamond's domination of comics distribution was solidified even further by the October 2011 closure of Haven, one of the last remaining independent distributors, and the announcement in early 2012 that Bud Plant, one of the pioneers in the distribution of graphic novels and comic-related art books, was calling it a day.

p. 147 "girl-geek and singles-night events": Comic-themed gatherings are underrated venues for meeting new partners. See this interesting report on the erotic undercurrents at the 2011 New York Comic-Con: http://www.slate.com/articles/double_x/doublex/2011/11/speed_dating_at_comic_con_why_it_s_great_for_women.html.

p. 147 "boys' club atmosphere": Some retailers apparently didn't get the memo. *Comic-Book Men*, a reality show that debuted in 2012 on AMC, produced by nerdlebrity filmmaker Kevin Smith and featuring his comic book store in New Jersey, perpetuates some of the most dire stereotypes of the business side of the hobby.

p. 147 "a new location called Little Island Comics": http://www.littleislandcomics.com/.

p. 147 "the rest of the community": http://www.comicsbeat.com/2011/09/05/littleisland-comics-north-americas-first-kid-focused-comics-shop-opens-tomorrow/.

p. 148 "shortly after the 2011 Comic-Con ended": http://www.comicsbeat.com/2011/08/21/breaking-atomic-comics-chain-closes/._

p. 152 "Mark Hamill": Yes, *that* Mark Hamill, best known as Luke Skywalker in the original *Star Wars* trilogy.

p. 152 "gamers who may or may not have any use for comics or animation": According to the Comic Book Resources website, *Batman: Arkham Asylum* was given a Guinness world record as the most critically acclaimed superhero game ever.

p. 155 "the current vogue for geek chic": The advertising world has taken note: a New York-based agency, the Bonfire Group, opened in early 2011 specifically to promote geek culture and branding.

p. 160 "the Ponzi scheme that is today's collectibles market": This story was reported and extensively documented by Daniel Best in his blog "20th Century Danny Boy," http://ohdannyboy.blogspot.com/2011/08/original-art-stories-steve-geppis.html.

p. 161 "literally wrote the book": Jerry Weist, *The Comic Art Price Guide* (second edition). Iona, WI: Krauss Publications, 2000.

p. 162   "most of the commerce takes place online and through back channels": The online forum the Collectors Society is one spot to observe the
behind-the-scenes conversations among this community: http://comics.
www.collectors-society.com/default.aspx.

p. 165   "crammed into their snug townhome": They would probably like me to
note that they've since moved to more spacious digs.

Chapter 6

p. 180   "handbook developed by Cruz and Hill in 2004": Which can, in theory,
be found here, although the site hasn't been updated in a while: http://
www.night-flight.com/secretorigin/.

p. 181   "under contract with the U.S. Army in the 1950s": Collected in a fine
edition in 2011: Eddie Campbell, ed., *PS: The Best of Preventative Maintenance Monthly* (Abrams Books, 2011).

p. 181   *"The Adventures of Johnny Bunko: The Last Career Guide You'll Ever
Need"* : Daniel Pink, illustrated by Rob Ten Pas, *The Adventures of
Johnny Bunko: The Last Career Guide You'll Ever Need* (New York: River-
head Books, 2008).

p. 181   "adapting business classics as graphic novels" :
http://www.forbes.com/sites/susanadams/2011/03/10
/now-you-can-read-business-books-as-comics/.

p. 182   "shelved at the Library of Congress": Comics are gaining acceptance at
the top of the library food chain: the Library of Congress;
http://www.tcj.com/introducing-the-small-press-expo-collection/.

p. 182   "merchandise, news, and book reviews in comics format":
See www.unshelved.com.

p. 183   "1996's *Palestine* by Joe Sacco" : Joe Sacco, *Palestine* (Seattle: Fantagraphics Books, 1996). This book received an American Book Award.

p. 183   "matter-of-fact true crime series, *A Treasury of Victorian Murder*": Collected in various formats by NBM Publishing.

p. 183   "the writers of the 1950s Beat Generation": Paul Buhle et al., *The Beats:
A Graphic History* (New York: Hill and Wang, 2010).

p. 184   "the needs of their communities or institutions": One excellent resource
is Stephen Weiner, *Faster than a Speeding Bullet: The Rise of the Graphic
Novel* (New York: NBM, 2003).

p. 184   "affection of many of today's leading literary lights for comic book culture": For an interesting take on this from the *Atlantic Monthly*, see http://www.theatlantic.com/entertainment/archive/2011/10 /how-zombies-and-superheroes-conquered-highbrow-fiction /246847/?single_page=true.

p. 189   "curated museum shows like the groundbreaking Masters of American Comics": http://hammer.ucla.edu/exhibitions/detail/exhibition_id/103.

p. 189   "R. C. Harvey": Some of his best aesthetic observations of the comics medium can be found in Robert C. Harvey, *The Art of the Comic Book* (Oxford: University of Mississippi Press, 1996).

p. 189   "Scott McCloud": Scott McCloud, *Understanding Comics: The Invisible Art* (New York: Harper Perennial, 1994).

p. 189   "Eisner himself": Eisner's treatises on comic aesthetics, *Comics and Sequential Art*; *Graphic Storytelling and Visual Narrative*; and *Expressive Anatomy* (with Peter Poplaski), are all worthy contributions to criticism from one of the medium's most accomplished practitioners.

p. 191   "Maurice Horn's monumental 800-page *World Encyclopedia of Comics*": Maurice Horn, *The World Encyclopedia of Comics* (New York: Chelsea House, 1976).

p. 195   "a first for such a high-profile title": As reported by ICv2: http://www.icv2.com/articles/news/21456.html.

p. 196   "competition with video games and movies for young mindshare and dollars": "Changing Habits Illustrate Decline of Indian Comics," *BBC News*, November 28, 11; http://www.bbc.co.uk/news/world-asia-15658311.

p. 196   "bring its superhero lineup to the subcontinent, with mixed results": A good rundown from local sources can be found at https://sites.google .com/site/gothamcomicsindia/blogs/marvelagainfailedinindia.

p. 197   "creating localization costs and complexity": Some question the value of localization with English literacy on the rise among youth; http://www.medianama.com/2009/03 /223-marvel-comics-to-focus-on-india-need-for-localization/.

p. 197   "betting heavily on this scenario is Liquid Comics": www.liquidcomics.com.

p. 197   "vast potential of India's high-tech, pop-crazy young readership": http://www.liquidcomics.com/press_release/Dec_05_2011.html.

p. 197   "create a new Indian superhero, Chakra—the Invincible": http://sciencefiction.com/2011/12/21 /stan-lee-creates-indian-comic-book-hero-chakra-the-invincible/.

p. 198 "Archie Comics has already employed in Latin America":
http://www.icv2.com/articles/news/20843.html.

p. 198 "the practical skills they need to create sustainable livelihoods": See
www.plainink.org for more information.

p. 200 "selling out in advance and hosting huge crowds": A firsthand account
can be found at https://sites.google.com/site/gothamcomicsindia
/comiccon-awalkthrough.

p. 200 "guests representing Europe and North America":
http://www.bdalger.net/.

p. 200 "ambassadors of comics culture in all its forms": In a related development on the domestic front, the Girl Geek Con, an unapologetically
female-centered fan event, sold out its two-day debut in Seattle in 2011,
signaling yet another advance in the development of the comics audience. A great firsthand account comes from professional comics writer
and guest of honor Gail Simone:
http://gailsimone.tumblr.com/post/11272833640
/some-personal-highlights-from-geek-girl-con.

p. 205 "the FAQ on the strip's website":
http://axecop.com/index.php/achome/story/.

p. 205 "a project called Trip City": http://welcometotripcity.com/, announced
at the Beat:
http://www.comicsbeat.com/2011/10/31/introducing-trip-city/.

p. 206 "his 2000 manifesto *Reinventing Comics*": Scott McCloud, *Reinventing
Comics: How Imagination and Technology Are Revolutionizing an Art
Form* (New York: William Morrow, 2000).

p. 206 "Jerry Holkins and Mike Krahulik's *Penny Arcade*": http://www.penny-
arcade.com/.

p. 206 "Pete Abrams's *Sluggy Freelance*": http://www.sluggy.com/.

p. 206 "Scott Kurtz's *PvP*": http://www.pvponline/.

p. 206 "a more-or-less webcomic on Jeff Kinney's 'Funbrain' site": http://www
.funbrain.com/journal/Journal.html?ThisJournalDay=1&ThisPage=2.

p. 206 "a world populated by glorified stick figures":
http://www.deadline.com/2011/12
/comedy-central-announces-2011-12-development-slate/#more-202206.

p. 208 "Lieber joined the discussion thread":
http://undergroundthecomic.com/4chan_thread_20614483.html.

p. 208   "artists who are trying to distinguish themselves in a crowded and competitive field" : Lieber blogged extensively about the experience and gave interviews to industry sites like Comic Book Resources: http://www.comicbookresources.com/?page = article&id = 29083.

p. 208   "what to do when that happens" : This account is adapted from an article I wrote in March 2011 at the site Internet Evolution: http://www.internetevolution.com/author .asp?section_id = 697&doc_id = 204863.

p. 208   "a deluxe edition from IDW" : http://www.kickstarter.com/projects/renaedeliz /womanthology-massive-all-female-comic-anthology?ref = card.

p. 208   "making the project commercially viable for the publisher" : Kickstarter has also proved problematic for certain kinds of projects, especially collaborations. A creator dispute threw a previously heralded Kickstarter project called *Ashes* into peril, raising troubling fundamental questions about the whole model. http://forbiddenplanet.co.uk/blog/2012 /an-ashes-update-jimmy-broxtons-off-the-book/.

p. 212   "by 2015, total tablet usage will top 82.1 million U.S. adults" : http://blogs.forrester.com/sarah_rotman_epps /11-01-04-us_tablet_sales_will_more_than_double_this_year.

p. 212   "more than 294 million units sold worldwide": http://www.reuters.com/article/2011/04/19 /us-tablets-research-idUSTRE73I16K20110419.

p. 212   "the Kindle Fire tablet in 2011": While tablets are still a bit pricey in the early 2010s, they are so effective as vehicles for the delivery of high-margin paid content that it is easy to see a day when providers or networks will give them away (or sell them for a nominal fee) as a means of locking in customers.

p. 212   "more than $2.8 billion by 2015, according to Forrester": http://www .forrester.com/rb/Research/ebook_buying_is_about_to_spiral_upward /q/id/57664/t/2.

p. 213   "files that ran only in their own application environments" : The security isn't foolproof, as some digital content is often "liberated" on sharing and torrent sites, but it represents a barrier to ordinary users.

p. 213   "restrictive terms of use governing digital comics": See http://www. comixology.com/terms for an example. Note that the terms license only the right to view the content, not the content itself. "Digital Content is licensed, not sold, to you by ComiXology. ComiXology reserves the right to revoke your license to Digital Content at any time for any reason."

p. 214   "service provider vanishes in the mist": The market got its first real taste of this problem in April 2012, when Graphicly announced it was closing its digital storefront and mothballing its reading application for Android and iOS devices to become a distribution service provider for the broader market for graphic e-books. See http//www.fastcocreate.com/1680464 /behind-a -pivot-graphicly-closes-marketplace-refocuses-business.

p. 216   "create critical mass around its platform": Smaller players like Panelfly, Wowio, and Longbox Digital are also fighting for share in a crowded market.

p. 216   "infusion of capital from private equity in November 2011": http://comicspl.us /iverse-media-announces-4-million-private-equity-funding-commitment/.

p. 216   "its potential for widespread industry adoption remain unclear": The rather complex iVerse/Diamond announcement from February 2012 was the subject of considerable discussion among industry observers. For example, see this clarifying report from Beat reporter Todd Allen: http://www.comicsbeat.com/2012/02/17 /diamonds-digital-distribution-program-the-actual-details/.

p. 219   "view them on the ComiXology app": For Steinberger's perspective on this, see http://www.suntimes.com/technology/ihnatko/8689560-452 /talking-the-amazon-fire-with-ComiXology.

p. 219   "ComiXology announced": "ComiXology Tops 50 Million Downloads." Press release issued by ComiXology, March 6, 2012. ComiXology updated its number to 60 million in April 2012.

p. 220   "a more-than-credible competitor overnight": Apple took a step in that direction in late February 2012, establishing a separate section of its iBookstore for comics and graphic novels, with a heavy emphasis on top-sellers from Marvel and Image. http://itunes.apple.com/us/genre/ books-comics-graphic-novels/id9026?mt=11, as reported in http://www.comicsbeat.com/2012/02/28 /itunes-launches-standalone-comics-section-of-ibookstore/.

p. 222   "titles that might not have enough viability in the direct market": DC announced its first "digital first" title, *Batman Beyond Unlimited* (a tie-in to the early 2000 animated series), in November 2011. It shipped in January 2012 for 99 cents as a digital edition only, and became available in print for $3.99 in February 2012, according to ICv2: http://www.icv2.com/articles/news/21518.html.

p. 222   "discounted pricing for complete story arcs": Marvel announced complete digital bundles (story arcs) from ComiXology in September 2011: http://robot6.comic/bookresources.com/2011/09 /marvel-offers-digital-bundles/.

p. 222   "monthly subscription model through the iVerse service": http://www.comicsbeat.com/2011/12/27 /sales-charts-unboxing-day-2011-and-a-surprising-discovery/.

p. 223   "sold more than 500,000 copies in print": http://www.hollywoodreporter .com/heat-vision/dc-comics-marvel-sales-figures-277720.

p. 225   "interact with the creators and one another": http://stumptowntradereview.com/2011/10 /this-is-how-digital-comics-should-work/.

p. 225   "a DVD that comes with the physical book": Art Spiegelman, *MetaMaus: A Look Inside a Modern Classic* (New York: Pantheon, 2011).

p. 225   "keeping it at an affordable price": http://www.publishersweekly.com /pw/by-topic/digital/content-and-e-books/article/49045-shanower--s-age-of-bronze-seen-app-goes-live-for-new-york-comic-con.html.

p. 226   "These do-it-yourself offerings outsold": http://www.nytimes .com/2011/10/10/business/media /for-archie-comics-a-return-to-superheroes.html?_r=1.

p. 226   "money comes through the tip jar, not the toll booth": Perhaps this is why DC and Marvel Entertainment are high-profile supporters of various legislative efforts to restrict content usage on the Internet.

p. 229   "polarized reactions": More so in the wake of his highly publicized November 2011 invective-tinged rant against the Occupy Wall Street movement that he posted on his blog, www.frankmillerink.com (the post was titled "Anarchy")—but that was still four months in the future when he appeared at the Dead Dog Party.

Chapter 7

p. 236   "known as scenario planning": Scenario planning was initially developed in the 1980s by a team of strategists working for Shell Oil who needed better risk models for determining future energy market conditions. Members of the team, including Peter Schwartz and Lawrence Wilkinson, later founded the consultancy Global Business Network and popularized scenario planning through books, workshops, and engagements. Large corporations, industry groups, and governments, including Microsoft, Procter & Gamble, Merck, and the nation of Singapore, use scenario planning to drive market, product, and competitive strategy.

p. 237   "a Marvel title called *What If?*": Most of these were written by Roy Thomas, the most continuity-oriented of his generation of writers, and many of the *What If* scenarios later ended up happening "for real" in the Marvel universe.

p. 247   "connected by networks and mobile devices": For a richer picture of this world, see my 2010 book, *Young World Rising.*

p. 252   "threatening to enemies of modernity and artistic experimentation": I address many of the problems of this scenario in an essay called "Entrepreneurship and Its Enemies," available in my 2011 e-book release, *Young World Shining.*

p. 257   "one of the great *X-Men* stories of the early 1980s": "Days of Future Past," by Chris Claremont and John Byrne, *Uncanny X-Men,* 141–142, Marvel Comics Group, January–February 1980.

ACKNOWLEDGMENTS ⫍⟶

I n 1977, when I was 10 years old, I was an avid reader of *The Spirit Magazine*, a collection of reprints of Will Eisner's classic 1940s stories published by Kitchen Sink Press. For some reason, I felt moved to dash off a letter of comment regarding the casting of a Spirit movie that was then under discussion ("James Garner as the Spirit, please"). I sent it to the publisher, a fellow named Denis Kitchen, who ran it in the next issue. It was the first time I saw my name in print, and I kind of liked it.

More than 30 years later, when I had some more to say about transmedia adaptations of comic book properties, I felt moved to dash off a 70,000-word manuscript. I sent it to my agent, a fellow named Denis Kitchen, and he saw it into print, this time through the good offices of Mary Glenn and her team at McGraw-Hill. You can't make this stuff up.

So thank you, Denis Kitchen (and partner John Lind), for encouraging me in this project and securing a place for it at warp speed. Thanks to everyone at McGraw-Hill for jumping on it so fast and being so supportive of such a weird, quixotic project. Thanks also to the late Will Eisner for inspiring a lifelong love and appreciation of comics, and for exemplifying the rare combination of creative talent and entrepreneurship that offers us hope for the future even in dark times. In this way as in so many others, Eisner was ahead of his time.

In navigating the treacherous complexities of the art, business, and universe of comics, I was fortunate to have the guidance of a few experts. Thanks to Batton Lash, Jackie Estrada, Dr. Robyn Hill, Chip Mosher, Chuck Rozanski, David Steinberger, Joe Ferrara, Micah Baldwin, Eddie Campbell, and Steve Lieber for your time, comments, guidance, and anecdotes. Special thanks to Chris Casos, G. Scott Tomlin, and the gang at Seattle's Comics Dungeon. I also want to thank Mic Messersmith and Emily Wydeven for allowing me to share their views and experiences at the Con.

On the business and futurism side, I am fortunate to be able to depend on Mike Dover, Daniel W. Rasmus, and Lawrence Wilkinson for thoughtful input and constructive criticism. I also got great feedback from Max Miller, Ivan Weiss, Guy Roadruck, and Thomas Kamber. Thanks for letting me bounce this stuff off you.

Henrik Andreasen, Jackie Estrada, Batton Lash, Kristi Long, Chip Mosher, Eunice Verstegen, and BOOM! Studios' Ivan Salazar were kind enough to give permission to use their photos. A special shout-out to Doug Kline, the mastermind behind PopCultureGeek .com and author of the essential *Unofficial San Diego Comic-Con Survival Guide*, for responding to my frenzied entreaties for decent pictures and coming through big-time. All photos are copyright by their respective owners.

In my research, I was helped immeasurably by being able to attend the ICv2 Future of Comics conference in July 2011, organized by Milton Griepp and his team, and the White Space conference at New York Comic Con in October 2011, run by Lance Fensterman and the good people at ReedPOP. Thanks to all the organizers, presenters, and attendees at those events.

Then there's the event at the center of this book, Comic-Con International: San Diego, which owes its success to the tireless efforts of executive director Fae Desmond, director of marketing David Glanzer, organization president John Rogers, and a cast of thousands. I hope this book provides ample evidence of the esteem in which Eunice and I hold your work, both personally and professionally. Comic-Con is an incomparable spectacle and an amazing example of entrepreneurial success.

One of the big challenges in writing this book was trying to stay on top of the fast-moving developments across the comics and pop culture industries. For the best news and commentary, I rely on Heidi MacDonald and her colleagues at The Beat; Tom Spurgeon at The Comics Reporter; the ICv2 Daily Insider email; the team at Comic Book Resources; and the "Has Boobs, Reads Comics" feed from The Nerdy Bird, Jill Pantozzi. I also tip my cap to groundbreaking comics futurist Scott McCloud and critic extraordinaire Douglas Wolk, who have both written articulate and essential books on the technological and aesthetic evolution of comics in the twenty-first century.

Thanks to my partners Guy Roadruck and Tracey Peyton, and to all of our team at our digital communications firm, MediaPlant, LLC, for once again indulging me in my "extracurricular" activities as an author in the midst of a busy season for the agency and our clients. I am also grateful to my students and colleagues at the University of Washington Master of Communication in Digital Media (MCDM) Program, where the future of storytelling, entrepreneurship, digital distribution, and media mashups is being written in real time.

Finally, my deepest and most profound thanks, with love and admiration, to my wife, Eunice. Her unfailing encouragement, critical eye, and insight helped make the manuscript stronger, but her companionship and enthusiasm have made Comic-Con—and everything else—a delight for all these years.

Rob Salkowitz
Seattle, WA
January 2, 2012

ABOUT THE AUTHOR

Rob Salkowitz attended his first con, the 1976 Delaware Valley Comic Art Convention, at age nine. He's been going to the San Diego Comic-Con since 1997. During the other 360 days of the year, he writes, speaks, and consults on issues related to the future of business and technology; serves as Director of Strategy and Content at MediaPlant, LLC, the Seattle-based communications firm he cofounded in 1999; teaches at the University of Washington MCDM (Masters in Communication/Digital Media) program; serves on the board of several nonprofits; writes for various online publications including *FastCompany* and *Internet Evolution*; and tweets up a storm @robsalk. He is the author of *Generation Blend: Managing Across the Technology Age Gap* (2008) and *Young World Rising: How Youth, Technology, and Entrepreneurship Are Changing the World from the Bottom Up* (2010), and coauthor, with Daniel W. Rasmus, of *Listening to the Future: Why It's Everybody's Business* (2009). Rob and his wife, Eunice Verstegen, live in Seattle, Washington.

For updates and additional content, "like" the book on Facebook at facebook.com/ComicConPopCulture.

For more info about Rob's projects, including contact information, go to www.robsalkowitz.com.